JUDICIAL POLICIES

JUDICIAL POLICIES

Implementation and Impact

Charles A. Johnson
Texas A&M University

Bradley C. Canon
University of Kentucky

A division of Congressional Quarterly Inc.
1414 22nd Street N.W., Washington, D.C. 20037

Library of Congress Cataloging in Publication Data

Johnson, Charles A., 1948-
    Judicial Policies.

    Includes indexes.
    1. Justice, Administration of—United States.
    2. Judicial process—United States. I. Canon,
Bradley C., 1937-   . II. Title.
KF8700.J63   1984   340'.11   83-26303
ISBN 0-87187-284-6

To my father, Robert A. Canon, who first interested me in law and politics

—B. C. C.

To my parents, Forrest and Marie Johnson, for their boundless encouragement

—C. A. J.

PREFACE

I n the wake of desegregation, expanded defendants' rights, legal-
ized abortion, and other controversial court decisions, political
scientists, legal scholars, and other researchers have begun paying
considerable attention to the implementation and impact of judicial
policies. Impact papers are presented at academic meetings and
appear in scholarly journals; a few case studies are available in book
form. Even magazines and newspapers sometimes follow up on the
impact of a judicial decision. But few people have stopped to take
general stock of our knowledge about what goes on after a court
renders a decision. Some textbooks that focus on the Supreme Court,
on the judicial process, or even on constitutional law devote their final
chapter to implementation and impact, but such coverage is illustrative rather than broadly structured and comprehensive. The fact is
that in recent years no one has really synthesized existing material on
the impact and implementation of judicial policies. The last such
effort was published in 1970 and is now out of print.

The absence of any comprehensive treatment of this literature
was quite frustrating in our teaching and research endeavors. We
often had to "wing it" in undergraduate classes for those periods
devoted to judicial impact. In graduate seminars our reading assign-
ments inadequately conveyed the breadth, scope, and approaches of
judicial impact research. Our research was hampered by the lack of a
book-length treatment of the literature that could link the findings
together. Conversations with colleagues indicated that we were not
alone in this frustration. As both of us are active in conducting
implementation and impact research, we decided to fill the void in the
judicial process literature and alleviate our frustration by writing this
book.

We have organized the synthesis according to a heuristic model
of populations and responses. We posit four categories of persons,
each of which stands in a particular relationship to a judicial policy;

these are the interpreting, implementing, consumer, and secondary populations. At the same time we posit two responses that affected persons must make when reacting to a judicial policy: the acceptance decision and the behavioral response decision. This model has the advantage of comprehensiveness. All reactions and all stages in the implementation and impact process are covered; no research is left out or included awkwardly. This organizational scheme links together in the same chapter the literature on people whose functions in the process are similar regardless of which judicial policy is involved and which theory, if any, is used.

Chapter 1 introduces the heuristic model—the populations and response sequences. Chapters 2 through 5 discuss the interpreting, implementing, consumer, and secondary populations in turn. In Chapter 6 we turn to theory development, focusing on nine theories— some formal, some not so formal—that have been offered to explain implementation and impact patterns; we look at the extent to which each has been verified by research. We then integrate the theories with the heuristic model and discuss the applicability of each theory to each population. In Chapter 7, our final chapter, we develop an overall assessment of the impact of judicial policies on American society. In this chapter we take two approaches. First we look at courts as entities within the political system and we examine research that assesses the abilities of particular courts to initiate or maintain major policies, especially in opposition to other political institutions. Then we focus on four major policy areas in American politics: freedom of expression, political and social equality, criminal justice, and economic policy; we offer a rough longitudinal assessment of the influence the judiciary has had in the formulation of public policy in each area.

Another goal for this book is to stimulate more research about the judicial implementation and impact process. There are numerous research opportunities awaiting the application of inexpensive efforts as well as more sophisticated designs. Judicial impact research was a burgeoning enterprise in the late 1960s and early 1970s but now seems to have lost momentum. We hope an overview mapping out what we do and do not know about judicial impact will foster greater attention to the field and perhaps suggest some specific research projects. This resurgence would be particularly appropriate now because of the increasing attention given in political science and public administration to the analysis of the implementation and impact of public policy, which is for the most part focused on legislation and executive decisions. Judicial policy *is* public policy. It should not be ignored or viewed as a fundamentally different area of research. We hope this overview will make an integration of judicial impact studies with other public policy studies easier and encourage public policy researchers to include court decisions in the ambit of their activities.

Finally, we want to emphasize two things in conjunction with our goals of filling a need and encouraging greater impact research. First, we believe that too much attention has been given to following up dramatic U.S. Supreme Court decisions such as *Brown v. Board of Education, Miranda v. Arizona,* and *Roe v. Wade.* A disproportionate amount of our impact knowledge comes from investigating the aftermath of just six or eight Supreme Court decisions. In part, perhaps, the loss of impact research momentum reflects the absence of Supreme Court decisions of the first rank during the last decade. But such decisions by their nature are exceptional. In focusing on the extraordinary, we have forgotten the ordinary. We believe a complete understanding of the processes in the implementation and impact of judicial policies must also include data about cases less heralded but nonetheless still important. Thus, where existing research or reasonable speculation permits, we make an effort in this book to focus on less dramatic Court decisions and on routine judicial areas such as antitrust law and product liability.

Second, we emphasize that not all judicial policy is made by the U.S. Supreme Court. Impact researchers are affected by the "upper court" myth as much as anyone. With a few notable exceptions, all their efforts are concentrated on the Supreme Court. There are more than 80 other appellate courts in the United States, as well as innumerable trial courts. They make policy too. We see no good theoretical or pragmatic reason to differentiate the study of their policies from that of Supreme Court policies. Thus, as far as possible we draw examples from other courts.

Many people contributed their time and energy to helping us turn a mass of undetailed ideas into pieces of manuscript and then put them together into what we hope is a complete and coherent book. We are particularly grateful to Robert L. Peabody of Johns Hopkins University, Lawrence Baum of Ohio State University, and Sheldon Goldman of the University of Massachusetts, who read a first draft of the manuscript. They saved us from several embarrassing errors and, even more important, made a number of valuable suggestions for organizing topics and illustrating points. Thanks go to Micheal Giles, now at Emory University, who read a first draft of Chapter 4. Jean Woy provided both general encouragement and specific guidance in the early stages of the book. At CQ Press Joanne Daniels maintained her valuable support and interest as we finished the book; Nola Healy

Lynch served as a thoroughly professional editor, whose advice and comments added much to the clarity and organization of this book. Carolyn England, Kim Hayden, and Betty Pasley typed drafts of various chapters at the University of Kentucky. At Texas A&M University Edna Lumpkin, Lisa Grubbs, Tammy Orth, and B. Wylbur typed chapter drafts. At both schools this was done with speed and efficiency. Thanks also go to our respective departments for the support that was necessary for long-distance coauthorship. Last but hardly least, we thank our wives, Rose Canon and Barbara Johnson, who kept cool heads during a process that lasted longer than either we or they anticipated.

Bradley C. Canon
Charles A. Johnson

CONTENTS

JUDICIAL POLICIES

CHAPTER ONE

Responses to Judicial Policies

John Marshall has made his decision, now let him enforce it.

—attributed to President Andrew Jackson

Does anybody know . . . where we can go to find light on what the practical consequences of these decisions have been?

—Justice Felix Frankfurter

Constitutional rights . . . are not to be sacrificed or yielded to the violence and disorder which have followed upon the actions of the Governor and Legislature.

—U.S. Supreme Court, *Cooper v. Aaron* (1958)

P resident Jackson's remark reveals an important insight—that judicial policies rarely implement themselves. Justice Frankfurter's comment also underscores the fact that once a judicial policy is announced a court may have little control over what the policy's consequences are. Finally, the Supreme Court's decision in *Cooper v. Aaron,* which overturned moves by Arkansas's governor and legislature to block school desegregation, illustrates the frequently political nature of the events that follow judicial decisions.

1

The basic premise of this book stems from observations such as those quoted above: judicial policies are not self-implementing, and implementing judicial policies is a political process. In virtually all instances, the courts that formulate policies must rely on other courts or on nonjudicial actors to translate those policies into action. Inevitably, just as making judicial policies is a political process, so too is the implementation of the policies—the issues are essentially political, and the actors are subject to political pressures.

STUDYING RESPONSES TO JUDICIAL POLICIES

This book examines the implementation and impact of judicial policies. There are important substantive and theoretical reasons for studying what may at first appear to be a very narrow part of the judicial process and for studying it as a political process instead of as a legal process. From the substantive perspective, few areas of the American political system remain untouched by judicial decision making. In our litigious society many disputes that have public policy ramifications are decided by the judiciary. Although they differ from legislative actions and executive orders in their origin, judicial policies are also public policies: they too must be implemented before disputes or problems are resolved, and they have an impact on the public. Racial segregation, for example, did not end with the announcement of *Brown v. Board of Education* in 1954. Ten years after the Supreme Court decided that separate but equal is inherently unequal, a great majority of the South's black students continued to attend overwhelmingly black schools. The Court's policy was given meaning only after considerable efforts by lower courts, the Department of Justice, the Department of Health, Education and Welfare, the Congress, and civil rights groups. Our knowledge about desegregation and the judiciary would be quite incomplete if we limited our analysis to the *Brown* decision. Knowing the events leading to a judicial decision and the substance of the decision gives us only a partial picture of the judicial process.

Studying the reaction to judicial policies is also important from a theoretical perspective. To a certain degree, evaluting the implementation of judicial policies is in the mainstream of the emerging field of policy analysis. Important theoretical questions in this field may be answered by studying the aftermath of judicial decisions: Why are some policies implemented while others are not? Why do some organizations change policies while others do not? Why do some policies have the intended impact while others fail to do so or have unintended consequences? The varied outcomes of judicial policies provide ample opportunities to examine the impact of public policies.

Responses to some court decisions have been immediate and implementation almost complete. For example, in the years following the Supreme Court's 1973 abortion decision in *Roe v. Wade,* several million women ended their pregnancies with legal abortions and new pro- and antiabortion groups emerged as powerful forces in our political system. By contrast, the events following *Brown v. Board of Education* demonstrate that the implementation of other decisions may be prolonged. And the Supreme Court's decision in *Abington School District v. Schempp* (1963), declaring prayers in public schools unconstitutional, is an example of a decision that has been implemented in varying degrees across the nation. Almost two decades after the decision, prayers continue as a daily practice in some of the nation's schools, while other school systems have dropped all religious activities. The aftermaths of these decisions and others raise important questions about the ability of the judiciary to make public policy effectively and about how individual citizens and political institutions relate to the judiciary. Moreover, studying the implementation of judicial decisions may shed some light on such longstanding issues as the relationship between law and human behavior and the role of the judiciary in our political system.

If studying the implementation of judicial policies is important, then we must study it as a political process. In a general sense, the implementation of *any* public policy is a political process. The ill-conceived notion that the administration of policy is apolitical has long since been discarded (if it was ever in vogue). Political scientist Michael Lipsky remarks on how postdecision factors may enter the implementation process: "There are many contexts in which the latitude of those charged with carrying out a policy is so substantial that studies of policy implementation should be turned on their heads. In these cases, policy is effectively 'made' by the people who implement it." [1]

As we will see in later chapters, many judicial decisions carry a great deal of latitude for interpretation and implementation. Political actors and institutions who follow through on these decisions make the judicial policy. Certainly, the judges who enforced desegregation in southern school districts or busing decisions anywhere were subject to political pressures from a variety of sources. Similar pressures affected school board decisions regarding the role of religion in schools. Even presidential politics may become intertwined with judicial policies, as did Richard Nixon's 1968 "law and order" presidential campaign criticizing the Supreme Court's criminal

3

justice decisions or the explosive issue of abortion in the 1980 presidential election. Like the Congress, the Supreme Court and lower courts must rely on others to translate policy into action. And like the processes of formulating legislative, executive, and judicial policies, the process of translating those decisions into action is often a political one subject to a variety of pressures from a variety of political actors in the system.

ROE V. WADE: A CASE STUDY OF JUDICIAL IMPACT

The best way to illustrate the political nature of the events that follow a judicial decision is to review the implementation and impact of a recent decision that remains controversial. We will use the Supreme Court's 1973 abortion decision in *Roe v. Wade* to show what may happen after a judicial policy is announced. Later in this chapter we will suggest a conceptual scheme by which the events following any judicial decision may be effectively organized and compared with the events following other judicial decisions.

The Decision

On Monday, January 22, 1973, Associate Justice Harry Blackmun announced the decision of the Court in two cases concerning the rights of women to end unwanted pregnancies with legal abortions, *Roe v. Wade* and *Doe v. Bolton.* According to Bob Woodward and Scott Armstrong's revealing account in *The Brethren,* this decision was the result of considerable conflict and compromise within the Court.[2] The decision came after almost a full year of research by Justice Blackmun, and the justices fully expected a public outcry after the decision was announced. They were not disappointed.

The cases before the Court challenged the laws prohibiting abortion in Texas and Georgia. The Court decided in favor of the plaintiffs in both cases—women who were identified only as Jane Roe and Mary Doe. The direct effect of the decision was to void the antiabortion laws in Texas and Georgia. Indirectly, of course, the Court also voided laws in every state that prohibited or limited abortion. The results and policy options for the states were summarized in the concluding parts of the majority opinion in *Roe:*

> 1. A state criminal abortion statute of the current Texas type, that excepts from criminality only a *lifesaving* procedure on behalf of the mother, without regard to pregnancy stage and without recognition of the other

interests involved, is violative of the Due Process Clause of the Fourteenth Amendment.

(a) For the stage prior to approximately the end of the first trimester, the abortion decision and its effectuation must be left to the medical judgment of the pregnant woman's attending physician.

(b) For the stage subsequent to approximately the end of the first trimester, the state, in promoting its interest in the health of the mother, may, if it chooses, regulate the abortion procedure in ways that are reasonably related to maternal health.

(c) For the stage subsequent to viability, the state in promoting its interest in the potentiality of human life may, if it chooses, regulate, and even proscribe, abortion except where it is necessary, in appropriate medical judgment, for the preservation of the life or health of the mother.[3]

In effect, the Supreme Court had given women the right to abortion on demand during the first two trimesters of pregnancy and had allowed the state to regulate abortions only to protect the mother's health during these two trimesters. The Court held that during the third trimester the state could regulate or even prohibit abortions, except where the life or the health of the mother was endangered.

Immediate Responses

On the day the Court announced the abortion decision, former president Lyndon B. Johnson died of a heart attack, and a few days before the Court's announcement, President Richard Nixon had announced the end of American military participation in the Vietnam War. These two events diminished the newsworthiness of the Court's decision in *Roe* and *Doe*. Instead of being the lead story in the weekly news magazines, the abortion decision received only limited coverage.[4] Nevertheless, the reactions from several corners of the political system were immediate, and they were mostly negative.

A few reactions were aimed directly at the justices. Woodward and Armstrong recount some of the reactions by noting that

thousands of letters poured into the Court. The guards had to set up a special sorting area in the basement with a huge box for each Justice. The most mail came to Blackmun, the decision's author, and to Brennan, the Court's only Catholic. Some letters compared the Justices to the Butchers of Dachau, child killers, immoral beasts, and Communists. A special ring of hell would be reserved for the Justices. Whole classes from Catholic schools wrote to denounce the Justices as murderers. "I really don't want to write this letter but my teacher made me," one child said. Minnesota Lutherans zeroed in on Blackmun. New Jersey Catholics called for Brennan's excommunication. Southern Baptists and other groups sent over a thousand bitter letters to Justice Hugo Black, who had died sixteen months earlier. Some letters and calls were death threats.[5]

But not all reactions were negative. The president of Planned Parenthood, Alan F. Guttmacher, called the decision a "courageous stroke for right to privacy and for the protection of a woman's physical and emotional health." A similar reaction came from women attorneys at the Center for Constitutional Rights, who cited the decision as a "victory for [the] women's liberation movement." [6] A more direct and personal reaction to the decision is reported in *The Brethren*. Several months after the abortion decision Justice Blackmun gave a speech at Emory University Law School, in Atlanta, Georgia, where a woman embraced him after his speech, saying, "I'll never be able to thank you for what you have done. I'll say no more. Thank you." Unknown to Blackmun at the time, this rare positive response came from "Mary Doe," the woman from Texas who had challenged the Texas abortion law.[7]

Reactions also came from members of Congress. A week after the Supreme Court's decision, Rep. Lawrence J. Hogan, R-Md., introduced the first of several "right to life" amendments to the U.S. Constitution. By November 1973 over two dozen resolutions to overturn some aspect of the Court's decision were introduced in Congress. Two of the proposals eventually enacted into law were added to the Health Programs Extension Act of 1973, which was amended to permit institutions receiving federal funds to refuse to perform abortions, and the 1973 Foreign Assistance Act, which was amended to prohibit the use of U.S. funds to pay for abortions overseas.[8]

Response was also immediate from women who sought abortions. In the first three months of 1973, 181,140 abortions were performed in the United States; and during the first year following the Supreme Court's decision a total of 742,460 abortions were performed nationwide. The overwhelming majority of abortions occurred in metropolitan areas, and 41 percent occurred in Middle Atlantic states. The variation in the number of abortions from state to state was considerable; the greatest number of abortions was performed in New York, a state that had previously liberalized its abortion law, while two states—Louisiana and North Dakota—reported no abortions during 1973.[9] Data from the first year of nationwide legal abortions suggest that almost one of every five pregnancies was terminated with an abortion.[10]

Whether a woman secured an abortion depended heavily on whether there was a physician or medical facility willing to provide abortion services. A study by Jon R. Bond and Charles A. Johnson found that fewer than half of the hospitals in their national sample changed abortion policies after *Roe*.[11] Indeed, for many hospitals in the sample (85.6 percent), the abortion issue was not a subject of heated staff or board discussions. The data seem to indicate that whether hospitals provided abortion services depended heavily on whether the hospital staff was in favor of abortions; factors such as community need or demand for abortion services and the hospital's financial situation were largely unrelated to the hospitals' decisions.

A national survey by the research division of Planned Parenthood, the Alan Guttmacher Institute, in 1973 revealed that less than one-third (30.1 percent) of the non-Catholic short-term general hospitals in the United States provided abortion services. Another survey revealed that 75 percent of the hospitals providing abortion services were privately controlled, rather than publicly controlled or government operated. In the year following the abortion decision, a relatively small number of nonhospital clinics provided abortion services (178 nationwide), and only a few physicians reported performing abortions in their offices (168 nationwide). Nonetheless, in the first year after the decision, the largest percentage of abortions occurred in clinics (44.5 percent), and most of the remaining abortions (41.1 percent) were performed in private hospitals.[12]

The Alan Guttmacher Institute concluded that in the 12 months following the Supreme Court's abortion decision, "the response of health institutions in many areas to the legalization of abortion in 1973 was so limited as to be tantamount to no response at all." [13] This widespread nonresponse had a considerable effect on *Roe v. Wade*'s impact—after being granted the *constitutional* right to an abortion, many women could not exercise that right because medical facilities in their communities refused to provide the services necessary to secure an abortion.

Later Responses

One year after the Supreme Court's announcement of the abortion decision, the first annual "March for Life" was held in Washington, D.C., to protest that decision. The demonstration gave direct evidence of political divisions created by the abortion decision. Battle lines were drawn by proponents and opponents of the Court's policy in several political arenas.

7

In the Senate a subcommittee began hearing testimony on several proposed constitutional amendments to overturn the decision. In the House a subcommittee chairman's refusal to hold similar hearings prompted the circulation of a discharge petition to force a constitutional amendment to the floor for consideration and vote. The discharge petition was 100 signatures short of the 218 required by House rules, but nevertheless the pressure continued. There were also moves in Congress to limit the federal government's support of abortions. Much of the activity centered on the federal funding of abortions under existing Medicaid programs. In 1974 and 1975 antiabortion forces unsuccessfully attempted to amend the annual appropriations bills for the Department of Labor and the Department of Health, Education and Welfare with restrictions on the use of federal funds for elective abortions. However, in 1976 Congress approved a restriction on Medicaid funding for abortions known as the Hyde Amendment (for its sponsor, Rep. Henry J. Hyde, R-Ill.). The amendment was the subject of considerable debate and political maneuvering; it passed easily in the House, but the Senate voted to kill it. After 11 weeks of stalemate in the conference committee, both houses finally compromised on language barring federal funding of abortions except where the life of the mother would be endangered if the fetus were carried to term. The provision came under attack immediately in the courts, and its implementation was delayed almost a full year, until August 1977.

Congress was not the only legislative body acting to restrict the implementation of the Supreme Court abortion decision. From 1973 through 1976, 34 states adopted laws relating to abortions.[14] Some of the laws concerned regulations that the Court indicated states could pass to protect the health of the mother—for example, requiring that abortions be performed by licensed physicians—and others called for reporting abortions to a state agency. Such laws were not considered to be restrictive or aimed at limiting the availability of abortions. Other laws, however, were clearly intended to limit the impact of the Court's decision or to discourage the use of abortions by women with unwanted pregnancies. Several states passed consent requirements under which the husband of a married woman or the parents of an unmarried minor would have to give their written approval before an abortion could be performed. A few states also required consultation or certification by a second physician during the third trimester. A majority of the states (29) adopted laws protecting physicians from discriminatory, disciplinary, or recriminatory actions if they refused to perform abortions, and 31 states adopted "conscience clause" laws specifically authorizing physicians to refuse to perform abortions.

Abortion opponents used the judicial process as well. The most celebrated case involved a Boston physician, Kenneth C. Edelin, who was indicted in June 1974 for manslaughter for causing the death of a fetus after an abortion he performed on a woman in the sixth or seventh month of her pregnancy. The trial of Dr. Edelin received national media coverage; *Newsweek* used the trial as a basis for a cover story entitled "Abortion and the Law."[15] Dr. Edelin was convicted of manslaughter by a jury in March 1975 and was sentenced to one year's probation, but the conviction was overturned by a state appellate court. Nonetheless, the immediate result of the conviction was to increase the caution of some hospitals and clinics in performing second trimester abortions. According to reports in the popular press after the conviction, hospitals in Pittsburgh, Detroit, and New York began limiting the stages of pregnancy during which they would perform abortions.[16]

In spite of intense opposition and various legal restrictions, the number of abortions performed in the United States continued to grow. By 1980 over 1.6 million legal abortions were performed annually. In contrast, the number of illegal abortions had shrunk from nearly 750,000 in 1969 to around 10,000 in 1980. Moreover, the increased emphasis on this issue had led to other gynecologic health improvements and to lower-cost services.[17]

As before, the overwhelming percentage of abortions were performed in metropolitan areas; one survey found that there were no facilities in 80 percent of the counties in the United States. Significantly, although the number of abortions continued to increase, the number of hospital facilities offering abortion services remained relatively constant. More and more, however, abortions were performed in clinics—the number of which nearly doubled during the three years following the Court's abortion decision.[18]

Four years after *Roe v. Wade,* the political struggles surrounding the abortion issue had spilled beyond the Congress, the states, and the judiciary. Pro- and antiabortion groups, for example, organized, and other political actors became involved. The National Right to Life Committee, meeting in a convention, applauded the House of Representative's vote for a ban on using Medicaid funds for abortions, and the leaders of the committee pledged to oppose the reelection of the representatives who had voted against the amendment.[19] Proabortion forces were also continuing their fight against limits on the implementation of the Court's decision. In August 1977, 27 women's and public interest groups sent a letter to President Carter expressing their support for the women in his administration who had publicly disassociated themselves from his advocacy of a ban on federally funded abortions.[20] Another political agency, the U.S. Commission on Civil Rights, issued a report in 1975 urging Congress to reject "anti-abortion legislation and amendments, and repeal those which have been enacted, which undermine the constitutional right to limit childbearing." [21]

Local politics were also affected. The Right to Life party formed in New York state and ran candidates for office. In other localities, candidates' stands on abortion were sometimes crucial to endorsements or support from blocs of voters. Even presidential politics was affected by the abortion controversy. Presidential candidates Gerald R. Ford and Jimmy Carter did not differ dramatically on the abortion issue, thus leading one elector from Washington state to withhold his electoral vote from President Ford, who had won the state. Mike Padden, the errant elector, cast his vote for Ronald Reagan because Ford had failed to take a strong stand against abortion.[22]

The Controversy Continues

The controversy over the abortion policy announced by the Supreme Court in 1973 and over how that policy was to be implemented continued unabated four years after the decision was announced. The intensity of the debate is best seen in Congress's annual consideration of amendments to appropriations bills deleting funds for abortion (for example, the Hyde Amendment). After compromising with the Senate in 1976, the House in 1977 adamantly insisted that no federal funds be used in any abortion procedures, even if the life of the mother was in danger. After five months of battling between the House and the Senate (whose version was less restrictive), Congress adopted an appropriations bill prohibiting federal expenditures for any *elective* abortion. The same language was adopted in 1978; in 1979 that language was altered to allow federal funding for abortions only to save the life of the mother or in cases of rape or incest, thus dropping the 1976 compromise provision allowing funding if two physicians agreed that the physical health of the mother would be damaged if the pregnancy continued. In addition, antiabortion riders were attached to six other appropriations bills and to two authorization bills in 1979.[23] Although Congress had not passed a constitutional amendment to overturn the 1973 Supreme Court decision, it had gone quite far to limit the impact of the original abortion decision.

While Congress enacted restrictions on abortion procedures, proabortion forces had some success in the judiciary. The Supreme Court anticipated several questions in *Roe v. Wade.* A footnote in the majority opinion indicated that questions about what rights a husband or a minor might have had not been raised in this case, so the Court need not now decide these issues.[24] Three years after *Roe,* the Supreme Court began refining its policy by addressing these and other issues.

One of the major cases came out of a challenge to several restrictive laws enacted in Missouri. Overturning several provisions of the law in question, the Court held that states could not require a woman to obtain her husband's consent (or parents' permission, in the instance of an unmarried minor) before having an abortion. Also, states could not proscribe the use of a particular method for abortions, nor could they require that physicians make an effort to save an aborted fetus as if the fetus were a premature baby (*Planned Parenthood of Central Missouri v. Danforth,* 1976). Three years later the Court ruled that minors may not be required to obtain the permission of a judicial officer prior to having an abortion (*Bellotti v. Baird,* 1979).

These decisions seemed to imply that states could not place limits on a woman's right to have an abortion. But the Court was not completely supportive of proabortion policies. In 1977 the Court held that states and municipalities could refuse to fund nontherapeutic abortions, even if they funded all other medical services (*Maher v. Roe,* 1977). And in 1980 the Court upheld by a five-to-four vote the constitutionality of the Hyde Amendment's prohibition of federal expenditures for elective abortions (*Harris v. McRae,* 1980). Justice Potter Stewart argued for the majority as follows:

> It simply does not follow that a woman's freedom of choice carries with it a constitutional entitlement to the financial resources to avail herself of the full range of protected choices.... Although government may not place obstacles in the path of a woman's exercise of her freedom of choice, it need not remove those not of its own creation. Indigency falls in the latter category.[25]

Because the operation of the Hyde Amendment had been enjoined pending the outcome of this suit, the effect of the Court's decision was almost immediate. The Department of Health and Human Services announced a fund cutoff date which, by their estimate, would reduce the projected number of federally funded abortions from 470,000 to less than 2,000 per year.[26] It appears, however, that there was a far smaller reduction in the actual number of abortions obtained by poor women.[27]

Following *Harris,* which was considered to be a victory for the antiabortion forces, the Court moved in 1983 to underscore its commitment to its original decision in *Roe v. Wade.* At issue were several sections of an Akron, Ohio, ordinance aimed at setting roadblocks to the provision and use of abortion services in that community. Items struck down by the Court included requirements that minors under the age of 15 obtain parental permission for an abortion, that women be informed in detail about fetal development and alternatives to abortion, that there be a 24-hour waiting period, and that fetal remains be given "humane" disposal (*Akron v. Akron Center for Reproductive Health*). Three justices—Sandra Day O'Connor, Byron White, and William Rehnquist—dissented in this case. However, at the same time the Court upheld a Missouri law requiring parental consent for "unemancipated" minors because there were detailed provisions for judicial approval of abortions where the lower court found that the minor was sufficiently mature to make this decision herself (*Planned Parenthood Association of Kansas City, Missouri v. Ashcroft*).

The embattled nature of the law and the Court in this area was perhaps best revealed by Justice Lewis Powell's majority opinion in the *Akron* case. In the opening paragraph of his opinion, Powell argued that *Roe* was now established law and that the doctrine of *stare decisis* ("let the decision stand," meaning that a precedent established in an earlier case is considered authoritative in the case at hand) required that the Court overturn the Akron ordinances, in spite of the continued arguments that the Court "erred in interpreting the Constitution." [28]

The continuing controversial nature of the abortion issue is also revealed in the general public's attitude on abortion. A Gallup poll on the abortion issue immediately prior to the Supreme Court's decision in 1973 found that 46 percent of the respondents favored permitting a woman "to go to a doctor to end pregnancy at any time during the first three months." Almost exactly the same percentage of the respondents, 45 percent, opposed granting such a right. [29] After the Court announced its decision, there was a slight jump in the proportion of the population favoring abortion, although the comparison is difficult to make precise because a different question was asked by the Gallup organization. However, a strong division in public opinion on abortion remained, as is indicated by the data in Table 1.1, which reports on another series of public opinion polls, conducted from 1972 to 1982. The question was whether a married woman should be permitted to obtain a legal abortion if she does not want any more children; as the table indicates, there was a jump in support

Table 1.1 Public Opinion Concerning Abortion (1972-1982)

Question: Please tell me whether or not you think it should be possible for a pregnant woman to obtain a legal abortion if she is married and does not want any more children.

Response	Year								
	1972	1973	1974	1975	1976	1977	1978	1980	1982
Yes	37.6%	46.9%	44.6%	43.6%	44.6%	44.0%	39.0%	45.2%	42.3%
No	57.1	50.5	50.5	51.9	52.0	51.5	57.8	50.7	49.1
Don't know/ no answer	5.3	3.4	4.9	4.3	3.5	4.5	3.2	4.2	4.6

Note: Columns may not total 100% due to rounding error.

Source: James A. Davis, *General Social Surveys, 1972-1982: Cumulative Codebook* (Chicago: National Opinion Research Center, 1982).

for abortions after the Court's decision in *Roe,* but thereafter public opinion has consistently remained sharply divided. Of course, Table 1.1 does not reflect the intensity with which the respondents held their views. It is generally believed that individuals opposed to abortion have the stronger feelings on the issue, which helps to explain their legislative successes.

In 1980 political conflict over abortion entered directly into the presidential campaign. While both Jimmy Carter and Ronald Reagan were personally opposed to abortion, their parties took opposing stands on the issue. The Republican platform recognized "differing views" on the abortion issue but supported a constitutional amendment "to restore protection of the right to life for unborn children." The platform also supported "congressional efforts to restrict the use of taxpayers' dollars for abortion." [30] The Democratic platform took the opposing point of view, expressing support for the 1973 decision "as the law of the land and opposing any constitutional amendment to restrict or overturn that decision." [31] Reagan's landslide victory— accompanied by a significant increase in the number of Republican representatives and the first Republican majority in the Senate in 26 years—gave renewed vigor to efforts to outlaw abortion. Senator Jesse Helms, R-N.C., introduced a measure by which Congress would declare that life begins at conception. He argued that such a law would undermine the logic of *Roe v. Wade,* which was premised on the belief that there was no consensus as to when life begins. Senator Orrin Hatch, R-Utah—chairman of the Senate Judiciary Committee, which considers constitutional amendments—pushed for an amendment that would give Congress and the states the power to regulate abortion or prohibit it altogether. (Hatch opposed abortion, but he felt that an amendment returning control to legislative bodies stood a better chance of being adopted than did one completely prohibiting abortion.) For various reasons, such as divisions within the antiabortionist ranks over strategy, the threat of a filibuster by senators favoring *Roe v. Wade,* and the press of other "Reagan reform" proposals, neither proposal passed. The opponents of abortion, however, are still very strong politically, and in the second decade after *Roe* it seems clear that the controversy it raised is not going to go away any time soon.

A MODEL OF THE IMPLEMENTATION
AND IMPACT OF JUDICIAL POLICIES

Chronicling the events that followed the Supreme Court's abortion decision gives some idea of the range of reactions and actors that may become involved in the implementation of a judicial decision. Similar case histories could be supplied for other court decisions. But our aim is not to study the aftermath of *every* judicial decision; instead, we want to make general statements about what has happened or may happen after *any* judicial decision. That is, we hope to move away from idiosyncratic, case-by-case or policy-by-policy analyses toward a general theoretical understanding of the events that may follow a judicial decision. The remainder of this book is devoted to explaining the responses one may encounter to any given judicial decision—who may react to the decisions and how; what types of reactions may occur; and what effects those reactions may have on the implementation of the judicial policy.

The first step in understanding any political process is to develop a conceptual foundation upon which explanations may be built. We will organize our presentation of what happens after a court decision around two major elements: the *actors* who may respond to the decision and the *responses* that these actors may make. Focusing on these two elements enables us to define more precisely who is reacting and how. In studying the responses to judicial policies we describe and attempt to explain the *behavior* following a court decision—specifically, what the behavior is, its antecedents, and its consequences. Hence, when we discuss "impact," we are describing general reactions following a judicial decision. When we discuss "implementation," we are describing the behavior of lower courts, government agencies, or other affected parties as it relates to enforcing a judicial

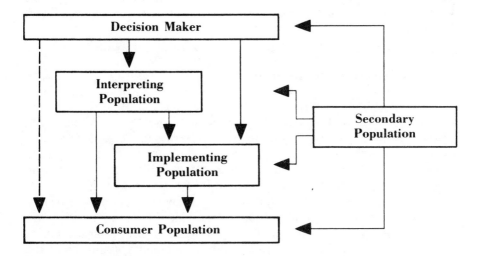

Figure 1.1 Populations and lines of communication involved in the implementation and impact of judicial policies. (Adapted from Charles A. Johnson, "The Implementation and Impact of Judicial Policies: A Heuristic Model," in *Public Law and Public Policy*, ed. John A. Gardiner [New York: Praeger, 1977], 107-126, with permission of the publisher.)

decision. When we discuss what many would call "compliance/noncompliance" or "evasion," we are describing behavior that is in some way consistent or inconsistent with the behavioral requirements of the judicial decision.

Figure 1.1 presents a schematic diagram of the different sets of actors, referred to as *populations,* that may respond to a judicial policy.[32] The organization of these populations is essentially a functional one, in which their roles in shaping the impact of judicial decisions and their influence on the ultimate impact of judicial policy differ. In addition to the four populations, Figure 1.1 also presents two broadly defined categories of responses in the response process: (1) acceptance decisions, which include attitude changes or nonchanges, and (2) behavioral responses, which include responses to the decision in terms of maintaining or changing policies and informal norms, as well as other types of actions. These include what is often termed *feedback behavior*—actions directed at the judiciary or other policy makers in the system and designed to alter or reinforce the judicial decision. We now turn to a discussion of these populations and their responses, illustrated with examples drawn from the events after the Supreme Court's abortion decision as well as other recent Supreme Court decisions.

The Interpreting Population

For any appellate court decision, the actor most often charged with responding to a decision is a particular lower court, often a trial court. Moreover, in our common law system many appellate court decisions become policies used in deciding future cases. In a general sense, therefore, a higher court's policy affects all lower courts within its jurisdiction. This set of courts (and in some instances government officials such as attorneys general) is known as the *interpreting population.* The interpreting population, as the name implies, responds to the policy decisions of a higher court by refining the policy announced by the higher court. Such refinements could have the effect of enlarging or of limiting the original policy. This population, in other words, interprets the meaning of the policy and develops the rules for matters not addressed in the original decision. Of course, all populations must "interpret" the decision in order to react to it. Interpretations of lower courts, however, are distinguished from the interpretations of others since theirs are viewed as authoritative in a legal sense by others in the political system. Hence, this population provides "official" interpretations of a court policy applicable to the other populations under their jurisdiction.

The Supreme Court's abortion decision launched the judiciary into a new area of the law, which required considerable refining before complete implementation. Shortly after the decision was announced, lower state and federal courts began hearing cases presenting issues that had not been directly addressed in the *Roe* or *Doe* opinions. In Florida, for example, the issue of a father's rights were raised by a father who brought legal action to restrain the mother of his unborn child from obtaining an abortion. The lower court denied relief and the Florida Supreme Court affirmed that decision, arguing that the Supreme Court's abortion decision was based on the mother's "right of privacy" (*Jones v. Smith,* 1973). The decision to terminate a pregnancy was, therefore, purely the right of the mother and could not be subject to interference by the state or private individuals.

Meanwhile, in Arizona, another matter was before the courts. Arizona law prohibited the advertisement of any medicine or procedures that facilitated abortions. New Times, Inc., a local publisher, was convicted under this statute and appealed to the state supreme court. The conviction was reversed, since the Arizona abortion statutes were found to be similar to the Texas statute struck down in *Roe v. Wade,* even though the issue before the court was different from that decided in the original abortion cases (*State v. New Times, Inc.,* 1973).

In each of these instances the issue before the court had not been addressed directly in the original decision. Consistent with the common law tradition, the lower courts had the responsibility of making authoritative interpretations of policy in light of the original Supreme Court decision. In their interpretations these courts could limit the application of the original policy, as did the Arizona trial court in convicting the publisher, or could facilitate its implementation, as did the Florida courts. Chapter 2 describes and offers explanations for the reactions of lower courts (and occasionally other agencies) that authoritatively interpret judicial decisions.

The Implementing Population

The lower courts usually apply a higher court's policy only in cases coming before them. Higher court policies and their interpretation by lower courts quite often affect a wider set of actors. We refer to this set of actors as the *implementing population.* In most instances, this population is made up of authorities whose behavior may be reinforced or sanctioned by the interpreting population. The implementing population usually performs a policing or servicing function in the political system—that is, implementors apply the system's rules to persons subject to their authority. Prominent examples of this population are police officers, prosecutors, university and public school officials, and welfare and social security workers. In many instances, the original policy and subsequent interpretations by lower courts are intended to set parameters on the behavior of the implementing population. A clear example of this activity involves decisions concerning police behavior with regard to the rights of criminal suspects.

Occasionally, the implementing population is composed of private individuals or institutions. This is the case when services provided by private concerns are the subject of a judicial policy. The best example of such a circumstance involves the Supreme Court's abortion decision, for which physicians and hospitals were the actual implementors. When the implementing population falls into this private classification they are usually under a different obligation from most public implementing populations. In the case of public implementing agencies, the court ordinarily *requires* that the agencies change behavior, stop a particular type of service, or provide some new service. Such was the obligation for school systems with regard to *Brown v. Board of Education* and the police with regard to *Miranda v. Arizona* (1966) and *Mapp v. Ohio* (1961). On the other hand, when private concerns are the implementing population, the compulsion to act affirmatively is substantially weaker, if it exists at all. For example, the abortion decision gave women the right to an abortion; hospitals could provide abortions, but hospitals and physicians were not obliged to provide abortion services against their will. Thus, affirmative action implementing a judicial policy by private implementing groups is most often voluntary.

The implementing population may vary from decision to decision. For criminal justice decisions, prosecutors, police officers, and defense attorneys are the primary implementors. For school prayer or busing decisions, the implementors are largely public school officials. Reapportionment decisions usually involve legislators as the implementing population. When judicial decisions require no action by government agencies, nongovernmental service agencies may implement decisions; alternatively, there may be no implementing population at all. As we mentioned in our earlier discussion, hospitals and individual physicians composed the primary implementing population for the abortion decision, although few of those capable of implementing the abortion decision actually did so by offering abortion services. And in a case such as *New York Times Co. v. Sullivan* (1964), which significantly decreased the applicability of libel law to public officials, there is no implementing population.

The degree to which a court decision actually benefits those it was intended to benefit depends on the actors and institutions who police the activities or provide the services called for in the decision. Women in communities where there were no physicians or hospitals willing to provide abortion services were effectively denied their newly granted right or were forced to go elsewhere to benefit from the judicial policy. As another example, where school officials sanctioned prayers after 1963, they often persisted for years.[33]

The reactions of various implementing populations to judicial policies have been extensively studied by social scientists and legal scholars. The results of these studies provide a basis for our discussion of implementing populations in Chapter 3.

The Consumer Population

Those for whom the policies are set forth by the court are identified as the *consumer population*. This population is the set of individuals (usually not affiliated with the government) who would or should receive benefits or suffer disabilities as a result of a judicial decision; that is, they gain or lose desired rights or resources. Criminal suspects, for example, benefit from judicial policies announced by the Supreme Court in *Miranda,* and black students in newly desegregated schools benefit from the *Brown* decision. In other instances, some consumer populations may not benefit from a judicial policy. For example, juvenile court defendants suffer from not being extended the right of trial by jury; stockholders may suffer when their corporation is split up as a result of an anti-trust ruling. And there are decisions under which members of the consumer population may either benefit or suffer, depending on their attitudes toward the policy. Under the *Schempp* decision on prayer in public schools, children who want to pray in public school suffer limitations and children who do not want to pray there gain benefits.

The consumer population, depending on the policy involved, may include the entire population of the political system, as with judicial decisions concerning general tax legislation. On the other hand, a very limited population may be directly involved, such as criminal suspects under arrest. When the policy affects a specific sector but supposedly is for the public good (for example, antitrust decisions), a distinction between direct and indirect consumption must sometimes be made.

Specifying the consumer population exactly may be troublesome in some cases. For example, few would dispute that women with unwanted pregnancies are the consumers for the Supreme Court's abortion decision. Those opposed to abortion would likely argue that unborn children are also consumers and receive negative benefits from the abortion decision. Others might argue that fathers of unborn children or parents of underaged, pregnant girls are part of the consumer population.

In studying the reactions of consumers to judicial policies, several questions need to be addressed. Do the potential consumers of a judicial policy know of the policy? If they know of the policy, why and how do they modify their attitudes or behavior because of it? What effect, if any, does the policy have on the attitudes and behavior of the consumer with regard to the judiciary or other political institutions? These questions and the issue of who may be identified as a member of the consumer population will be considered in Chapter 4.

The Secondary Population

The populations we have discussed so far are those directly affected by a judicial policy or its implementation. The *secondary population* is a residual one. It consists of everyone who is not in the interpreting, implementing, or consumer population. Members of the secondary population are not directly affected by a judicial policy; however, some may react to a policy or its implementation. This reaction usually takes the form of some type of feedback directed toward the original policy maker, another policy maker, the implementing population, or the consumer population.

The secondary population may be divided into four subpopulations: government officials, interest groups, the media, and the public at large. First, there are *government officials.* This subpopulation includes legislators and executive officers who are not immediately affected by the decision. Though usually unaffected directly, these individuals are often in a position to support or hinder the implementation of the original policy. This subpopulation is distinguished from other secondary subpopulations in that its members have direct, legitimate authority in the political system, and they are often the recipients of political pressure from the public. The second subpopulation is *interest groups,* which are often activated by court policies even when they are not directly affected by them. Subsequent actions by these groups may facilitate or block effective implementation of the judicial policy. The third subpopulation is the *media,* which communicate the substance of judicial policies to potentially affected populations. Included here are general and specialized media, which may affect implementation by editorial stance or simply by the way of reporting judicial policies. Media attention to a policy, descriptions of reactions to it, and support or criticism of it can play a large role in determining the amount and direction of feedback behavior. The fourth subpopulation consists of members of the *public at large,* insofar as they do not fall within the consumer population. The most important segment of this subpopulation is attentive citizens—those who are most aware of a judicial policy. This segment includes individuals who may be related to the consumer population (for example, parents of students affected by school prayer decisions), politically active individuals (for example, political party workers), and perhaps knowledgeable or alert individuals.

For the Supreme Court's abortion decision, the secondary population is large and quite varied. Recall from our chronicle of the events following *Roe* that although there were apparently some minor moves in public opinion regarding abortions, most of the reaction came from interest groups and government officials. As to the former, existing institutions or groups such as the Catholic church and many Protestant denominations vigorously denounced the decision, while organizations such as Planned Parenthood, the National Organization for Women, and the American Civil Liberties Union supported it. New groups on both sides devoted solely to the abortion issue also developed quickly. The efforts of these groups produced additional litigation, intensive lobbying, electoral maneuvering, and attempts to mobilize public opinion. Government officials also reacted to the abortion decision by passing restrictive laws, issuing restrictive orders, or, in a few cases, adopting policies that provided opportunities for women to obtain abortions. A fundamental issue for some government officials after *Roe* was whether the government should aid in the implementation of the policy by funding the abortions of poor women. With the eventual approval of the Supreme Court, Congress and several states restricted funding for elective abortions for poor women.

Legislative and executive officials may have considerable influence on the implementation of a judicial policy, even though they are not members of the implementing population (that is, they do not provide policing or implementing services). Legislatures, for instance, may be generous or stinting in appropriating money to carry out a policy, as in funding legal services for the poor. The president and state governors may use their appointing authority to select officials with power over members of the implementing population; or they may use their personal or official influence to encourage either maximum or minimum cooperation in the implementing process, as well as to mobilize public opinion. The reactions of secondary populations and how they may influence the implementation of judicial decisions are considered in Chapter 5.

Fluidity and Linkage among Populations

The basis for the foregoing classification of populations is primarily functional. We may, therefore, on some occasions find that particular individuals are members of different populations in different circumstances. For example, it is entirely possible for an attorney general to be an interpreter for one judicial policy and an implementor for another. In the former instance, the attorney general would be issuing an authoritative, legally binding statement interpreting a judicial decision; in the latter instance, the attorney general would be charged with the responsibility of applying a judicial policy to some consumer population or of carrying out some order of the court. It is also possible that courts as members of the interpreting population may occasionally be in a position to direct the implementation of judicial policy. Such may be the case when a judge takes direct charge of the implementation of a school desegregation order, as happened in Boston in the 1970s. Teachers are implementors of the prayer decision and consumers of decisions affecting funding levels of public schools. Obviously, private citizens are in both consumer and secondary populations, depending on the nature of the judicial policy.

Attorneys constitute a special set of participants whose function may vary from one setting to another. By and large, this subpopulation is composed of lawyers who practice before various judicial bodies. These attorneys may insist that other participants follow or implement rules promulgated by a higher court. When they assert the rights of criminal suspects or protect citizens whose constitutional rights have been violated, attorneys are playing a role as quasi-members of the implementing population.

Perhaps even more often, attorneys are called upon to give their interpretations of judicial policies for potential consumers, implementing groups, and, occasionally, secondary groups such as interested citizens or legislative bodies. Such interpretations are not official like those of the interpreting population; however, on many occasions these interpretations are likely to be final, since paying clients assume that the attorneys give a reasoned and fair interpretation of a court decision. Unfortunately, we have no way of knowing how frequently attorneys are called upon to intrepret judicial decisions or how frequently their interpretations are accepted and effectively become final, but it is reasonable to assume that such interpretations play an important role in accounting for the reactions of others to judicial policies. Attorneys also serve as interpreters of judicial policies for courts themselves. Because judges cannot read and interpret all higher court policies, they frequently rely on attorneys' briefs to inform them of relevant cases and, sometimes, rival interpretations of those cases.

In a broad sense, attorneys performing these functions serve as linkages between various populations. They provide a link for the communication of decisions downward from higher courts to relevant actors as well as being unofficial interpreters of these decisions. Their linkage activities may also prompt new litigation or feedback to the courts or other agencies, which, in turn, may affect the implementation of a decision.

Acceptance Decisions and Behavioral Responses

We are interested in the responses to judicial policies by all of the populations identified above. We may observe a large variety of responses to judicial decisions, so precise distinctions are difficult to make. Nonetheless, we believe two general categories of responses are captured in the concepts of acceptance decisions and behavioral responses.

The *acceptance decision* involves psychological reactions to a judicial policy, which may be generalized in terms of accepting or rejecting the policy. The acceptance decision is shaped by several psychological dimensions: intensity of attitude, regard for the policy-making court, perceptions of the consequences of the decision, and the respondent's own role in society.

The intensity of a person's *attitude toward the policy* prior to the court's decision can be important. Most white southerners, for example, were extremely hostile toward policies of racial integration before *Brown;* thus their unwillingness to accept the decision was not surprising. Many people had similarly intense attitudes about abortion and about prayers in the public schools. Many blacks, feminists, and civil libertarians, respectively, had equally intense attitudes in favor of these policies. For most policies, though, feelings are not so intense. Few people feel strongly about such issues as the size and composition of juries, new doctrines in libel law, or the application of the First Amendment guarantees to commercial advertising. In such instances the acceptance decision is less likely to be governed by prior attitudes.

Another dimension involves *regard for the court* making the decision. People who view the Supreme Court favorably may be more inclined to accept a decision as legitimate and proper. Those who generally view the Court negatively or who believe it has usurped too much authority may transfer these views to particular decisions that the Court makes.

A third dimension relates to a person's *perception of the consequences* of a decision. Those who may not quarrel with a decision in the abstract but believe it will have a serious and detrimental effect on society may be reluctant to accept it. In the 1950s, for example, many citizens feared that the Supreme Court's decisions granting due process to suspected subversives dismissed from government employment would aid the spread of Communism;

more recently, many people were disturbed about the exclusion of illegally seized evidence from criminal trials, fearing that criminals might often go without punishment.

Finally, acceptance decisions are shaped by a *person's own role in society.* An ambitious judge or attorney general may be reluctant to accept (publicly, at least) an unpopular judicial policy for fear that it will harm his or her career. Corporate officers or citizens may be unwilling to accept a decision if they think it will reduce their profits or cause them great inconvenience. Conversely, people may accept quite willingly decisions that are popular with the public or that bring them financial or other benefits.

Behavioral responses involve reactions that may be seen or recorded and that may determine the extent to which a court policy is actually realized. These responses are often closely linked to acceptance decisions. Persons who do not accept a judicial policy are likely to engage in behavior designed to defeat the policy or minimize its impact. They will interpret it narrowly, try to avoid implementing it, and refuse or evade its consumption. Those who accept a policy are likely to be more faithful or even enthusiastic in interpreting, implementing, and consuming it. Of course, nonacceptors may not always be in a position to ignore a decision or refuse completely to comply with it. Some behavioral responses may be adjusted to meet the decision's requirements while other, less visible, behavioral responses may more truly reflect their unwillingness to accept the decision. Conversely, acceptors may for reasons of inertia never fully adjust their behavioral responses to a new judicial policy.

Policy changes concern changes in rules, formal norms within an organization, or even informal rules regarding behavior within an organization. Police departments may, for example, adopt formal policies against illegal searches, but may informally wink at violations. Schools may devise strategies to comply with the letter but not the spirit of the Supreme Court's school prayer decision in *Schempp.* Policy changes may also include changes in organizational structure or function. As indicated previously, the delivery of health care services related to abortion changed after *Roe v. Wade* to the extent that currently most abortion services are provided by clinics, not hospitals.

Another dimension of behavioral responses is the activities involved in carrying out the policy. These actions by interpreting and implementing populations may benefit or disadvantage the consumer population; in turn, the consumer population may respond by using, ignoring, or avoiding the policy. (The behavioral responses of the secondary population are usually manifest in the form of feedback behavior, which is discussed below.) We must examine these actions, in addition to such formal responses as written policies, because written policies sometimes bear little relation to a population's behavior.

Feedback behavior is another behavioral response to a judicial policy. It is directed toward the originator of the policy or some other policy-making agency. The purpose of feedback behavior is usually to provide support for or make demands upon other political institutions regarding the judicial policy. Almost immediately after the Supreme Court announced its abortion decision, feedback in the form of letters to the justices began. Also, some members of Congress let the Court know of their displeasure with the abortion decision by introducing amendments to the Constitution to overturn *Roe.* Frequent manifestations of displeasure, as well as some of support, by various interest groups have been directed at the Court and other political institutions, such as Congress and state legislatures. In varying degrees, these attempts at feedback have led to modifications of the policy—as we can see in the Court's approval of the Hyde Amendment passed by Congress, which terminated federal payment for abortions for poor women.

SUMMARY

In this chapter we have introduced the notion that judicial decisions are not self-implementing; courts must frequently rely on other courts or on nonjudicial actors in the political system to turn law into action. Moreover, the implementation of judicial decisions is a political process; the actors upon whom courts must rely to translate law into action are usually *political* actors and are subject to political pressures as they allocate resources to implement a judicial decision. The events and actors following the Supreme Court's 1973 abortion decisions illustrate the initial premises underlying the remainder of this book.

NOTES

1. Michael Lipsky, "Implementation on Its Head," in *American Politics and Public Policy,* ed. Walter Burnham and Martha Weinberg (Cambridge, Mass.: MIT Press, 1978), 390-402, as cited in Robert T. Nakamura and Frank Smallwood, *The Politics of Policy Implementation* (New York: St. Martins Press, 1980), 19.

2. Bob Woodward and Scott Armstrong, *The Brethren: Inside the Supreme Court* (New York: Simon and Schuster, 1979).
3. *Roe v. Wade,* 410 U.S. 113 (1973) at 164-165.
4. See, for example, "Abortion on Demand," *Time,* January 29, 1973, 46-47.
5. Woodward and Armstrong, *The Brethren,* 238-239.
6. "Cardinals Shocked—Reaction Mixed," *New York Times,* January 23, 1973, 1, 20.
7. Woodward and Armstrong, *The Brethren,* 240. The authors may have been in error reporting this incident, since "Mary Doe" challenged the Georgia abortion statute, not the Texas statute.
8. David Loomis, "Abortion: Should Constitution Be Amended?" *Congressional Quarterly Weekly Report,* May 3, 1975, 919.
9. Alan Guttmacher Institute, *Abortion 1974-1975: Need and Services in the United States* (New York: Planned Parenthood Federation of America, 1976).
10. Alan Guttmacher Institute, *Abortion 1975* (New York: Planned Parenthood Federation of America, 1975), 62.
11. Jon R. Bond and Charles A. Johnson, "Implementing a Permissive Policy: Hospital Abortion Services after *Roe v. Wade,*" *American Journal of Political Science* 26 (February 1982): 1-24.
12. Alan Guttmacher Institute, *Abortion 1975,* 62.
13. Ibid., 11.
14. Charles A. Johnson and Jon R. Bond, "Coercive and Noncoercive Abortion Deterrence Policies: A Comparative State Analysis," *Law and Policy Quarterly* 2 (January 1980): 106-128.
15. "Abortion and the Law," *Newsweek,* March 3, 1975, 18-30.
16. Ibid., 18.
17. Willard Cates, Jr., "Legal Abortion: The Public Health Record," *Science* 215 (1982): 1586-1590.
18. Ellen Sullivan, Christopher Tietze, and Joy G. Dryfoos, "Legal Abortion in the United States, 1975-1976," *Family Planning Perspectives* 9 (May/June 1977).
19. "Abortion Foes Look to Ultimate Victory," *New York Times,* June 19, 1977, 24.
20. "Carter's Appointees Who Opposed Him on Abortion Hailed," *New York Times,* August 16, 1977, 31.
21. United States Commission on Civil Rights, *Constitutional Aspects of the Right to Limit Childbearing: A Report of the United States Commission on Civil Rights* (April 1975), 101.
22. Matt Pinkus, "Carter's Narrow Victory Brings Electoral College under Renewed Scrutiny," *Congressional Quarterly Weekly Report,* December 18, 1976, 3330.
23. For a history of this legislation see Peg O'Hara, "Congress and the Hyde Amendment," *Congressional Quarterly Weekly Report,* April 19, 1980, 1038-1039.
24. *Roe v. Wade,* 410 U.S. 113 (1973) at 165, n. 67.
25. *Harris v. McRae,* 448 U.S. 297 (1980) at 316.
26. Harrison Donnelley, "Decision Seen Generating More Politics Than New Laws," *Congressional Quarterly Weekly Report,* July 5, 1980, 1863.

27. "Curbs on Medicaid Abortions Found Not to Deter the Poor," *New York Times,* September 4, 1981, 1.
28. *Akron v. Akron Center for Reproductive Health,* 103 Sup.Ct. 2481 (1983) at 2487.
29. George Gallup, *The Gallup Poll: Public Opinion 1972-1977* (Wilmington, Del.: Scholarly Resources, 1978), 94.
30. Donald Bruce Johnson, *National Party Platforms, 1840-1976,* 1980 supp. (Urbana: University of Illinois Press, 1982), 183.
31. Ibid., 47.
32. This model is drawn from Charles A. Johnson, "The Implementation and Impact of Judicial Policies: A Heuristic Model," in *Public Law and Public Policy,* ed. John A. Gardiner (New York: Praeger, 1977), 107-126.
33. Kenneth M. Dolbeare and Phillip E. Hammond, *The School Prayer Decisions: From Court Policy to Local Practice* (Chicago: University of Chicago Press, 1971).

CHAPTER TWO

The Interpreting Population

I mportant policy announcements almost always require interpretation by someone other than the policy maker. Only occasionally may a policy be so simple and straightforward that no additional interpretation is required; "Keep off the grass" is a policy that requires little or no interpretation. Most policies, however, have greater scope and sophistication. They are made to govern society or large institutions within it and often focus on complex and perhaps interrelated circumstances. Sometimes such policies cannot easily be applied to local situations or unanticipated events, and the policy-making person or organization is rarely available for an immediate interpretation. Other persons, then, must interpret the policy in question, at least temporarily.

This chapter focuses on the population that interprets judicial policy. The actions of this population are the first link in the chain of events that gives a judicial decision its impact. Members of other populations, particularly the implementing population, look to the interpreting population for guidance and are often subject to authoritative commands by the interpreting population. Quite often it is only after this population has interpreted a particular policy that the other populations feel that they are free to—or that it is necessary for them to—implement, consume, or react to a judicial decision.

The interpreting population is readily identifiable and remains quite stable from one judicial policy to another. (As we will show in subsequent chapters, these characteristics do not pertain to the other populations.) Broadly speaking, the interpreting population is composed of those persons whose regular function in society is telling others what judicial decisions mean. Lawyers who interpret a decision for their clients are in this category—especially if the clients act upon the advice and do not go to court. Attorneys general and other officials who regularly interpret court decisions are also included. And, of course, so are judges.

Judges are the heart of the interpreting population. Judges' interpretations—unlike those of lawyers, attorneys general, and others—are authoritative, that is, they must be obeyed under threat of penalty; they are not merely a form of advice. (Occasionally, state attorneys general can issue interpretations that are legally binding unless overruled by a court. For example, Michigan's attorney general recently nullified the state's ban on advertising brands and prices of alcoholic beverages after finding that it violated the U.S. Supreme Court's decisions extending First Amendment protection to commercial speech.) [1] Because of the special interpretive status of judges and because there is virtually no literature about how interpretations by nonjudges affect the impact of decisions, we will focus on judges in this chapter. We will not distinguish between trial and appellate judges, since all (except for the justices on the U.S. Supreme Court) must interpret the decisions of higher courts.

It will be useful to review briefly the structure of courts in the United States. (A simplified diagram is shown in Figure 2.1.) Bear in mind that this is a very simple description of the system; the particular titles of the courts are not as important as their functions relative to each other, and, in fact, courts with similar names in different states may have generally different jurisdictions. The judicial hierarchy is divided between federal and state courts and between appellate and trial courts; there are two levels of appellate courts for the federal level and for about half the states. It is possible for a case originating in a state trial court of general jurisdiction to go through as many as three appeals. State supreme court decisions regarding state statutes or common law are final, except where a federal question is involved; then a case will go from a state supreme court to the U.S. Supreme Court—the ultimate judicial policy maker. Any court to which a case is appealed is a higher court for that case; thus an appellate court may be sometimes designated a higher court (in relation to a trial court, for example) and sometimes a lower court (in relation to another appellate court or to a supreme court). We are most interested here in the interpretation by a lower court of a higher court's policy; we have not attempted to describe such matters as the U.S. Supreme Court's original jurisdiction, the transfer of cases from state to federal courts, state courts that have both trial and appellate

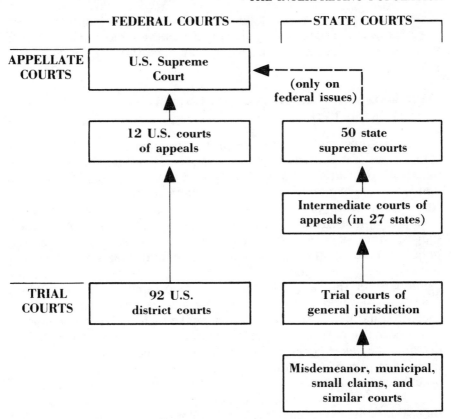

Figure 2.1 Simplified diagram of American court system.

functions, courts with special subject-matter jurisdiction, and exceptions to the ordinary route of appeals.[2]

Once a case is decided by the state supreme court or the U.S. Supreme Court, a policy has been made. All courts lower in the hierarchy must attempt to apply the policy to relevant cases, interpreting the policy as necessary to fit the circumstances at hand. The process most often starts in the first trial court a case is brought to; the trial court judge must make an initial interpretation and transmit the policy to interested persons outside the judicial hierarchy, particularly lawyers and litigants. Each appellate court in turn interprets the policies of higher courts and transmits policies to lower courts.

In this chapter we first discuss some of the reasons lower court judges must interpret higher court policy. Next, we turn to an analysis of the freedoms of and limitations on lower court judges who must interpret higher court policies. Finally, we consider research concerning the responses of judges and look at some explanations of why judges respond as they do when they must interpret higher court policies.

WHY AND WHEN JUDICIAL POLICIES MUST BE INTERPRETED

Judicial policies require interpretation under a variety of circumstances and for a variety of reasons. Some policies (for example, antitrust and labor relations laws) are by nature complex. The opinions—the explanations that accompany court decisions— written for certain cases involve very sophisticated reasoning. Moreover, because opinions usually come from an appellate court with several judges, vague phrases may be used to cover differences between the judges. Some opinions may require interpretation or elaboration because one or more controversial implications of the decision are not dealt with in the original opinion. Indeed, since judicial opinions usually occur as a result of a dispute between two parties over a specific situation, most court opinions make little effort to announce a comprehensive policy. But even if the opinion does more than settle a dispute, the decision and opinion do not stand alone. Rather, the decision is part of a broader policy and thus must be enmeshed with other decisions, ones that may have different outcomes and rationales.

One of the major reasons judicial policies must be interpreted is that situations arise that were not contemplated by the higher court when the original policy was announced. It simply may not be clear how a policy should be applied to new technological developments, legislation, or social trends. Lower court judges could, for example, be called upon to decide whether a Supreme Court decision upholding a moratorium on mortgage payments announced during the depression of the 1930s (*Home Building & Loan Association v. Blaisdell,* 1934) applies to more prosperous times. Or in the near future, lower court judges will probably have to decide whether the decision permitting the patenting of genetically engineered microorganisms (*Diamond v. Chakrabarty,* 1980) means that more advanced life forms may be patented.

Further interpretation is needed when a higher court announces a policy that either opens a new area of the law or changes previous policies. The *Diamond* case mentioned above is an example of the former situation; the switch in policy announced in the *Mapp v. Ohio* (1961) decision provides a good illustration of the latter situation. The *Mapp* decision applied the exclusionary rule to state action, thus requiring state courts to enforce the constitutional prohibition against unreasonable search and seizure by the police. After 1961 many state courts quickly developed interpretations of *Mapp* for a variety of search and seizure situations. As we will discuss later in the chapter, the state supreme courts frequently diverged in their interpretation of the requirements of *Mapp.* Thus, the circumstances under which citizens enjoyed the protection of *Mapp* varied from one state to another.

FREEDOM AND CONSTRAINTS IN INTERPRETING JUDICIAL DECISIONS

Infrequency of Appeals

As in any hierarchical organization, a lower court's interpretation is subject to modification or reversal by the policy-making court. But, for several reasons, reversal does not happen very often. First, losing parties in the lower court often lack the resources or optimism to appeal. Only a small percentage of state trial court decisions are appealed; the proportion is greater at the federal level, but here, too, many parties accept the initial decision. Second, even if the loser appeals, the policy-making court may not want to hear the case. The U.S. Supreme Court and the majority of state supreme courts can pick and choose what cases they review. About 6,000 losing parties, for instance, ask the Supreme Court to review their cases every year; the Court does so for about 250 of them. In the remaining cases, the lower court decisions, many of which have interpreted Supreme Court policy, become final. Third, occasionally the situation producing the legal dispute ends (or becomes *moot,* in legal terminology) before an appeal can occur; thus the lower court's interpretation becomes the effective one. Lower court decisions enjoining or allowing political or racial parades or protests fall into this category. In 1963, for instance, a Birmingham, Alabama, trial judge banned the Reverend Martin Luther King, Jr.'s, Easter Day antisegregation parade. Four years later the Supreme Court said that the trial judge's interpretation of the Court's First Amendment policies had been erroneous; but the Court could hardly restore the enjoined parade (*Walker v. City of Birmingham,* 1967). A planned American Nazi party march through heavily Jewish Skokie, Illinois, was similarly thwarted by local judges in 1976.

Thus, most lower court interpretations of high court policies, rather than being steps on the way to final decisions, are often the final decisions themselves. Only in cases that involve important issues with rather widespread application is there a serious likelihood of review by the policy-making court.

Weakness of Removal Power

In most bureaucracies, the ultimate constraint on a defiant subordinate is the possibility of losing his or her job. Supervisors tolerate modest deviation from their policies because some latitude is inherent in the system, but they can always insist on obedience when the deviation becomes unacceptable.

In the judiciary, however, the primary mechanism for controlling subordinates is not the removal power. Policy-making courts seldom have the legal authority to dismiss lower court judges. The latter are elected or appointed for set terms and can be removed only by the legislative branch through the ponderous process of impeachment. In the federal system, the removal of a judge by impeachment has occurred only four times, the last in 1936. But no adequate substitute for impeachment has been developed (see *Chandler v. 10th Circuit Judicial Council,* 1970).

Successful impeachment is almost as rare at the state level as at the federal level. To make judicial discipline more efficient, several states have made constitutional changes permitting the state supreme court or a judicial removal commission to suspend or remove judges. Impeachment or removal issues usually involve a judge's corruption or untoward behavior rather than his or her misinterpretation of higher court decisions. Of course, in many states judges can be removed by defeat at the polls, or in some states even by a recall election. But it would be unseemly and violate judicial ethics for a state supreme court to advocate defeat of a trial judge or sponsor a recall election because of resistance to its policies. Moreover, a local judge's deviant interpretations may well be quite popular with his or her constituents.

In short, unlike a bureaucracy, a policy-making court cannot easily remove a lower court judge who is stubborn about adhering to an unwarranted interpretation of its policy. The higher court, can, of course, reverse a lower court's interpretation, provided that the losing party appeals. If the lower court judge remains stubborn, the higher court can enforce its will through a *writ of mandamus* (a directive from a higher court to a lower court carrying a contempt penalty for noncompliance). The Supreme Court has twice threatened lower court judges with this writ in recent years (*United States v. Haley,* 1962; *In re Herndon,* 1969).

Professionalism and Legal Obligation

While higher courts cannot dismiss lower court judges and generally must rely on the voluntary adherence of lower court judges in their interpretive activities, there are other factors pushing judges toward a conscientious interpretation of higher court policies. One important factor is professionalism. A judge is selected, ostensibly at least, because of his or her outstanding understanding of the law. The expectation of legal competence is reinforced in various ways. For a judge to write an opinion that is poorly researched or reasoned or that patently misinterprets a higher court policy would undermine the judge's self-image as well as his or her reputation among other judges. In other words, judges become concerned about their evaluation as professionals—about the respect of lawyers and other judges with whom they interact. Moreover, when the decisions are published, the judge knows that his or her interpretation of relevant precedents will be subject to scrutiny from distant fellow judges as well as from lawyers and commentators in legal journals around the nation. Nearly all decisions are published from U.S. courts of appeals, state supreme courts, and intermediate courts of appeals in states that have them. Even many trial court opinions for important cases in federal and state courts are published nationally. The published opinion lies at the heart of judges' professionalism; it is where they demonstrate their professional skills by fashioning a well-reasoned opinion. A central aspect of this professionalism is rendering an honest interpretation of the law as handed down by a higher court.

One indication of a judge's high level of professionalism is the relatively low frequency with which his or her decisions are reversed. While all judges suffer reversals on occasion, frequent reversal is usually seen as a sign by the bench and the bar that the judge either cannot or will not meet professional standards. Not only can such a perception undermine a judge's reputation, it can preclude opportunities for career advancement. One of the most telling criticisms of G. Harrold Carswell, whom then President Richard Nixon nominated to a vacant Supreme Court seat in 1971, was the extremely high reversal rate Carswell had as a U.S. district judge in Florida. His nomination was rejected by the Senate. Ordinarily, judges with abnormal reversal rates are "shot down" before the nomination stage, often due to information provided by bar association committees.

Not just fellow judges but also others in the political system expect judges to interpret higher court policy fairly and without bias. Judges are isolated and deliberately protected from the pressures of interest groups. When appearing in court, judges wear special

35

garments and are accorded clear physical and verbal symbols of deference. In addition, societal and legal norms drastically restrict contact with judges concerning pending litigation. All communications must occur in standard legal forms (pleadings, briefs, oral arguments, and so on), available to the opposing party for rebuttal and substantively limited to legally relevant facts and arguments. Resorting to back-room pleas or special information is strictly forbidden; violations of the norm against such contacts lead to a contempt-of-court citation. In other words, the need for judges to follow existing legal policy is strongly encouraged, and society strives to reinforce their sense of professionalism by protecting judges against daily reminders of the political and social interests that bear on their decisions.

In recognition of the fact that they must decide cases according to the law, all judges take an oath to support the Constitution; state judges are also bound to support the constitution of their home state. Although there was some debate in the early years of the Republic, it is now universally understood that the U.S. Supreme Court is the final authoritative interpreter of the meaning of the U.S. Constitution. Likewise, state supreme courts have the final authority in interpreting state constitutions. Thus, judges are bound by their oaths of office to abide by the policies of these higher courts insofar as they stem from constitutional interpretation. This sense of duty can be a powerful reinforcement to a judge who is formulating a decision that goes against social or political pressures—or even against his or her own better judgment.

Comments by a Pennsylvania federal judge explaining his decision to prohibit religious exercises in the local public schools illustrate the impact of role expectations: "It may be elucidating and inspirational to have Bible readings and prayer recitations in school, and it may well be what an overwhelming majority of the pupils and parents in the school district desire. I may even agree that it would be most beneficial to the student to have these exercises, but I can do nothing more than observe the dictates of our law as interpreted by the United States Supreme Court." [3]

Indeed, professionalism and legal obligation can often be used to deflect hostility from a lower court judge who applies an unpopular judicial policy. State judges in eastern Kentucky, for example, must sometimes apply the Kentucky Supreme Court's "broad form" mineral deed interpretation, which often permits the strip mining of coal over the objections of owners of the surface land. As one judge said:

I go to great lengths to explain to people that it is the duty of the trial judge to follow case law as set by the [Kentucky] Supreme Court as long as the supreme court says the broad form deed is law and that the ... coal companies have all these rights that in many instances may be detrimental to the general public, the trial judge still has to uphold the broad form deed.[4]

A similar situation sometimes occurs in criminal cases where a trial judge may have to throw out charges against a clearly guilty defendant. An appellate court can reinforce this sense of professionalism through praise, as for example, the Oklahoma Court of Criminal Appeals once did when commending a trial judge for "courageously following the law as laid down by the Supreme Court of the United States, even though it is not always a popular thing to do." [5]

Integrity of the Judicial System

One of the most important reasons for judicial adherence to high court policies is that widespread failure to apply them would lead to a breakdown of the judicial system. Since judges are part of that system, its breakdown would, of course, adversely affect their own status and authority. Judges who publicly defy or evade their superiors' policies must realize that they are inviting similar treatment from those subject to their own rulings. Moreover, such behavior affects the overall legitimacy of judicial authority. If the special competence of judges to interpret the law is accepted by the public, judges may obtain compliance—however reluctant—with unpopular policies. However, if such competence is, in effect, disputed by the judges themselves, laymen can be expected to pick up cues and behave accordingly. The risks inherent in defiance were cogently recognized when Louisiana Supreme Court Justice Mack Barham dissented from his colleagues' overt unwillingness to apply a U.S. Supreme Court search and seizure decision. Justice Barham wrote:

> We, sitting as the Supreme Court of Louisiana attack with harsh and condemning language our state appellate courts below us for daring to deviate from, or even to question, our jurisprudence. . . . Yet we, who under our oath must obey the supremacy clause of the United States Constitution and respond to the United States Supreme Court decisions, tell that court of final supremacy that we will act on federal issues as we see fit—its pronouncements to the contrary notwithstanding.[6]

The justice then pointedly concluded his dissent by urging Louisiana's trial judges and district attorneys to abide *not* by his colleagues' decision but by the search and seizure policy interpretations of the U.S. Court of Appeals for the Fifth Circuit and the two Louisiana federal district courts.

To summarize, factors such as judicial professionalism, a sense of duty imposed by others, and a fear of undermining the judicial system are strong constraints that keep lower court judges from rendering careless or seriously deviant interpretations of higher court policies. These factors hold the judicial system together and enable it to transmit judicial policy from Washington or the state capitals to the implementing populations without too much distortion or loss of meaning. It should be emphasized that most of the time judges make a conscientious and reasoned effort to interpret and apply the policies of higher courts. In making such efforts, judges occasionally misinterpret ambiguous or poorly articulated policies; sometimes a judge can do little more than make an intelligent guess about what the policy-making court intends. Such guesses may well reflect the judge's own biases or peculiarities of reasoning. But there are also some occasions when judges unduly limit or expand judicial policies. Judges are, after all, political actors, and they often have strong views on public policy. The following section examines the methods by which judges may limit or expand higher court policies.

INTERPRETIVE RESPONSES BY JUDGES

The Continuum of Acceptance

As we noted in Chapter 1, when members of the interpreting population face the likelihood of having to interpret a court case or policy, they must make certain decisions about how to do it. The initial decision is an attitudinal one: they decide whether to accept the policy as something they can live with. Then, depending upon the nature of their acceptance decision, they must adjust their behavior accordingly. Judges' acceptance and behavior are not very different from those of political party officials who must decide whether to support the party convention's nominee for president and, if so, how enthusiastically. Any policy may be limited or expanded by various methods, and judges' behavior basically consists of choosing and using those methods.

A judge's acceptance decision is one of degree, reflecting his or her overall enthusiasm for the higher court's policy. It will fall somewhere on a continuum, as is illustrated in Figure 2.2. Most reactions will fall in what can be called "the zone of indifference," [7] which means that the judge has a neutral, or at least not a strong, reaction to the policy. Within the zone of indifference, in other words, the judge's sense of professionalism and obligation will overcome any personal reaction he or she might have to the higher court's policy.

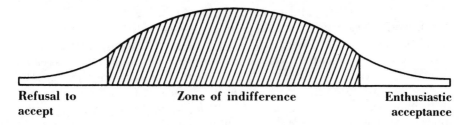

| Refusal to accept | Zone of indifference | Enthusiastic acceptance |

Figure 2.2 The continuum of acceptance of judicial policies.

On occasion a judge's reaction falls outside the zone of indifference. If a judge is very enthusiastic about a policy, he or she may interpret the policy broadly, pushing its logic to the limit and praising it in the opinion. This happened frequently in the 1930s, when many federal district judges broadly interpreted several Supreme Court decisions (for example, *Schechter Poultry Corp. v. United States* [1935], *United States v. Butler* [1936], and *Carter v. Carter Coal Co.* [1936]) limiting or emasculating crucial New Deal programs.[8]

On the other side of the zone are the reactions of a judge who refuses to accept a higher court policy. At the extreme a judge might overtly defy the higher court, but more often he or she will try to evade its mandate or will interpret the policy as narrowly as possible. Following the Supreme Court's acceptance of New Deal programs in 1937, many federal district judges who previously had been happy about the Supreme Court's policies regarding the New Deal became less willing to interpret the Court's decisions broadly.

Once a judge has decided to what extent to accept a judicial policy, he or she then must adjust interpretive behavior accordingly. When the policy falls within a judge's zone of indifference, he or she will usually give it a conscientious and reasonable interpretation. Judges who accept the policy enthusiastically may render interpretations that expand the scope or depth of the higher court's decision. Judges who refuse to accept a higher court's policy or who do so only in a pro forma sense will try to avoid applying the policy any more than necessary.

Techniques of Nonacceptance

A judge who does not accept a higher court policy has three basic options: defiance, avoidance, and limited application.

Defiance. By *defiance* we mean that the judge simply does not apply the policy in cases coming before the court. Overt defiance is highly unprofessional and threatening to the judicial system; thus it is a relatively rare event. Donald Songer, in his study of federal courts of appeals compliance with *Miranda v. Arizona* (1966) during 1968, found only one instance of clear noncompliance out of 120 cases studied.[9] Defiance may be slightly more frequent in trial courts. Desegregation brought out considerable trial court defiance; in one extreme case, a Birmingham, Alabama, municipal judge not only refused to follow Supreme Court decisions desegregating municipal facilities but also declared the Fourteenth Amendment unconstitutional.[10] But trial court defiance is by no means confined to the South. A Schenectady, New York, judge announced that the contention that he was obliged to abide by the Supreme Court's opinion in *Bowles v. Willingham* (1944) upholding the Wartime Rent Control Act was without merit, and did not do so.[11] Even federal judges can be defiant. In 1958 Judge Whitfield Davidson of Texas obstinately refused to follow the Supreme Court's decision in *Wickard v. Filburn* (1942), which upheld the crop production limitation of the Agricultural Adjustment Act. In general, the effects of such defiance are overcome if the losing party pursues the issue, but appeal can be a long process. Over four years passed before the Supreme Court restored operation of the federal agricultural programs in northern Texas by threatening Judge Davidson with a writ of mandamus (*United States v. Haley,* 1962).

Defiance need not be overt—in some situations, a lower court judge will simply ignore the higher court's policy. Again, this is easiest to do at the trial court level; appellate court opinions are available to the public, so ignoring policy is considered to be overt defiance and unprofessional behavior. Trial courts are better shielded from professional and public scrutiny, however, and in many cases—especially those involving misdemeanor courts with lay judges—there is virtually no norm of strict adherence to judicial policy. In the 1940s and 1950s, for example, it was common practice for trial courts to order hitchhikers and vagrants to leave town, even though the Supreme Court had clearly established the rights of all citizens, even indigent ones, to travel and relocate (*Edwards v. California,* 1941). More recently, some juvenile court judges who were well aware of the *In re Gault* decision (1967) nonetheless continued to deny minors the right of counsel or other due process requirements in their court.[12]

Avoidance. When defiance is inconvenient or unseemly, a lower court can try to avoid having to interpret and apply an unacceptable higher court policy. Generally this is accomplished by disposing of a threatening case through procedural or technical considerations so that the court will not have to consider it on its merits. Rules of judicial procedure are not as inflexible as a layman might imagine; judges have considerable discretion in their invocation of precedent. By and large, such rules are "Janus-faced" (to use Karl Llewellyn's term)[13] and can be applied to obtain almost any result the judge desires. Two common judicial criteria that are flexible enough to allow avoidance tactics are standing to sue and mootness. Theoretically, in order to sue someone a plaintiff must show that he or she has suffered or is about to suffer an injury; failure to do so will lead to dismissal of the suit. In the same vein, if the issue is resolved before the trial or passes the point where the court can do anything about it, the case is considered moot and the complaint is subject to dismissal. Nonetheless, courts do accept cases where the plaintiffs have patently suffered no injury or where the issue is obviously moot. Scholars have shown rather clearly that the standards here are not at all certain and are subject to considerable manipulation.[14] Thus on some occasions a lower court judge has sufficient discretion to dismiss a suit that otherwise might force him or her to apply an unacceptable policy.

Another strategy is for a judge to decide that the crucial language of a precedent he or she dislikes is *dicta* (the part of an opinion that does not contribute to the central logic of the decision). In traditional jurisprudence, dicta, while useful as guidance, are not considered binding. Indeed, the Supreme Court has at times rejected language in some of its previous opinions as dicta without repudiating the precedent as a whole. But what constitutes dicta is not always clear. If one court's core logic is another's dicta, then nothing can be considered absolutely binding and a desperate lower court judge can find dicta almost anywhere.

A judge can also decide that the plaintiff has sought the wrong remedy—for example, contract instead of tort or the 1866 Civil Rights Act rather than the 1968 Fair Housing Law. Alternatively, a judge can find that the appellant failed to raise a crucial point of law at the trial (when many criminal defendants may have had inexperienced or unenthusiastic lawyers). In 1955, for instance, the Georgia Supreme Court (*Williams v. State,* 1955) allowed a black defendant to go to the electric chair because at the trial he failed to challenge a selection process that had produced an all-white jury, even though that process had been held unconstitutional by the U.S. Supreme Court. The doctrine of *equitable abstention* (waiting for a state court construction of statutes under constitutional attack) is also sometimes useful in avoiding the application of an unacceptable judicial policy. For instance, some federal courts refused to declare state segregation laws unconstitutional because the laws had not been fully interpreted by the state courts. Eventually, the Supreme Court put an end to this avoidance tactic (*Bailey v. Patterson,* 1962).

Avoidance tactics, of course, serve only to delay implementation. Sooner or later a case will come along that cannot be avoided through procedural maneuvering. However, avoidance tactics certainly can forestall the impact of a disliked judicial policy for some time.

Besides resorting to legal procedures or technicalities, a court can resort to foot dragging, which means that the lower court simply takes its time about implementing the higher court's policy. Southern judges resorted to this tactic frequently in desegregation cases. The Florida Supreme Court, for example, recognized its obligation to allow blacks to attend the state's all-white universities, but it delayed ordering the integration of universities for several years while surveys about integration were conducted and plans for its accomplishment were drawn up. The original plaintiff, in fact, never attended the University of Florida.[15] Using similar tactics, some federal district judges ordered school districts to desegregate—six to eight years in the future. Federal judges in Mississippi sometimes waited months or even years before granting motions requiring local voting registrars to produce documents relevant to lawsuits having to do with the rights of blacks to vote.[16]

While disposing of cases on procedural grounds and foot dragging may be found in a variety of cases, these tactics are generally limited to situations where a judicial policy requires considerable change. Lower courts cannot easily avoid those judicial policies upholding the status quo or allowing change at the discretion of implementing or consumer populations. The abortion decision, for example, could not be avoided by lower courts, since this decision does not *require* the state to do anything, but merely *allows* women and doctors to take some action. Thus the burden of going to court rests with the opponents of the abortion policy—or with the state— and not with the policy's beneficiaries.

Another avoidance tactic available to state courts faced with the possibility of applying a Supreme Court policy is to decide the case on state grounds rather on than federal grounds. State constitutions generally have provisions similar to those found in the Bill of Rights of the U.S. Constitution; thus a state court can decide a civil liberties case on state constitutional grounds and avoid having to subscribe to the Supreme Court's narrow interpretation of a similar provision of the federal constitution. State courts, however, cannot interpret a state civil liberties guarantee *more narrowly* than the Supreme Court has interpreted a similar federal constitutional provision, since the U.S. Constitution protects most rights against encroachment by the states as well as by the federal government. But state courts can construe their constitutional provisions more liberally. For instance, when the Supreme Court ruled that there was no First Amendment right to picket or distribute literature at privately owned shopping malls (*Lloyd Corporation, Ltd. v. Tanner,* 1972), the California Supreme Court decided that such a right existed under the freedom of speech guarantee in the California constitution (*Robins v. Pruneyard Shopping Center,* 1979 and 1980). Subsequently, lower courts in several states have found similar requirements in their state constitutions.[17] For example, New York State's highest court overturned a ban on topless entertainment as violative of the state free speech guarantee, even though the U.S. Supreme Court had earlier upheld the ban against a First Amendment challenge.[18] In the criminal justice area, Donald Wilkes has found that several state supreme courts—particularly California's—have avoided applying more conservative Burger court interpretations of the Bill of Rights by this strategy, although most state supreme courts have not followed this route.[19] Such state court liberalism is not new. In the 1920s about 20 state supreme courts adopted the exclusionary rule as an interpretation of their own constitutions' guarantees against unreasonable search and seizure; the U.S. Supreme Court did not interpret the federal constitution this way until 1961 (*Mapp v. Ohio*).

Limited Application. A judge who does not accept a higher court's decision, but who cannot or will not defy or avoid it, can limit its application. Limiting the application of precedent or doctrine is not in itself a manifestation of hostility. In any court case, lawyers for both sides cite a variety of precedents in their arguments; a judge could not normally accept all of the precedents as being applicable and still come to a meaningful decision. The heart of an appellate opinion is an explanation of why the judge accepts the applicability of some precedents or doctrines and limits that of others. Often, however, the relevance of a precedent to a case under consideration can be strongly argued. In such situations, a judge's finding that the precedent is not a controlling one most likely reflects his or her unwillingess to accept it.

One method of limiting a precedent is to stress factual differences between it and the situation the judge is called upon to resolve. In legal terminology this is called *distinguishing* the precedent. At times such distinctions can be all but meaningless. For example, in 1968 the Supreme Court held that teachers could not be fired for exercising their First Amendment rights in a school policy dispute (*Pickering v. Board of Education*). The next year, the Alaska Supreme Court upheld the firing of two teachers who were leading a campaign to oust the local superintendent (*Watts v. Seward School Board,* 1969). The Alaska court distinguished the two cases by noting that the teachers in *Watts* had made false and reckless statements, whereas those involved in *Pickering* had made substantive charges. Generally speaking, however, lower courts do not resort to making minor factual distinctions unless they are adamantly unwilling to accept a higher court's precedent and can find no more plausible means of evading its application.

Sometimes the factual differences between a precedent and the case at hand are significant enough that a judge may fairly distinguish the cases. However, there may be times when these factual differences are less important in light of an overall view of the higher court's decision or the direction of its policy development. A classic example of a judge's ignoring the direction of an emerging policy is the refusal of federal district judge John Bell Timmerman of South Carolina to acknowledge the relevance of *Brown v. Board of Education* (1954) to a suit seeking the desegregation of city buses. Noting that *Brown* had stressed the importance of equal educational opportunities to the development of the skills and personality of black people, Judge Timmerman disdainfully remarked, "One's personality is not developed on a bus." [20] Few observers, however—including, we suspect, Judge Timmerman himself—had any real doubts that the fundamental thrust of the *Brown* decision was that segregation in general, not just segregation in schools, was unconstitutional.

In a reversal of roles, but using what amounts to the same strategy, a lower court may declare that distinctions deemed important by the policy-making court are insignificant. When the Supreme Court ruled that oaths forswearing membership in or support of the Communist party or other subversive groups (which many states required of their employees in the 1950s) were unconstitutional because they made no exception for unknowing or inadvertent membership or support (*Weiman v. Updegraff,* 1952), several lower courts simply intepreted the oaths to incorporate such an exception. Similarly, after *Miller v. California* (1973) set forth fairly clear standards that state obscenity statutes had to meet, nearly a dozen state supreme courts merely reinterpreted the rather vague and ambiguous wording of their state laws so that they met the *Miller* standards. In effect, these courts rewrote the law to make it consistent with current Supreme Court policy rather than finding the law unconstitutional and awaiting the possible passage of a new one by the legislature.

When it is not feasible to focus on factual distinctions, a judge can intepret the precedent in question very narrowly. The judge may observe the letter but not the spirit of the decision. After the Supreme Court held in *Shelley v. Kraemer* (1948) that state courts could not enforce restrictive convenants (written neighborhood agreements not to sell property to certain racial groups) by injunction because such contracts were contrary to public policy, several state courts held that *Shelley* did not preclude neighbors from filing a damage suit against a former neighbor who had sold his home to a black person. Indeed, at times lower courts will openly admit that they are interpreting a higher court decision as narrowly as possible. Such tactics are found especially in interpretations of some of the Supreme Court's decisions expanding the rights of criminal suspects or defendants. Fearful of the real political consequences of applying precedents that would be likely to enable seemingly guilty persons to escape punishment, several state supreme courts announced that they would interpret such decisions "in the interests of the realistic administration of criminal investigations" or so as to forestall "disastrous social consequences." [21]

At the extreme, a lower court may in effect "reinterpret" a precedent to mean something different from what the policy-making court intended or what most neutral observers believe it means. Some lower courts or attorneys general interpreted the Supreme Court school prayer decision (*Abington School District v. Schempp,* 1963) to mean that prayers in school were unconstitutional only if they were compulsory. Others held that prayers were unconstitutional only if they seemed to have a denominational origin or slant.

A variant of the reinterpretation strategy is for a lower court to feign inability to understand what the higher court said. A deputy state attorney general in Indiana, when asked how he reconciled the continuation of prayers in public schools with federal court decisions to the contrary, replied, "Federal laws? Nobody understands federal laws." [22] Even appellate judges will sometimes blithely say they cannot figure out what the Supreme Court is doing and go their own way.

Such behavior, if carried too far, becomes defiance. However, the language of a decision may be ambiguous or contradict previous decisions, thus making the interpreting population unsure about the exact nature of the policy. Under such conditions, a judge who does not like the policy can easily limit its scope without appearing to be particularly defiant.

Rather than choosing to make a substantively limited or distorted interpretation of an unacceptable higher court decision, a court can give it a narrow, situational interpretation. One method is for the lower court to give the higher court decision a prospective application only (one that is not applicable to events prior to the date of the decision). Most decisions are retrospective; a prospective interpretation is contrary to the norms of both common law and constitutional interpretation and can usually be taken as a sign of hostility to the precedent. It is fair to note, however, that in some situations a retrospective application of a new policy can be highly inequitable to some individuals or even dysfunctional to society. In a few situations, the Supreme Court has explicitly permitted lower courts to adopt a policy of prospective application only. *Miranda v. Arizona* (1966) is one such example. An alternative method is to hold a precedent inapplicable to certain classes of people. Texas courts, for instance, refused to apply the Supreme Court's decision forbidding discrimination against blacks in the jury selection process (*Norris v. Alabama,* 1935) to persons of Mexican descent until directly ordered to do so by the Supreme Court (*Hernandez v. Texas,* 1954).

Techniques of Expansion

At the other end of the continuum, lower court judges can sometimes be quite enthusiastic in their acceptance of a higher court policy. An enthusiastic judge will try to give such a decision an expanded interpretation, thus following a policy opposite that of a judge who is unwilling to accept it as precedent.

One technique of expansion is to apply a precedent to situations where coverage seems ambiguous. Judicial policies traditionally refrain from addressing questions of application not raised in the case. As we noted in our Chapter 1 chronology of events following the abortion decision, many such issues arise sooner or later in the lower courts. Examples of an enthusiastic application of a precedent by lower court judges are not hard to find. For instance, after the Supreme Court's ruling that defendants in juvenile courts had a constitutional right to be represented by counsel and to confront witnesses against them (*In re Gault,* 1967), the Rhode Island family court held that juvenile defendants had a constitutional right to trial by jury (*In re Rindell,* 1968), a right accorded by virtually no other lower court and one that the Supreme Court later said was not constitutionally required (*McKeiver v. Pennsylvania,* 1971). Similarly, several Supreme Court decisions outlawing sex discrimination in areas such as social security and military dependency benefits were cited by some state courts as authority for decisions ordering that girls be allowed to play on high school varsity football teams (*Commonwealth v. Pennsylvania Interscholastic Association,* 1975; *Darrin v. Gould,* 1975).

Lower court enthusiasm for higher court policies has perhaps been noticeable in the area of busing to achieve racial balance in the public schools. Because busing orders must be suited to the situation in a particular school district, the Supreme Court has been unwilling to set specific nationwide policies or even to exercise very much control over the scope and detail of policies established by federal courts. Consequently, federal judges in some northern cities issued orders requiring busing for a greater number of pupils over a greater geographical area than was probably necessary to meet integration criteria set forth in various Supreme Court decisions. Indeed, lower court judges in Detroit, Dayton, and Pasadena (California) went so far that the Supreme Court rejected their plans (*Milliken v. Bradley,* 1974; *Dayton (Ohio) Board of Education v. Brinkman,* 1977; *Pasadena City Board of Education v. Spangler,* 1976).

Another technique lower court judges may use to expand a judicial policy is to apply it to a different policy area. Of course, judicial decisions often seem to rest on premises or to advance principles that transcend the immediate subject matter. Nonetheless, courts are usually rather cautious about transferring the applicability of precedents to wholly new areas of jurisprudence, as this tends to upset the stability of the law. When a lower court is willing to transfer a policy to any significant degree, it manifests a clear enthusiasm for the judicial policy. For example, the abortion decision of 1973 is in the civil liberties area of jurisprudence, more specifically, as a right of privacy. However, courts in New York and Texas have let it expand into torts as well by holding that parents of children born with defects stemming from the wife's measles during pregnancy could sue the gynecologist for not counseling an abortion (*Jacobs v. Theimer,* 1975; *Park v. Chessin,* 1977). Another example can be found in the expanded application of *Griswold v. Connecticut* (1965), where the Supreme Court held a Connecticut law forbidding the sale or use of contraceptive devices to be unconstitutional. The rationale behind *Griswold* was that married couples had a constitutional right of privacy. In subsequent years, a number of lower courts have used the right of privacy articulated in *Griswold* to overturn rules limiting the length of male public school students' hair, specifying a dress code for public employees, and requiring applicants for government jobs to take psychological tests.

At times, lower court applications of a precedent are based not upon its general premise or principle but upon a particular phrase that may be taken out of context. Most notable, perhaps, is Justice William O. Douglas's uncharacteristic statement, "We are a religious people whose institutions presuppose a Supreme Being," [23] found in *Zorach v. Clausen* (1952), a case upholding released-time programs for offering off-campus religious education to public school students. Lower court judges cited this statement as justification for upholding practices such as the singing of religious songs or having priests or nuns clothed in religious garments teaching in public schools. One federal district court went so far as to use Douglas's statement to deny citizenship to an unchurched alien.[24]

Thus, by broadly interpreting the meaning of a policy, judges may expand it in order to resolve new questions in the same issue area or to decide cases in other issue areas. In expanding the policy, judges may use any of a number of aspects of a case, including the holding, the logic, or even a key phrase in the majority opinion.

FACTORS AFFECTING LOWER COURT INTERPRETATIONS

So far we have discussed why judicial policies must be interpreted and who interprets them. We have also described the range of a lower court's possible responses to a higher court's decision and how these responses can be incorporated into particular interpretations. Now we will turn to the work of scholars in the field of judicial policy and summarize their explanations of why judges' responses are negative, neutral, or positive. Generally, scholars focus on explaining behavioral responses rather than acceptance decisions, that is, they are concerned with what the judges decide or what they say in their opinions, rather than with their attitudes toward the policies. The reason for focusing on behavior instead of attitudes is simple—judges rarely respond to inquiries about their attitudes toward the Supreme Court and other judicial bodies, or toward the policies they announce. Because judges are bound by some of the norms discussed in the previous section, one cannot take what judges say in their opinions as representative of their personal attitudes. Thus, until researchers focus exclusively on attitudes of judges relative to higher court policies, we can discuss only their behavioral responses.

Explanations of why a judge may react positively or negatively to a higher court policy tend to emphasize three factors: the policy itself, the environment within which the interpretation takes place, and the personality of the judge. Some of the characteristics of a policy that may affect interpretation are its clarity, the form of its transmission, and its perceived legitimacy and authority. The environment includes the social and political pressures that might affect the decision making of a lower court judge. The personality of a judge, especially his or her attitudes and policy preferences, will also affect interpretation. Empirical research relating to judicial policy interpretation has supported each of these factors to some extent, and none has emerged as most important.

Policy Characteristics

Clarity of the Policy.   To the extent that an opinion is ambiguous, vague, or poorly articulated, it is more likely to produce dissimilar lower court interpretations. That is, the clarity of a judicial decision or policy may affect the scope of interpretations substantially. Finding unclear decisions, even by the U.S. Supreme Court, is not a difficult task.

Judicial decisions may lack clarity for a variety of reasons. Some decisions and policies are ambiguous because the issue before the policy-making court is complex or the subject matter is difficult to resolve in a judicial opinion. Judicial policy regarding obscenity is one area, for example, where policy making is difficult and often leads to decisions lacking the clarity needed to guide lower court judges. In this issue area, it is simply impossible to fashion a precise judicial policy defining obscene material. Phrases such as "patently offensive" or "without serious redeeming value" necessarily leave room for subjective interpretation among judges, even those who are more or less indifferent to the substance of the Supreme Court's policy.

Sometimes appellate court opinions are unclear because the court may be sharply divided in its reasoning. This division may result either in a single majority opinion that has to accommodate the divergent views of several judges or in several opinions, none of which has majority support on the court. The Supreme Court's initial busing decision in *Swann v. Charlotte-Mecklenburg County Board of Education* (1971), although unanimous, was rather confusing. It was characterized by one lower court judge as being full of "a lot of conflicting language. It's almost as if there were two sets of view laid side by side." [25] Occasionally Supreme Court judges themselves openly disagree on what one of their opinions means. Following its 1979 decision in *Gannett Co. v. DePasquale,* declaring that the public and press may be excluded from a pretrial hearing in order to avoid publicity prejudicial to the defendant, several justices publicly differed about whether the decision permitted the closing of criminal trials at the request of the defendant. In such circumstances, it would be unlikely that lower court judges would follow a common interpretation—and, needless to say, they did not. Access to criminal trials varied from jurisdiction to jurisdiction until the Supreme Court came back to clarify the matter in *Richmond Newspapers, Inc. v. Virginia* (1980).

Multiple opinions also tend to cloud the intentions and expectations of a policy-making court. In the Pentagon Papers case (*New York Times Co. v. United States,* 1971), for example, every justice wrote an opinion. Thus, while the result was clear—lifting the injunction against the *New York Times* and leading to the continued publication of the Pentagon Papers—the general policy regarding conditions under which the government could enjoin publication of sensitive material remained uncertain. Thus, eight years later a federal district judge had little guidance when the government asked him to enjoin publication of an issue of *Progressive Magazine* that contained an article on how to build a hydrogen bomb (*United States v. The Progressive, Inc.,* 1979). *Regents of University of California v. Bakke* (1978) provides another example of divided thinking on the Court. In that case, the Court experienced a four-one-four split; the man in the middle, Justice Lewis F. Powell, Jr., wrote an opinion whose overall theme was not supported by any other member of the Court, although each of its component parts was supported by one or the other of the groups of four. Such a configuration provided little or no guidance to lower court judges in the area of affirmative action policy.

Complex subject matter and divided reasoning on a court are sometimes indicative of another difficulty that leads to less than clear court policies: the overall policy goals may be unclear because of a disagreement on the court, a change in policy by the court, or the development of different, and ultimately conflicting, lines of precedents. Clearly, when judges disagree, goals cannot emerge unambiguously; but even if there is apparent agreement on policy, the overall goals of the policy-making court may remain somewhat unclear to lower court judges. When a higher court's attitude on a question changes significantly, but not to the extent of overturning prior policy, lower court judges face a dilemma. The *Brown v. Board of Education* decision did not, for example, explicitly overturn *Plessy v. Ferguson* (1896); as we noted previously, at least one lower court judge attempted to use *Plessy* to uphold segregation on buses in a southern city. Because the Court sometimes fails to disavow prior decisions, one commentator concludes that "lower courts have greatly increased opportunities to explore the logical frontiers of current decisions and to judge the validity of past precedent. The activism of the Supreme Court has resulted in the delegation of substantial line drawing powers to the lower courts." [26]

Clarity is also occasionally problematic because the higher court simply fails to provide consistent, continuing cues to lower courts about the interpretations of important policies. Several authors have criticized the Supreme Court for not following up its decision in *Brown v. Board of Education* with more decisions stating precisely what levels of desegregation should be achieved by local school boards or explaining the phrase "with all deliberate speed." [27] Lower courts were essentially on their own to interpret that decision as they believed the Court wanted it interpreted. Not surprisingly, lower court interpretations varied considerably, and implementation of the decision in many jurisdictions was slow.

John Gruhl's research on liberal decisions of lower federal courts provides one example of response to consistent and continual policy development. The Supreme Court changed libel law dramatically in *New York Times Co. v. Sullivan* (1964); Gruhl details how lower federal courts had applied this and subsequent decisions through 1974. He notes that while the decisions of the Court in this area "were not exceptionally clear, . . . lower courts did not seem troubled by this lack of clarity." [28] Also, the opinions of the Court were not for the most part supported by large majorities on the Court. However, while neither especially clear nor widely supported, the decisions of the Court were consistent with each other. Gruhl comments,

> The Supreme Court handed down a series of decisions [through 1972], each of which reinforced the preceding ones. In the series of cases it had clarified and expanded the principles which it announced in *New York Times*. And, importantly, it had ruled in favor of the defendant in every one of these decisions. Thus the Court had continually emphasized its commitment to the *Times* doctrine. [29]

Gruhl found 100 percent compliance with *New York Times* in federal courts of appeals libel cases through 1974 and speculates that Supreme Court consistency from decision to decision achieved greater compliance than may have been obtained if merely one or two unanimous decisions had been rendered by the Court.

Somewhat related to the problems of consistency are difficulties that arise when different lines of precedents have different emphases. Carol Jenson's study of state supreme court reactions to Supreme Court rulings in internal security cases over a 50-year period provides a good illustration of what events are likely when two different Supreme Court policies give lower courts considerable room to interpret judicial policy. Jenson studies lower court decisions among the 50 state courts as well as the development of internal security cases at the U.S. Supreme Court level. She maintains that the Supreme Court allowed two lines of precedents to develop in this area—one line that approved state security measures and another that protected political speech from state interference. As Jenson points out, the development of these two lines of precedents was piecemeal, and the Supreme Court did not overturn earlier cases, which tended to support state security measures. As a result of these dual lines of authority, "state courts that did not accept the Supreme Court doctrine of protected political speech selected the alternative lines of precedents." [30] Thus, while the Supreme Court's apparent goal of protecting political speech was relatively well defined, the presence of prior, limiting decisions that had not been disavowed by the Court provided considerable leeway for lower courts that wished to evade or avoid the policy.

Even if the higher court's decision is clearly written, unanimously supported by the court, and related to a clear policy objective, any single decision will probably not answer all questions about the scope of its applicability. The Supreme Court's decision establishing the exclusionary rule in search and seizure (*Mapp v. Ohio,* 1961) is a good example. While the opinion announced the rule as a constitutional mandate, it left many questions about the scope and applicability of the rule unanswered. Table 2.1 illustrates the uncertainty that followed during the 1960s in the state courts. Eventually the Supreme Court settled some of the uncertainties, but others remain open questions to this day. Until answers are forthcoming, lower courts are left to make whatever inferences they can from the language of the original decision.

Michael Combs's research on how nonsouthern federal courts of appeal handled desegregation decisions illustrates the variation one may find if critical questions about major policies go unanswered by the Supreme Court. [31] Studying decisions by nonsouthern courts of appeal between the time of *Brown v. Board of Education* (1954) and *Milliken v. Bradley* (1974), Combs concludes that these courts had considerable latitude in their own decision making because many important questions about northern desegregation had not yet been resolved by the Supreme Court. Combs finds that the net effect of this latitude was the regionalization of constitutional rights: some circuit courts gave narrow interpretations to the applicability of desegregation orders in their circuit, while others clearly went beyond the Supreme Court's intentions in expanding the application of desegregation policies in various localities. None of the court of appeals decisions were noncompliant in themselves, but

Table 2.1 State Supreme Court Decisions on Applicability of *Mapp v. Ohio* to Various Situations, 1961-1969

Legal question before state supreme court	Number of states applying exclusionary rule	Number of states not applying exclusionary rule
1. Does failure of the defendant to make a timely motion for supression of illegally seized evidence waive his or her right to invoke the exclusionary rule later?	2	21
2. Can one spouse waive the Fourth Amendment rights of the other and consent to a search of the home?	4	16
3. Is evidence secured during a routine noncriminal search—a building inspection for example—admissible in criminal prosecutions?	1	4
4. Is *Mapp* retroactive? That is, does it apply to cases where the trial occurred before the Supreme Court's decision?	5	11
5. Is evidence secured from one who was stopped for "suspicious behavior" admissible under the Fourth Amendment?	3	6
6. Are searchs of automobiles following a traffic arrest valid?	4	7
7. Must appellate courts overturn convictions in which illegally obtained evidence was introduced but did not constitute a vital or major proportion of the evidence upon which the verdict was based?	3	5
8. Does a defendant who does not reside in the premises from which the evidence was illegally seized have standing to object to its admission?	12	16

(Continued)

Table 2.1   (Continued)

Legal question before state supreme court	Number of states applying exclusionary rule	Number of states not applying exclusionary rule
9. Are warrants issued or searches made on the basis of anonymous tips valid?	3	3
10. Can evidence be admitted which is secured in good faith but nonetheless illegally (that is, the warrant is later determined to be void)?	3	3
11. When a defendant is under arrest or in custody, is a waiver of Fourth Amendment rights presumed to have been coerced and thus void unless the state can rebut the presumption?	8	5
12. Is testimony about illegally seized evidence admissible?	6	1
13. Is evidence seized in the course of an invalid arrest admissible?	5	1

Source: Adapted from Bradley Canon, "Reactions of State Supreme Courts to a U.S. Supreme Court Civil Liberties Decision," *Law and Society Review* 8 (1973): 115-117, by permission.

the range of responses to similar policy questions was considerable.

Thus, whether a higher court decision or policy is clearly articulated may have a substantial effect on lower court interpretations. Conscientious judges frequently have to make their own best guesses about how to interpret a judicial policy and apply it to a particular set of circumstances not considered by a higher court. The greater the ambiguity of the case or the policy, the wider the range of possible interpretations. Ironically, interpretations are also less likely to be noncompliant, since noncompliance is difficult to define for ambiguous decisions or policies.

Communication of the Policy.   In order for a judicial policy to be accurately interpreted, the text of the policy must be available to the interpreting population. Equally important, the members of that population must read and consider the statement of policy. In most bureaucracies policies are set forth in memos that are directly disseminated to all appropriate persons in the lower echelons. In our judicial system, however, the court decisions that embody judicial policies are merely made available to the public; the deciding court makes no effort either to inform lower courts (other than the one from which the specific case was appealed) of its decisions directly or even to ensure that lower court judges have access to a copy of the policy statement.

Ordinarily, judicial opinions are available to judges in such places as courthouse libraries. In some rural areas, however, this is not true; for example, throughout Wyoming's 97,000 square miles there are only three sets of U.S. Supreme Court decisions publicly available.[32] Also, many judges—especially justices of the peace or those presiding over juvenile or probate courts—are not lawyers and serve on only a part-time basis. Lay judges often have little interest or skill in reading judicial opinions or any other legal material. As one California justice of the peace put it, "I don't know anything more about the law than a hog does about the Fourth of July." [33] Some try. Holding court in an insurance agency or even a private home, some justices of the peace will keep a copy of *You and the Law* by the editors of *Reader's Digest* handy.[34] As an extreme (we hope) illustration of the lack of legal knowledge in some local courts, we offer the following questioning of a justice of the peace in the mountains of eastern Kentucky by a lawyer whose client the justice had found guilty:

Q.: Are you familiar with the Fourteenth Amendment to the Constitution of the United States, as to what it provides?

J.P.: Yes, sir.

Q.: What does it provide?

J.P.: Right off hand I don't . . . something about judicial. I think one of them is judicial procedure or something or another. I'm not for sure.

Q.: Do you think the Fourteenth Amendment . . . deals with judicial procedure?

J.P.: Right off hand, I couldn't tell you.

Q.: Are you familiar with the term "due process of law" or "equal protection of the law?"

J.P.: Yes, sir.

Q.: In legal meaning?

J.P.: No, that's beyond me.

Q.: Are you familiar with the rights accorded to a defendant as accused in a criminal case under the Fourteenth Amendment?

J.P.: As I previously said, I don't know . . . exactly understand this Fourteenth Amendment. I know part of it.

Q.: Are you familiar with the *Supreme Court Reports* of the United States Supreme Court?
J.P.: I am familiar with some of them, but I don't agree with all of them.
Q.: What is your understanding with respect to the effect that a judge should give between conflicting rulings made by the Kentucky Court of Appeals and the Supreme Court of the United States? Do you understand the question?
J.P.: No, I really don't. I don't think I know.[35]

One investigation by Bradley C. Canon and Kenneth Kolson determined that around 40 percent of Kentucky's mostly nonlawyer juvenile court judges had not heard of the Supreme Court's landmark decision concerning the rights of juveniles, *In re Gault* (1967), three years after it was announced.[36] *Gault* held that juvenile defendants had a constitutionally guaranteed right of free counsel if indigent, as well as protection against compulsory self-incrimination. Moreover, many of the judges who had heard of *Gault* could describe it only in the vaguest terms.

Even professional judges whose chambers are directly across the hall from a law library may not hear about or read about all higher court decisions relevant to a case before them. Like most busy professionals, judges tend to read only as they need to. Research by John Paul Ryan and his colleagues indicates that the typical state court trial judge spends less than one hour per day keeping up with the law.[37] The judges' expectation is that the contending attorneys will discuss relevant cases in their briefs or oral arguments. The degree to which relevant materials may be found in the briefs largely depends on the competence and resources of the attorneys. This varies considerably, but Chief Justice Warren Burger once estimated that one-third to one-half of the nation's attorneys were not competent to conduct a trial.[38] The not infrequent failure of attorneys to cite a case or develop a strong interpretive argument concerning it can result in a judge's being unaware of the case or at least of its implications. This is especially true in trial courts, where judges do not have law clerks to do research for them.

We do not want to overemphasize the extent of these failures of awareness and understanding. Almost universally on appellate courts and to a large degree in trial courts of general jurisdiction, judges do know about relevant decisions. Nonetheless, we should remember that the communication of information about judicial decisions is not an automatic process and that it may work very poorly at the lowest echelons of the judicial hierarchy.

Perceived Legitimacy of the Policy. While the clarity and communication of the policy may affect the range of interpretations accorded to a decision, the direction of those interpretations (positive or negative) may be substantially influenced by the perceived legitimacy of the policy. A lower court may refuse to accept a judicial decision because the judge believes the higher court lacks the right to make such a decision. Such a belief questions the legitimacy of the higher court's ruling. The concept of legitimacy has several dimensions that we will discuss more fully in Chapter 6. Here we are particularly concerned with how a lower court perceives the legitimacy of a policy made by a higher court; such perceptions may depend on whether the lower court acknowledges the right of the higher court even to make policy in a certain broad area of the law.

Questions about the legitimacy of Supreme Court policies are most frequently raised in state courts. These courts naturally resent any Supreme Court decisions that they believe invade their jurisdiction. Indeed, Spencer Roane, Chief Justice of the Virginia Supreme Court in the early 1800s, argued strenuously that his court was not obligated to abide by Supreme Court interpretations of the Constitution, but could interpret that document in its own light (see *Martin v. Hunter's Lessee* [1816] and *Cohens v. Virginia* [1821] for a discussion of these arguments). Of course, the contentions of Roane and other state court justices never prevailed and were no longer seriously argued after the Civil War. While the supremacy of the Supreme Court is conceded by virtually every lower court judge, one still finds an occasional case where such judges accuse the Supreme Court of moving beyond its constitutional bounds. Such arguments were raised after the Supreme Court announced *Brown v. Board of Education,* the reapportionment decisions in the 1960s, and some interpretations of the Fourteenth Amendment extending protection to citizens against various actions of the state. In 1983, for example, an Alabama federal district judge permitted the state to continue prayers in the public schools because he believed the Supreme Court's incorporation into the Fourteenth Amendment of the principle of the separation of church and state lacked any constitutional foundation (*Jaffree v. Board of School Commissioners of Mobile County*). Likewise, in a 1968 criminal case, the Utah Supreme Court announced that the Fourteenth Amendment applied only to racial equality cases (if indeed it was constitutional at all) and hinted that the U.S. Supreme Court was permeated by subversives (*Dyett v. Turner*). The Utah court likened itself to a galley slave and said it would row in accord with the decisions of the nation's highest court only under the compulsion of the judicial whip and lash.[39]

The debate about the legitimate authority of the Supreme Court is frequently philosophical, and the actual effects of perceived legitimacy are difficult to assess, especially since most modern-day judges do not state bluntly that they are rejecting a policy or giving it a narrow application because they doubt the right of the Supreme Court to make such a policy.

Perceptions about Support for the Policy.   Lower court judges may also believe a policy lacks sufficient authority, depending on the level of support the policy has on the higher court. Lower court judges may be suspicious of policies that lack majority support on a policy-making court, since such policies are likely to be changed; a decision rendered with a close vote may be altered when new judges come on the court or when one of the original majority changes sides.

A close vote and the presence of dissenting opinions may also raise questions about the legal correctness of the higher court's decision. A close vote may indicate that a sizable dissenting group on the court believes that another policy may be equally as reasonable and respectable as the one adopted, especially if persuasive dissenting opinions accompany the majority opinion. Lower court judges might therefore assume that the prevailing policy does not necessarily represent good law and be encouraged to interpret narrowly or ignore the policy, hoping that by the time any appeals of their own decisions are resolved, a new majority will reverse the policy.

To avoid questions about legitimacy and support on the Supreme Court, Chief Justice Earl Warren strived to obtain unanimity of both vote and opinion in the 1954 decision desegregating southern schools.[40] Southern judges were not going to like the decision regardless of the vote, but it was hoped that they might accord it minimal acceptance if they knew that the Supreme Court was united in desegregation policy. Indeed, the Supreme Court apparently attached such great importance to imparting legitimacy by unity that major desegregation decisions were unanimous for almost two decades after *Brown v. Board of Education.*

It is unclear whether, in general, the unanimity of a court—or other efforts to increase the legitimacy of a court's policy, such as discouraging dissent or having a majority opinion written by the chief justice—actually makes a difference in how lower court judges respond to judicial policies. Instances where the closeness of the vote or the dubious future of a precedent affect lower court decisions are occasionally found. A dramatic instance occurred in the 1940s; in 1942 three Supreme Court justices publicly regretted their votes in *Minersville School District v. Gobitis* (1940), a decision upholding a compulsory flag salute law in Pennsylvania. (The three signaled their change of mind in a dissenting opinion in an unrelated case, *Jones v.*

Opelika [1942].) Two other justices in the *Gobitis* majority were no longer on the Court when a challenge to a similar law in West Virginia arose. Court of Appeals Judge John J. Parker noted the change in attitudes by the justices and declared the law unconstitutional in spite of the *Gobitis* ruling. On appeal to the Supreme Court, Parker's analysis proved correct and his decision was upheld (*West Virginia State Board of Education v. Barnette*, 1943).

Other instances of lower court disavowal of Supreme Court precedent due to questions about the authority of the precedent because a case failed to have a substantial majority—or any majority at all—have frequently been noted. Research by Charles Johnson provides some evidence that these instances may be the exceptions rather than the rule. Analyzing the citations by lower federal courts from 1963 to 1967 to 347 decisions announced by the U.S. Supreme Court from 1961 to 1963, Johnson found that "the degree of Supreme Court support or non-support for a particular case has little or no bearing on eventual treatment of that case by lower courts." [41] This analysis used several indicators of support—size of the deciding majority, number of justices supporting the majority opinion, size of the dissenting minority; Johnson also considered the presence of dissenting opinions and whether the chief justice wrote the majority opinion. Citations reported in *Shepard's Citations* classifying treatments as either positive ("compliant") or negative ("evasive") were uncorrelated with these indicators of support or legitimacy.

Thus, it is not clear that majority votes implying support for or lending legitimacy to a particular policy have a systematic effect on lower court responses. On some occasions, a four-to-three vote on the Supreme Court is cited as a justification for defiance;[42] on other occasions, a unanimous vote appears to carry great weight. But there is no systematic evidence about the degree to which such factors make a difference in lower courts' interpretive behavior.

Environmental Pressures on Interpreting Populations

Judges are products of a political world, and they frequently render decisions in highly political environments. Among state judges, whether elected or appointed, politics plays a central role in the selection of individuals as members of the interpreting population. Similarly, federal judges are also the products of a political process. Federal district judges are often effectively selected by a U.S. senator from the state that contains the federal district court, if there is a senator from the same party as the president. (Such senators can effectively force presidential consultation because of senatorial courtesy—a tradition whereby the Senate refuses to confirm presidential appointments to positions in a senator's state if the senator declares that the appointee is "personally obnoxious.") And if there are no senators of the president's party from a state, the president frequently turns to local supporters or party officials for nominations. As a result, most presidential appointees to the federal bench are from the president's party and have extensive political backgrounds.

Because most judges come to the bench through a political process, it should not be surprising that their decisions are frequently related to, if not motivated by, their partisan background. (We look at the influence of these partisan characteristics in the next section of this chapter.) But because judges are products of a political process they are also sensitive to political and social pressures from their environment. Research on judicial decision making suggests that environmental pressures may substantially influence lower court decisions in several areas. Studies by Beverly Blair Cook, for example, show that the willingness of U.S. district court judges to convict and sentence draft evaders during the Vietnam War era varied with local opinion about the war.[43] The district of northern California, where opposition to the war was widespread and vocal, was particularly noted for its leniency. Another study, by James Kuklinski and John Stanga, found that the severity of California judges' sentences for marijuana-related crimes was greater in the Los Angeles—San Diego area than in the San Francisco Bay area, reflecting differing regional attitudes toward drugs as expressed in a statewide referendum on the abolition of marijuana laws.[44] Further, in a study of criminal sentences by James Gibson, Iowa judges were shown to be sensitive to community expectations about sanctions. Judges serving different communities had different patterns of sentencing convicted felons, depending on their perceptions of community needs and attitudes.[45]

While these studies involve the decisions of judges who were implementing legislative policy about crime and justice, there is no major difference in this context between the interpretation of statutes and the interpretation of judicial policies. If pressures from the environment affect one set of decisions, they might be expected to affect other, similar decisions.

Research on the impact of judicial decisions points to several sources of pressure that may be brought to bear on judges or other members of the interpreting population. At least three major environmental features appear to influence how judges interpret higher court policies: (1) the policy preferences of significant others in the judge's political or social life, (2) different constituency demands or role expectations concerning how a judge should respond to higher court policies, and (3) the impact a policy may have if implemented in the judge's local community, especially if it could be disruptive. These three factors often tend to reinforce one another; however, we will treat them separately even though they may not be so easily separated in real life.

Significant Others in the Judge's Environment. Judges are both political and social creatures, and other individuals in their political and social systems may substantially influence their thinking about judicial policy. We refer to these individuals as *significant others.* Some of these individuals may be important for the judge's continued well-being as a judge or for eventual promotions to higher level courts. In some cases, the significant others could be political party leaders who play a key role in the nomination and selection of state judges. Sometimes the significant others may be the voters at large, and for some federal judges they may be particular senators. Judges do not, of course, always listen to the policy preferences of significant others, but for that they occasionally must pay a price. In California, where until recently incumbent judges were rarely challenged, the Law and Order Campaign Committee sprang up in the late 1970s and was successful in defeating several incumbent trial judges whose application of Supreme Court criminal law precedents such as *Miranda v. Arizona* (1966) rendered them "soft on crime" in the committee's eyes.[46] In fact, California's Chief Justice Rose Bird only narrowly won retention in 1978 in a campaign in which the main issue was judicial laxity on crime.

At the federal level, Judge J. Skelly Wright's firm stand in desegregating the New Orleans school system as a U.S. district judge in 1960 rendered him so unpopular locally that Louisiana's U.S. senators used senatorial courtesy to veto his prospective appointment to the Fifth Circuit Court of Appeals. Eventually he was appointed to the Court of Appeals for the District of Columbia, a circuit beyond the reach of southern senators. Similarly, President Herbert Hoover's nomination of Judge John J. Parker to the Supreme Court was rejected by the Senate because of organized labor's objections to Parker's interpretation of several high court antilabor precedents during his service as court of appeals judge—interpretations that appeared to be consistent with the Supreme Court's intended policy. But narrow interpretations may also limit a judge's mobility in particular situations, as in the case of President Nixon's nomination of Judge G. Harrold Carswell to the Supreme Court. The Senate rejected Carswell for several reasons, one of which was his reluctance to give more than a minimal interpretation to desegregation decisions.

In addition to pressures, real or imagined, from political sources, pressures from nonpolitical or social sources may also influence interpretations of higher court decisions. Most judges have longstanding ties with their local communities—most federal judges were born and educated in the state they serve in, for example. A judge's interaction with friends and neighbors makes him or her intimately aware of local values and opinions. Like most human beings, judges are reluctant to offend community sentiments and risk the loss of friendships and perhaps the diminution of respectability. Even if such pressures are not actively applied, judges may semiconsciously anticipate their possibility.

The impact of social pressures on interpretations of higher court decisions is well illustrated by responses to *Brown v. Board of Education* among southern judges. Segregation, of course, was a way of life in the South; it permeated all community affairs. One scholar, Jack Peltason, vividly described the pressures on federal judges below the Mason-Dixon line:

> The District judge is very much a part of the life of the South. He must eventually leave his chambers and when he does he attends a Rotary lunch or stops off at the club to drink with men outraged by what they consider "judicial tyranny." A judge who makes rulings adverse to segregation is not so likely to be honored by testimonial dinners, or to read flattering editorials in the local press, or to partake in the fellowship at the club. He will no longer be invited to certain homes; former friends will avoid him when they meet him on the street.[47]

These social pressures can be effective. Federal District Judge J. Waites Waring of South Carolina was cut off from Charleston society, into which he had been born, after making several desegregation decisions. He eventually felt so isolated that he resigned the judgeship and moved from the state.[48] Sometimes pressures were substantial even if there was some distance between the affected community and the judge. When he ordered widespread busing in the Louisville, Kentucky, school system (after a court of appeals reversed his earlier, less pervasive order), Judge James F. Gordon found that "an awful lot of white people didn't talk to me," even though he lived in a community over 100 miles from Louisville. He particularly noted that "the organized bar never met its obligation to defend me. You see, I was just standing alone pretty well."[49] Speaking of the era immediately following the announcement of *Brown,* Jack Peltason also noted:

> There are less gentle pressures, too. Judges . . . have been forced to discontinue the public listing of their telephone number to avoid anonymous

and obscene telephone calls made round the clock. Their mail has been loaded with threatening letters. Some have been forced to seek police protection for themselves and their families.[50]

Some judges can resist such pressures. In his book *Unlikely Heroes,* Jack Bass focuses on four judges of the Fifth Circuit Court of Appeals (located in the Deep South) who served during the height of the controversy over desegregation. Although they received much abuse, they faithfully implemented *Brown* and subsequent Supreme Court decisions, often taking direct action to negate district court evasion or delaying tactics. It may be significant, however, that two of these judges were raised outside the South and that three of the four were Republicans—at a time when the South was solidly Democratic.[51]

The Influence of Constituency Expectations on Judges. Some of the environmental influences we have mentioned involve personal contacts between a judge and significant others—political allies as well as personal friends and neighbors. A judge may also feel pressure to implement judicial policies differently, depending on the different constituencies he or she serves or the perceived expectations others may have of him or her as a judicial officer.

The idea that judges serve different constituencies was advanced by Richard Richardson and Kenneth Vines as a result of their study of federal district and court of appeals judges.[52] These authors suggest that federal court of appeals judges are frequently caught between two sets of expectations, one stemming from a democratic subculture that ties the court to regional values and expectations and a second stemming from a legal subculture that ties the court to national values and expectations. J. Woodford Howard's study of federal courts of appeals in the District of Columbia, the Second Circuit, and the Fifth Circuit supports the idea that conflicting expectations influence judicial interpretations of Supreme Court policy:

> Each premise of decision, to be sure, was qualified by competing considerations. The judges not only felt obligated to obey the Supreme Court but also to assist in legal growth, and their psychic independence was probably too strong for frequent rule by anticipated reactions of the U.S. Supreme Court. They identified themselves with a national community, and regional reference groups, especially in the South. Informal norms are national in scope but regionally enforced.[53]

Federal district courts, while influenced by national legal norms, are more local courts and are even more susceptible to local or popular pressures. Federal Judge John Miller of Arkansas emphasized the relationship between local values and judges in addressing the desegregation issue in the 1950s: "Judges must speak for the will of the people." [54]

The impact of different constituencies is also apparent in differences between state courts and federal courts as interpreting groups. Several authors hypothesize that federal courts are more likely to implement Supreme Court policies fairly and correctly than are most state courts. The reasons for this are presumably that federal judges are more socialized to national legal norms and soon loosen their ties to local political systems.

Evidence concerning differences in the implementation of judicial policy between state and federal courts is somewhat divided. One study, by Edward Beiser, of lower court responses to the Supreme Court's reapportionment decision in *Baker v. Carr* (1962) evaluated state and federal court differences on several dimensions. Beiser's analysis demonstrated that state courts were *not* more critical of the Supreme Court's decision, and that state courts were just as likely as federal courts to give broad interpretations to this decision. His findings were surprising, since many scholars expected state courts to be more susceptible to political pressures, making them more conservative and timid in the political thicket of reapportionment. Beiser offers a possible explanation for these negligible differences by suggesting, "Careful selection by litigants of courts in which they sought benefits from *Baker v. Carr* may have prevented such differences from occurring." [55]

A later study on a different issue by Kenneth Haas partly corrected for the problem of selectivity by considering how federal courts of appeals and state supreme courts dealt with nine questions concerning the implementation of *Johnson v. Avery* (1969). This Supreme Court decision held that state prisoners have a general right to legal counsel and legal assistance, but did not specify explicitly how that right could be exercised, thus leaving it up to lower courts to define the rights precisely. Haas found that the federal courts of appeals were more inclined to decide in favor of the prisoner than were the state appellate courts. Out of 40 decisions by federal courts, 27 "strengthened the ability of inmates to secure judicial redress of their grievances. However, only 6 of the 22 responses from state appellate courts constituted a victory for prisoners." Perhaps more telling, according to Haas, there were no instances "where a state supreme court resolved a particular question in a liberal manner while the federal appeals court encompassing that state responded in a conservative fashion." Thus, for a variety of reasons, Haas concludes that "state judges can be expected to respond to different and more salient nonjudicial pressures when dealing with questions of rights of politically unpopular litigants." [56]

The Influence of Policy Consequences on Judges. We can best see how environmental pressures affect judges' interpretations if we focus on policies with potentially dramatic consequences. If lower court interpretations of higher court policies mean that substantial changes are required in the community and if those changes are viewed negatively by the community, then there may be substantial incentives for local judges not to implement the judicial policies. We have previously cited the reluctance of southern judges to implement the *Brown* decision in the late 1950s and early 1960s due to their perceptions of community opposition to the Supreme Court's desegregation decision.

A study of the desegregation decisions of southern federal district judges from the late 1960s to the early 1970s brings into focus the effects of potential disruption. This study, by Micheal Giles and Thomas Walker, finds a relationship between location of the court and location of the school system under desegregation orders by the judge. Giles and Walker found that if the court was in the school district under supervision, then levels of segregation were likely to be substantially higher than if the court and school district were in different localities. The researchers offer several explanations for this finding, but the most plausible one seems to be that when "faced with desegregating his own community, a judge may be more concerned with public reaction than when dealing with an outlying area." [57] Thus, when the level of disruption may be great—as it might be when massive changes are ordered for large communities, which usually have federal district courts—then interpretations and the implementation of judicial policies may be more consistent with local preferences.

Another, more direct evaluation of whether levels of disruption affect the responses of interpreting groups was made by G. Alan Tarr, who studied state supreme court reactions to a series of U.S. Supreme Court decisions concerning religious exercises in the public schools. Tarr tests the hypothesis that "response depends fundamentally on judicial perceptions of the effects the impact that alternative responses would have on state policy and/or practices within the state." [58] Essentially, the hypothesis is that the greater the disruption a decision would have on state practices, the greater the probability that responses would be noncompliant. Tarr evaluates the hypothesis by classifying states into those with widespread and longstanding school religious practices and those where the practices were either new or localized. The first category of states had approximately 70 percent compliant responses, whereas the second category had approximately 96 percent compliant responses. Another analysis, which included only cases where the state courts had to choose between noncompliance and the invalidation of state programs, revealed a more dramatic difference. In states where schoolhouse religious practices were widespread and longstanding, the compliance rate was 20 percent, while in the other states the compliance rate was 90 percent.[59] In a related analysis, Tarr also finds that noncompliant decisions are directly related to the incidence of schoolhouse religious practices within the state. Essentially, the greater the religious activities within the state's public schools, the less likely the state supreme court was to interpret the U.S. Supreme Court's decisions such as *Schempp* to require substantial change. Thus, Tarr concludes that compliance is greater "when invalidation of state or local programs is unlikely to have substantial effects felt by larger segments of the state populace."[60]

Judicial Attitudes and Interpreting Decisions

Besides being subject to environmental pressures, a judge's interpretations of policy can be influenced by his or her political attitude. Most often, judges will try to be detached in their application of the law, but they are intellectually active individuals who usually have opinions—often vigorous ones—on legal issues of the day. Where ambiguity and limited language in a policy-making court's opinion allow, individual opinions are likely to make their way into a lower court judge's interpretation. Strongly held individual opinions may even override environmental pressures for positive or negative interpretations of a policy.

At least two kinds of personal attitudes may come into play when a lower court judge interprets a higher court's decisions. First, attitudes about a relevant prior policy may be important, especially if a judge is committed to the policy. Second, the individual policy preferences of judges may leave their mark on judicial interpretations of policy. If the judge is favorably disposed toward a higher court policy, then his or her interpretations may be more expansive or positive than the norm; the reverse would be true for judges unfavorably disposed toward a policy.

Commitments to Prior Policies by Judges. Judges may be committed to policies in their jurisdiction for several reasons. First, the policies may be consistent with the judges' personal values. Second, the policies may be consistent with environmental pressures that constrain the judge. Third, even if the policy itself falls into the zone of indifference for a particular judge, continuing with the policy is easier than making major changes. In such situations judges would prefer to deal with the existing policies or to deal only with minor, incremental changes instead of with massive, fundamental changes.

The hypothesis that prior policy commitments influence lower court reactions to higher court decisions was advanced by Neil Romans, who studied state supreme court responses to the Supreme Court's decisions in *Escobedo v. Illinois* (1964) and *Miranda* (1966). Romans asserts that the *Escobedo* ruling, which held that criminal defendants should be provided an attorney in the pretrial stages of the judicial process, was vague about when and under what circumstances the attorney should be supplied. Romans found that after *Escobedo,* and before the more definitive *Miranda* decision, state supreme courts frequently refused to abandon their previous positions, in spite of an obvious liberal push from the U.S. Supreme Court. Romans argues that "short of a clear command from the Supreme Court, state supreme courts would continue to assert their traditional policy positions and distinguish Supreme Court decisions as narrowly as possible to prevent fundamental changes in their policy positions." [61]

Romans also found further evidence that lower courts may become committed to their own policies. After the *Miranda* decision, which precisely stated the rights of criminal suspects, many of the courts that had previously been conservative in the area of criminal rights revised their policies accordingly. However, state courts that had until then been innovative and liberal became very conservative, giving limited interpretations to the *Miranda* decision. Romans explains this unusual finding by suggesting that there was "a feeling of institutional loyalty within the innovative courts—a strong spirit of independence and resistance to outside interference in their policy making. These courts had developed a commitment to the policies that they had been evolving on their own and seemed to resent attempted interference from the outside forces with what they felt were adequate procedural safeguards for criminal suspects." [62]

The hypothesis that courts may react negatively to liberal higher court decisions if they have been innovative in the same policy area was also tested by Tarr in his research on the responses of state supreme courts to the U.S. Supreme Court's religious decisions. In contrast to Romans, Tarr found that courts that maintained a policy of greater separation of church and state, a position Tarr views as being innovative, were more compliant than courts that had allowed closer relations between church and state. Moreover, there was no relationship between a lower court's having made a number of decisions concerning church-state relations and that court's noncompliance, even though the court presumably could be expected to remain committed to its established policy. Tarr concludes that the lack of any relationship reinforced the hypothesis that the degree of anticipated disruption (p. 66) explains lower court reluctance to interpret Supreme Court decisions fully.[63]

Why Romans and Tarr derive completely different findings is unclear. Both authors deal with Supreme Court decisions that were essentially liberal in issue areas where conservative policies had prevailed before. Both authors study state supreme courts rendering decisions during roughly the same period of time—the 1960s. And both issues were highly salient in the legal community as well as the general public. Other scholars have also produced conflicting results. David Manwaring's study of California court implementation of *Mapp v. Ohio* found that innovative courts were reluctant to abandon their positions in the face of a liberal policy by the Supreme Court.[64] But Bradley C. Canon found that limited or expansive state supreme court interpretations of *Mapp* were unrelated to whether the state had adopted the exclusionary rule before the U.S. Supreme Court.[65]

Personal Policy Preferences of Judges. Over the past two decades political scientists have developed a large body of research about the impact of judges' attitudes and policy preferences on judicial decisions. Most of this research focuses on appellate court judges, particularly Supreme Court justices; however, some research suggests that on occasions lower court judges are also influenced by personal policy preferences. Researchers find, for example, that sentences imposed upon criminals by trial courts are influenced by the attitudes of judges. While many lower court decisions do not concern the interpretation and implementation of judicial policy directly, findings linking attitudes and behavior are at least suggestive of the potential influence judges' attitudes may have on their responses to higher court policy.

Beyond the occasional outburst from a lower court judge who is interpreting a higher court's decision, it is very difficult to demonstrate a link between a judge's attitude and his or her interpretive behavior. Some observers reach the conclusion that attitudes are important on the basis of indirect evidence. Lawrence Baum states, "On standards of patent validity, policies of the courts of appeal and district courts are significantly related. However, this relationship is far from perfect, indicating a substantial gap between the two levels of courts and their decisional tendencies." Since he found that Supreme Court decisions had little impact on lower court patent decisions, and since external forces were minimal in the area of patent policy, Baum concludes that "the most important . . . factor may be judges' own preferences." [66] In another study, J. Woodford Howard asked court of appeals judges: "In reaching decisions, how influential are these factors?" Judges were to evaluate a number of considerations, including personal attitudes, precedents, and the nature of the parties and attorneys. Nearly all of the judges (32 of 35) indicated that "precedent when clear and relevant" was very important, and this factor ranked at the top of the decision-making considerations. In a follow-up question, Howard asked: "When precedents are absent or ambiguous, what do you do?" To this question, most judges selected the choice "dictates of justice" (chosen by 26 of 35 judges).[67] Presumably, if these judges believed a clear, applicable precedent did not exist, then *their* notions of justice guided the decision before them.

A few researchers have attempted to test the impact of judges' personal policy preferences on lower court interpretations of higher court decisions by linking the interpretations to the judges' social and political backgrounds.[68] Such efforts have produced mixed results. Tarr, for example, found no relationship between background characteristics, such as urbanization of birthplace or religious affiliation, and support for the Supreme Court's religious decisions. He found a moderately weak relationship between party affiliation and judicial responses: Republican judges were more likely to comply with the Supreme Court's religious decisions than were Democratic judges.[69]

The studies by Richardson and Vines and by Giles and Walker also produced mixed results. Richardson and Vines found that Democratic and Republican judges' civil rights decision making differed dramatically during the 1950s and 1960s, but the direction of the relationship was not what many expected. Democratic judges were more conservative than were Republican judges, a relationship explained by the stronger links Democratic judges had with the southern culture and political system.[70] Giles and Walker did not find such a relationship for judges deciding school desegregation cases in the late 1960s and early 1970s.[71]

A later study by Susan Heike of school desegregation decisions made between 1954 and 1975 for all federal district court judges confirmed both of these findings. Heike's analysis reconfirmed the findings of Richardson and Vines that judges with social and political backgrounds tying them to the South tended to render segregationist decisions in the years from 1954 to 1963. However, judges appointed after 1963 were more inclined to render desegregationist decisions, while judges serving both before and after 1963 shifted slightly in favor of desegregation.[72]

Finally, a study by Kathleen Barber on the behavior of judges deciding reapportionment cases on state supreme courts after *Baker v. Carr* (1962) found that partisan backgrounds played a major role in how this decision was interpreted. Barber found that when judges in Michigan and Ohio were faced with choices that benefited either the Democratic or the Republican party, only 5 of 27 cast at least one vote inconsistent with their party position. In Michigan 8 of 11 supreme court judges voted their party line consistently; in Ohio 6 of 7 state supreme court judges voted with their party. Barber also noted that 4 out of 6 federal judges ruling on apportionment in the two states voted for interpretations that enhanced their parties' legislative strength.[73]

SUMMARY

The interpreting population exists because judicial decisions almost always generate further questions or problems about their meaning as they are applied to particular circumstances. Thus the actions of this population constitute the first link in the chain of events that develops the impact of judicial policies. Lower court judges are the heart of this population, since lower court interpretations are authoritative. This chapter has focused on their responses to higher court decisions.

Several factors result in freedom for and constraints on lower court judges in their interpretive role. One important source of freedom is that most lower court decisions are final; only a minority of cases are appealed. Another factor is that higher court judges cannot fire lower court judges for incompetent or even deliberate misinterpretations. However, lower court judges usually feel constrained to make honest interpretive efforts out of a sense of professionalism, legal obligation, and regard for their own reputation. Moreover, they realize that the legal system would fall apart if lower court judges did not generally abide by higher court rulings.

A judge's willingness to accept a higher court decision depends upon whether it falls within his or her "zone of indifference." For most judges, the zone is broad enough to encompass the great majority of judicial policies. But some decisions—usually in emotional issue areas such as desegregation—fall outside the zone. In cases where a judge refuses to accept a higher court decision, he or she can interpret it extremely narrowly, try to avoid having to acknowledge or interpret it at all, or, in rare instances, engage in overtly defiant behavior. On the other side of the zone, a judge who is highly enthusiastic about a higher court decision can expand its meaning or coverage well beyond its original parameters.

Several factors affect lower court interpretations. Clarity of the decision(s) setting forth the policy is an important factor. Ambiguous or vague statements, multiple opinions, inconsistent precedents, and the like make the task of interpretation difficult and leave more room for discretion. Second, there is no systematic method for communicating higher court policies; at times they are not accurately communicated to the lowest judicial levels. Third, a lower court will not abide by a policy it believes is not legitimate—one it believes the higher court has no right to make. Finally, a lower court may refuse to follow a decision whose authority seems tenuous, such as one made by a plurality vote or one that appears to have lost majority support on the higher court after a change in judges.

Lower court interpretations often respond to actual or perceived pressures from the local political and social environment. Concerns about reelection or reappointment, adverse publicity, and reactions from social peers affect the nature of lower court interpretations of unpopular higher court policies. This is particularly true when there are marked political and cultural differences between the higher court's environment and that of the lower court—as occurred in the desegregation cases in the 1950s and 1960s.

The attitudes of lower court judges are also important in explaining their acceptance of and response to higher court decisions. Courts already committed to prior policies of their own making are often more reluctant to accept different policies wholeheartedly than are courts with no preexisting policies. And, of course, the personal preferences of judges with regard to the policies at issue are highly important in shaping their interpretive responses.

NOTES

1. "Michigan Ban on Ads for Alcohol Struck Down," *Lexington (Ky.) Herald-Leader,* February 7, 1982, B-7.
2. See, for example, Howard Ball, *Courts and Politics: The Federal Judicial System* (Englewood Cliffs, N.J.: Prentice-Hall, 1980), pt. 2; and Henry R. Glick, *Courts, Politics and Justice* (New York: McGraw-Hill, 1983), ch. 2.
3. Frank Sorauf, *The Wall of Separation: The Constitutional Politics of Church and State* (Princeton, N.J.: Princeton University Press, 1976), 216-217.

4. "Judges with Coal Interests Are Controversial," *Lexington (Ky.) Herald-Leader,* July 13, 1980, A-12.

5. *State v. Harp,* 457 P.2d 800 (Okla. Crim. App. 1969) at 806.

6. *LeBlanc v. Henderson,* 259 So.2d 557 (La. 1972) at 566.

7. The concept of the zone of indifference was introduced by Chester I. Barnard in *The Functions of the Executive* (Cambridge, Mass.: Harvard University Press, 1938). G. Alan Tarr has also used this concept in relation to judicial impact in *Judicial Impact and State Supreme Courts* (Lexington, Mass.: Lexington Books, 1977), 86.

8. See, for example, Robert H. Jackson, *The Struggle for Judicial Supremacy* (New York: Knopf, 1941), esp. ch. 1 and 9; and Jack Peltason, *Federal Courts in the Political Process* (New York: Random House, 1955), 46-48.

9. Donald R. Songer, "The Impact of the Supreme Court on Outcomes in U.S. Courts of Appeals: A Comparison of Four Issue Areas" (Paper delivered at the 55th Annual Meeting of the Southern Political Science Association, Birmingham, Ala., November 1983), 6.

10. "22 Negroes Fined in Bus Bias Case," *New York Times,* March 22, 1957, 14.

11. See Note, "Lower Court Disavowal of Supreme Court Precedent," *Virginia Law Review* 60 (1974): 495. Other examples of trial court refusals to apply Supreme Court decisions can be found in this article.

12. See Bradley C. Canon and Kenneth Kolson, "Compliance with Gault in Rural America: The Case of Kentucky," *Journal of Family Law* 10 (1971): 300-326; and Norman Lefstein, Vaughn Stapleton, and Lee Tietelbaum, "In Search of Juvenile Justice: *Gault* and Its Implementation," *Law and Society Review* 3 (May 1969): 491-560.

13. See Karl Llewellyn, *The Bramble Bush* (New York: Oceana, 1951), 68.

14. See, for example, Karen Orren, "Standing to Sue: Interest Group Conflict in the Federal Courts," *American Political Science Review* 70 (1976): 723-741.

15. Eight court orders involving the delay are reprinted in "Virgil Hawkins Goes to Law," in *Courts, Judges, and Politics,* ed. Walter Murphy and C. Herman Pritchett (New York: Random House, 1961), 606-617.

16. Bernard Stern, "Judge William Harold Cox and the Right to Vote in Clarke County, Mississippi," in *Southern Justice,* ed. Leon Friedman (New York: Pantheon, 1965), 165-186.

17. "Shopping Malls Protest Intrusion by Protesters," *New York Times,* July 19, 1983, 13.

18. "High Court Lets Stand Topless Ruling in New York," *New York Times,* June 2, 1982, 15.

19. Donald Wilkes, "The New Federalism in Criminal Procedure: State Court Evasions of the Burger Court," *Kentucky Law Journal* 62 (1974): 421-451.

20. *Flemming v. South Carolina Gas and Electric Co.,* 128 F.Supp. 469 (D.S.C., 1956) at 470.

21. See Bradley C. Canon, "Organizational Contumacy in the Transmission of Judicial Policies: The *Mapp, Escobedo, Miranda,* and *Gault* Cases," *Villanova Law Review* 20 (November 1974): 50-79.

22. Kenneth Dolbeare and Phillip Hammond, *The School Prayer Decisions* (Chicago: University of Chicago Press, 1971), 52.

23. *Zorach v. Clausen,* 343 U.S. 306 (1952) at 313.

24. Frank Sorauf, "*Zorach versus Clausen:* The Impact of a Supreme Court Decision," *American Political Science Review* 53 (September 1959): 789.

25. Bob Woodward and Scott Armstrong, *The Brethren: Inside the Supreme Court* (New York: Simon and Schuster, 1979), 112.

26. Note, "Lower Court Disavowal," 499.

27. See Stephen Wasby, Anthony D'Amato, and Rosemary Metrailer, *Desegregation From Brown to Alexander* (Carbondale, Ill.: Southern Illinois University Press, 1977).

28. John Gruhl, "The Supreme Court's Impact on the Law of Libel: Compliance by Lower Federal Courts," *Western Political Quarterly* 33 (December 1980): 518.

29. Ibid.

30. Carol E. Jenson, *The Network of Control: State Supreme Courts and State Security Statutes, 1920-1970* (Westport, Conn.: Greenwood Press, 1982), 91.

31. Michael Combs, "Courts of Appeals and Northern School Desegregation: Questions, Answers, and Public Policy" (Paper delivered at the 39th Annual Meeting of the Midwest Political Science Association, Cincinnati, Ohio, April 1981).

32. Stephen Wasby, "The Communication of the Supreme Court's Criminal Procedure Decisions," *Villanova Law Review* 18 (June 1973): 1090.

33. Donald Jackson, *Judges* (New York: Atheneum, 1974), 46.

34. Ibid, 36.

35. Quotation from Walter Murphy and C. Herman Pritchett, eds., *Courts, Judges, and Politics,* 3d ed. (New York: Random House, 1979), 159-160.

36. Canon and Kolson, "Compliance with Gault."

37. John Paul Ryan et al., *American Trial Judges: Their Workstyles and Performance* (New York: Free Press, 1980), 35.

38. "Chief Justice Burger Proposes First Steps toward Certification of Trial Advocacy Specialists," *American Bar Association Journal* 60 (February 1974): 173-174.

39. See Canon, "Organizational Contumacy," for further discussion of state court perceptions of illegitimate U.S. Supreme Court decisions.

40. See S. Sidney Ulmer, "Earl Warren and the Desegregation Cases," *Journal of Politics* 33 (August 1971): 689-701.

41. Charles A. Johnson, "Lower Court Reactions to Supreme Court Decisions: A Quantitative Examination," *American Journal of Political Science* 23 (November 1979): 802.

42. See J. F. Davis and W. L. Reynold, "Judicial Cripples: Plurality Opinions in the Supreme Court," *Duke Law Journal* 1974 (1974): 59-86.

43. Beverly Blair Cook, "Public Opinion and Federal Judicial Policy," *American Journal of Political Science* 21 (August 1977): 567-600.

44. James Kuklinski and John E. Stanga, "Political Participation and Government Responsiveness: The Behavior of California Superior Courts," *American Political Science Review* 73 (December 1979): 1090-1099.

45. James Gibson, "Environmental Constraints on the Behavior of Judges: A Representational Model of Judicial Decision Making," *Law and Society Review* 14 (Winter 1980): 343-370.

46. Dona Cochran, "Why So Many Judges Are Going Down to Defeat," *California Journal,* September 1980, 359-360.

47. Jack L. Peltason, *Fifty-eight Lonely Men: Federal Judges and School Desegregation* (New York: Harcourt, Brace and World, 1961), 9.

48. Ibid., 10.

49. "The Busing Judge: A Reminiscence," *Louisville Courier Journal,* September 21, 1980, 17.

50. Peltason, *Fifty-eight Lonely Men,* 10.

51. Jack Bass, *Unlikely Heroes* (New York: Simon and Schuster, 1981).

52. Richard Richardson and Kenneth Vines, *The Politics of the Federal Courts: Lower Courts in the United States* (Boston: Little, Brown, 1970).

53. J. Woodford Howard, *Courts of Appeals in the Federal Judicial System: A Study of the Second, Fifth, and District of Columbia* (Princeton: Princeton University Press, 1981).

54. Peltason, *Fifty-eight Lonely Men,* 197.

55. Edward Beiser, "A Comparative Analysis of State and Federal Judicial Behavior: The Reapportionment Cases," *American Political Science Review* 62 (September 1968): 794. Werner Grunbaum and Lettie Wenner, "Comparing Environmental Litigation in State and Federal Courts," *Publius* 10 (1980): 129-142, have also found state courts equally if not more willing to enforce environmental restrictions on business.

56. Kenneth Haas, "Supreme Court Prisoners' Rights Decisions and the Lower Federal and State Courts: A Comparative Analysis" (Paper delivered at the 37th Annual Meeting of the Midwest Political Science Association, Chicago, Ill., April 1979), 27, 30.

57. Micheal Giles and Thomas Walker, "Judicial Policy-Making and Southern School Segregation," *Journal of Politics* 37 (May 1975): 932.

58. Tarr, *Judicial Impact and State Supreme Courts,* 105.

59. Ibid., 117.

60. Ibid., 75, 117.

61. Neil Romans, "The Role of State Supreme Courts in Judicial Impact Analysis," *Western Political Quarterly* 27 (March 1974): 51.

62. Ibid., 58-59.

63. Tarr, *Judicial Impact and State Supreme Courts,* 117-120.

64. David Manwaring, "The Impact of *Mapp v. Ohio,*" in *The Supreme Court as Policy-Maker: Three Studies on the Impact of Judicial Decisions,* ed. David Everson (Carbondale, Ill.: Public Affairs Research Bureau, Southern Illinois University, 1968).

65. Bradley C. Canon, "Reactions of State Supreme Courts to a U.S. Supreme Court Civil Liberties Decision," *Law and Society Review* 8 (Fall 1973): 109-134.

66. Lawrence Baum, "Responses of Federal District Judges to Court of Appeals Policies: An Exploration," *Western Political Quarterly* 33 (June 1980): 223, 224.

67. Howard, *Courts of Appeals,* 165.

68. For a discussion of the extensive literature on the influence of backgrounds on judicial decision making see C. Neal Tate, "Personal Attribute Models of the Voting Behavior of U.S. Supreme Court Justices: Liberalism in Civil Liberties and Economic Liberties Decisions, 1946-1978," *American Political Science Review* 75 (June 1981): 355-367; and Sheldon Goldman and Thomas P. Jahnige, *The Federal Courts as a Political System,* 2d ed. (New York: Harper and Row, 1976), esp. ch. 4 and 5.
69. Tarr, *Judicial Impact and State Supreme Courts,* 57-83.
70. Richardson and Vines, *The Politics of the Federal Courts,* 80-112.
71. Giles and Walker, "Judicial Policy-Making."
72. Susan Heike, "Federal District Judges and School Desegregation: Social Background Factors Reconsidered" (Paper delivered at the 50th Annual Meeting of the Southern Political Science Association, Atlanta, Ga., November 1978).
73. Kathleen L. Barber, "Partisan Values in the Lower Courts: Reapportionment in Ohio and Michigan," *Case Western Reserve Law Review* 20 (1969):406-407.

CHAPTER THREE

The Implementing Population

T raditionally, political scientists have paid a great deal of attention to the antecedents of public policies and to the announced policies themselves. But in recent years researchers have broadened their interests to include the consequences of a policy. The results of these new analyses are striking. Whether one examines the aftermath of executive, of legislative, or of judicial decisions, the results seem to be the same—policy implementation is never straightforward, and the *actual* impact of a policy is rarely the same as its *intended* impact.

In our discussion of the aftermath of the Supreme Court's 1973 abortion decision (pp. 5-14) we touched on the wide range of events that may follow a judicial decision. In Chapter 2 we explored the role of lower courts in the impact of judicial decisions and found that lower courts—which, in theory, are obliged to follow the policies of higher courts—do not necessarily interpret policies faithfully. This chapter concerns the actors who are one step further removed from the sources of judicial policy. We call these actors the implementing population because members of this population usually carry on the day-to-day tasks of translating executive, legislative, *and* judicial policies into action.

The membership of the implementing population is quite diverse. Although it is a mistake to dismiss the influence of individuals acting alone in implementing public policy, in most cases implementation is a group effort by some bureaucratic organization. Implementing groups range from major departments of the federal government to local school officials. The population is composed of individuals and institutions with different motivations and preferences from those of the legislators, executives, and judges who originated the public policies. In addition, the implementors are subject to a variety of pressures that may not influence the original policy makers.

Since these groups implement legislative, executive, and judicial policies, statements about their behavior regarding judicial policy may also apply to their reactions to legislative and executive policies. School boards, for example, must respond to demands on a variety of issues from state education offices, state legislatures, the U.S. Departments of Education and Justice, and occasionally a state or federal court. Although there has been little research on the matter, there is reason to believe that school boards, and perhaps more generally any implementing group, respond differently to different superior policy makers.[1]

The ways in which implementing groups respond to executive and legislative mandates are beyond the scope of this book, since we are interested in the impact of judicial policies. However, it is important to note that compared to the implementation of executive and legislative policies, that of judicial policies is likely to be very problematic. This difference can be traced to the relationship between the courts and most members of the implementing population.

THE JUDICIARY AND THE IMPLEMENTING POPULATION

Variations in the implementation of public policies and differences between the intended and the actual consequences of a policy may be the result of several factors. The capacity of the court to shape the implementation process is one factor particularly relevant to the relationship between the judiciary and the implementing population. Using an implementation model proposed by Paul Sabatier and Daniel Mazanian, Lawrence Baum argues that the courts are in a weak position to exercise sufficient influence over the behavior of implementors. He points out that the reason for the courts' weak position is twofold: first, "courts are imprisoned within the adjudicative process," and second, "courts lack some very important legal powers ... the judiciary does not control the sword or the purse."[2] The effects of these two factors are substantial and underscore the tenuous nature of the relationship between judicial bodies and implementing groups.

Legislatures and executives may initiate a policy and investigate its implementation at their discretion. However, courts must wait until a case is filed in order to render a policy announcement, and later they must also wait for additional cases to review a policy's implementation. For example, the Supreme Court announced in several decisions (*McCollum v. Board of Education,* 1948; *Abington School District v. Schempp,* 1963) that religious activities in public schools must be curtailed. However, many school systems continued religious exercises simply because no one initiated litigation to stop them. Local courts could not order schools to stop the religious activities in the absence of a properly initiated suit. If the implementing group is not challenged or if it is successful in keeping the issue out of the courts, then court influence on the group is quite limited.

Another source of difficulty in the relationship between implementing groups and the judiciary is that a policy itself may be incomplete, unclear, or contradictory. Judicial policies stemming from a court decision are usually limited by the facts of a case and the applicable case law; rarely will a single decision completely outline a policy for implementing groups to follow. Also, because of the norms of the judicial process, especially the requirement that only real cases in controversy will be decided by the courts, implementing groups cannot easily return to a court for clarification of a policy. These agencies must, therefore, frequently interpret a judicial policy before carrying it into action. Of course, unlike the interpretations of judicial policies rendered by lower courts, interpretations by implementing groups do not have authoritative force. But even though an implementing group's interpretation may not be authoritative or correct, in order to be reversed it must first be challenged in court, something that does not occur in many policy areas. If the original statement of a judicial policy is unclear or ambiguous—as is the case with many lower court decisions—implementing groups are more or less free to interpret and implement the policy as they wish, until their actions are challenged and reversed in court.

A further difficulty that is unique to judicial policies is that the institutional powers of the judiciary usually limit the court's selection of who implements a judicial policy, how it is done, and with what resources. Thus the judiciary is for the most part forced to work with existing implementing groups. To compound the problem, the groups that implement the policies are frequently parties to the decision. If the implementing group loses its case, then it must immediately execute a decision against which it fought for weeks, months, or even years. Even if the implementing group is not directly involved in the litigation, it may have commitments to a policy similar to that of a participant in the original lawsuit. Hence, the judiciary frequently has no choice except to rely on implementing groups that have opposed the policy being adopted by the court.

Courts cannot often choose implementing agencies, and only rarely are they in a position to select personnel for those agencies. Attorneys appointed by the court, usually called *special masters,* are occasionally used to oversee the implementation of a decision, but normally masters work with a particular implementing agency and a particular set of administrators.

While courts may not select implementing groups or appoint personnel in those groups, they do have the power to impose fines and jail sentences. If an implementing group is ordered to carry out a particular policy but fails to do so, its members may be cited for contempt of court. Being convicted of contempt could result in daily fines or in jail sentences for the offending parties. While the powers stemming from the ability to bring contempt procedures are substantial, courts are quite reluctant to use them. Most judges explore all other alternatives before initiating contempt proceedings. The size and diversity of some implementing groups make the first step difficult—citing numerous members of a department of government for contempt is difficult logistically. Moreover, contempt citations may be problematic for political persons—for example, citing a governor or a legislature for contempt is difficult politically for a state or even a federal judge. A judge may be deterred by the complicated logistics of citing members of a group, such as an entire government department or a large group of teachers, for contempt; the size and diversity of the organization make the proceedings very cumbersome. In other instances, a judge may find it difficult and potentially damaging to his or her career to cite politicians for contempt because doing so may enflame public opinion against the court or the policy. For example, Mississippi Governor Ross Barnett's contempt citation from a federal district court for refusing to admit black applicant James Meredith to the University of Mississippi in 1962 was overturned (see *Barnett v. United States,* 1964). Still, implementors do not treat the prospect of contempt citations lightly. In all but the most extreme situations, officials will seek to avoid them through at least minimal compliance and tacit compromises.

The relationship between any policy-making group and any implementing group is likely to be tenuous. But the procedural constraints of the judicial process and the limited powers of the judiciary make the relationship between the judiciary and relevant implementing groups especially tentative. Of course, it is wrong to infer that few judicial policies are ever implemented; most are, at least to some extent. The fact is that implementation varies from group to group and from policy to policy. The remainder of this chapter is devoted to understanding why these variations occur.

IMPLEMENTING GROUPS AS ORGANIZATIONS

Courts decide matters involving a variety of policy areas, including criminal justice, economic regulation, civil liberties, civil rights, and election disputes. Not all decisions require implementation by someone other than the parties immediately involved in the court suit, but many decisions have policy implications that affect others in the political system. Commonly, almost all implementing groups are organizations, regardless of the policy area involved, the number of implementing groups affected, or the size of the groups expected to respond to the judicial policy. Most are public organizations—public agencies at the federal, state, or local level—but a few are private organizations, as were some of the hospitals that responded to the Supreme Court's abortion decision. In our efforts to understand implementing groups, the work of organizational theorists and researchers about how these groups respond to demands for change is especially relevant.

Organizational responses to judicial decisions arise out of a series of complex factors, including an organization's commitment to existing programs and policies and its wish to conserve resources for agency-defined goals.[3] These factors often constitute inertial forces that undercut attempts to change policies and practices. However, agencies also want to avoid sanctions for failure to change programs and policies. Hence, if a court decision requires change, that change is not likely to follow without some resistance, unless the effects of inertial forces are overcome or unless the change furthers the organization's pursuit of agency-defined goals.

Organizational theorists tell us that organizations faced with demands for change engage in at least three activities: they interpret and decide to accept or reject the demands; they search for ways to meet those demands as well as for ways to circumvent them; and, if necessary, they change policies and practices in order to satisfy the demands for change while retaining as many of the organization's original goals as possible.[4] The last two activities are what we call *program adjustments.*

Interpreting Judicial Decisions

We noted in Chapter 2 that judicial decisions often need interpretation. Lower courts have the responsibility of giving official interpretations to the judicial decisions of higher courts. However, even lower courts cannot anticipate all of the day-to-day circumstances under which judicial policies may be applicable; and while lower courts are giving meaning to the original decisions of higher courts, the implementing population is still expected to institute the changes required by the higher courts. Hence, implementing agencies often must themselves interpret judicial decisions, and only sometimes with the help of lower court elaborations. Of course, the interpretations of implementing groups are not authoritative and do not have the status of a law. However, because many interpretations by implementing agencies go unchallenged, they often have the same effect as official interpretations by lower courts.

An agency's acceptance of a judicial decision is a function of what the agency believes the court is requiring, that is, of the agency's interpretation. Kenneth Dolbeare and Phillip Hammond, for example, suggest that the rural and small-town school officials they interviewed gave limited interpretations to the Supreme Court's school prayer decision in *Schempp*. The officials saw it as banning the *establishment* of religion in public schools, but not as limiting the *free exercise* of religion. Hence, their discussions about the changes that ought to be made in the school system concerned the "amount of religion allowed by the Court." This interpretation was characterized by Dolbeare and Hammond as follows: "The state shall not require religious exercises; the state shall respect religious diversity; and therefore its public schools shall protect the religious rights of all students." [5] Because officials believed that their schools did not sanction "official" prayers and that the existing prayer procedures were not "coercive," it follows that no action by the school board was required to ensure compliance with *Schempp*.

Other researchers who examined the reactions of school systems to *Schempp* also found that interpretations of this decision were directly related to the system's behavioral responses. William Muir reports that the implementation of the school prayer decision in the school district he studied was based largely on the interpretations of the school board.[6] In this instance, however, the interpretations resulted in a ban on all religious activities in the local schools. Studies by Richard Johnson and by Robert Birkby also show that diverse interpretations of *Schempp* affected its impact in various communities.[7] The interpretation of the decisions finally adopted by the officials largely dictated the alternatives later considered by the organizations. The major difference between cases in which narrow or incorrect interpretations are given to judicial decisions and instances in which generally correct or broad interpretations are given is that one or more of the authoritative figures in the organization have been in fundamental agreement with the judicial policy.

In general, when a judicial decision receives an incorrect or narrow interpretation, no authoritative figure in the implementing organization is in agreement with the policy; when a decision receives a generally correct or broad interpretation, one or more of these figures are in fundamental agreement with the policy. Except for a few officials who came to their positions after the Court had acted, no officials in Dolbeare and Hammond's study had eagerly accepted the school prayer decisions. In the school systems studied by Muir and by Johnson, however, many officials were sympathetic with the Court's actions to remove religion from the public schools. Even in these systems, however, if the school superintendent in one system and the school board's attorney in the other system had not given the *Schempp* decision an accurate and favorable interpretation, then those systems probably would not have discontinued prayers. It is significant that both of these officials dealt with their systems from a position of strength and thus were able to persuade and cajole others in the systems to accept their interpretations.

The Search Process

An integral part of evaluating a judicial policy, except in the few instances when an agency accepts or rejects a decision at the very outset, is obtaining information about the decision and about alternative courses of action for the agency. Anthony Downs, among others, refers to this information-gathering process as a *search process*.[8] Of course, the search process will be influenced by the goals and preferences of the agency's officials, to the extent that ultimately an incomplete picture of the demands and alternatives emerges. But no matter how imperfect the process is, it affects the implementation of policy in concrete ways, and we need to understand how the search is conducted.

Since administrative officials usually wish to conserve resources as well as to avoid sanctions, one of their first considerations is to determine whether the court-mandated changes compromise or conflict with agency goals and preferences. If, in the agency's judgment, the mandates of the court do not significantly alter existing policies, then the agency may continue its activities much as it did before the court decision, making only minor changes in policies or procedures. The agency's decision concerning whether the court's demands are acceptable will depend on at least two factors: the perceived difference between the existing program and that suggested by the court, and the commitment of the agency to the existing program. The less compatible the existing policies are with those suggested by the court, the greater the change that will probably be required by the judicial policy. In such a situation, compromise in agency goals and preferences will be called for. An agency that is faced with an incompatible court decision, rather than adopting the court's policy immediately, will initiate a search for alternatives to consider.

The degree to which an agency is committed to a particular policy or program may also affect the initial response and subsequent search for alternatives. It is difficult to abandon a program to which an agency is highly committed. Southern state governments were vehement supporters of racial segregation, which had been practiced for several generations. Similarly, many school boards had an unshakable belief in the importance of school prayer. Thus, immediate change is not likely under most circumstances. Instead, the agency is more likely to initiate a search for alternatives.

The threat and potential severity of sanctions are other considerations that affect the initiation and scope of a search by an agency responding to a court decision. If a court policy is not immediately acceptable to an agency and if the probability of enforcement is low, then the agency is not likely to engage in an extensive search because any search costs time and money—which are usually limited for most agencies. On the other hand, if officials believe the probability of enforcement to be high, then the search will be wider and will cover a full range of interpretations and alternatives. The severity of sanctions would have a similar impact on any decision to institute a search for alternatives—the greater the probability of severe sanctions, the greater the search activity.

Neal Milner examined differences in the search behavior of four police departments in Wisconsin in his study of the impact of the Supreme Court's decision requiring that criminal suspects be informed of their rights (*Miranda v. Arizona,* 1966). He reports that since most departments and individual officers believed that *Miranda* would result in major changes in the rules governing police behavior, each of the four departments sought out information from legal sources or law enforcement organizations regarding the implications of *Miranda.*[9] Which and how many information sources a department consulted was influenced by the professionalism of the department as well as whether it believed local criminal defense attorneys would enforce the *Miranda* standards. The more professional departments relied extensively on national sources for information (for example, the FBI); the departments in cities with an aggressive defense bar gathered more information.

Not unexpectedly, attorneys within implementing organizations and professional associations tend to dominate the search process for most agencies. Milner reports that the police departments he studied stayed within the department or the law enforcement organizations as far as possible to obtain interpretations and alternative responses to *Miranda.* Similarly, in the school prayer area, Muir reports that the one attorney who was a member of the school board he studied was largely responsible for structuring the alternatives after *Schempp.* In most instances, the net effect of the search process is to produce narrow interpretations and a limited number of alternatives that tend to be consistent with existing policy preferences and agency practices or that minimize the necessary changes.

PROGRAM ADJUSTMENTS AFTER JUDICIAL DECISIONS

Adjustments by an agency after an adverse court decision may involve a variety of changes in policies, procedures, and practices. An agency's response to such a decision can usually be assigned to one of three categories: noncompliance, evidenced by the lack of change in policies, procedures, or practices; evasion, which may include cosmetic changes in policies, procedures, or practices; and compliance, characterized by adjustments to conform to the decision. Of course, as we noted in Chapter 2, categorizing a response is not always an easy matter, especially if there is some ambiguity about what precisely the court expects an agency to do after the decision. Nevertheless, although the categories are rough, they serve at least as useful reference points in discussing the behavioral responses of organizations to judicial policies.

Obviously, our explanation of the behavioral adjustments made by agencies must be considered in the context of their decision to agree or disagree with a decision—their acceptance decision. Presumably, an agency that agrees with a decision is likely to be compliant, as is one that decides to abide by an adverse decision (perhaps because the decision falls within its zone of indifference). But because of other factors affecting their responses, even when they make similar acceptance decisions organizations may adopt different behavioral responses. After considerable speculation and empirical research by some social scientists, explanations of responses usually tend to emphasize one or more of the following features: the communication and clarity of the judicial decision, the policy setting within which the implementing group is expected to respond, and the internal dynamics of the organization implementing the decision. Whether one of these attributes is more important than another is not clear because researchers have not so far compared the influence of these factors in controlled situations.

Communication of the Decision

Just as the clarity and transmission of a judicial policy affect lower court interpretations of that policy (Chapter 2), so do they affect the behavior of implementing groups. In examining the implementation of judicial policies, scholars usually focus on two aspects of the communication process: the clarity of the decision itself and the sources of information used by the implementing agencies to understand the judicial policy.

Even the clearest decision can pose problems. Some Supreme Court decisions, such as *Miranda,* are quite specific about what the police were expected to do. Arresting officers were to read criminal suspects a list of rights that the Court outlined precisely. Nonetheless, there was some initial confusion about the requirements. Michael Wald et al., for example, found that compliance with *Miranda* in New Haven, Connecticut, increased over a several-month period as officers became familiar with the requirements of that decision.[10] The clarity of the *Miranda* decision is often contrasted with the uncertainty stemming from *Mapp v. Ohio* (1961), which was intended to discourage unreasonable search and seizure by state and local authorities. Michael Murphy, former police commissioner of New York City, joined others who argued that the noncompliance with *Mapp* was partially a function of confusion by individual officers about what was expected of them in conducting a search, especially since "the courts have not been able to formulate rules which are adequate guidelines for practical application on the firing line."[11]

The implementation of the *Brown v. Board of Education* decisions in 1954 and 1955 apparently was also affected by the characteristics of the decisions and how they were announced. This case involved two separate opinions, sometimes referred to as *Brown I* and *Brown II. Brown I* held that separate but equal educational facilities were unlawful; the implementation issues associated with that decision were addressed in *Brown II,* announced one year later. Stephen Wasby, Anthony D'Amato, and Rosemary Metrailer argue that the Court's decision to have a second set of arguments "meant that it [the Supreme Court] had already decided that there would be a later implementation opinion that would not be cast in terms of immediate rights, but rather, would involve the court system in a slow process of supervising school boards so that desegregation could proceed 'with all deliberate speed.' "[12] Several criticisms of this decision are summarized by Wasby and his colleagues. First, *Brown II* allowed too much time for desegregation efforts, especially since no specific deadlines were implied. Second, no clear guidelines regarding what was expected were provided for the lower courts that would have to implement the order. Third, *Brown II* was too much concerned with the difficulties of implementation and too little concerned with the principles articulated in *Brown I*. Last, the decision provided a list of factors that lower courts could consider as reasons for delaying the implementation process. In sum, the *Brown II* decision did not provide specific instructions, was not persuasive, and described how *Brown I* could be evaded, at least in the short term. Further, for almost a decade the Court did not issue any other general rulings regarding the implementation of *Brown I* to guide lower courts or school boards in this issue area.[13]

It is unlikely that *any* opinion in the desegregation cases would have been sufficiently persuasive or clear to prompt positive responses from southern public officials, especially in light of their strong commitment to segregated education and their willingness to oppose desegregation with all "legal" and "honorable" means. Nevertheless, since specific instructions were not given to lower court judges, school officials had no specific goals or timetables toward which to work. Moreover, the Supreme Court itself provided a list of circumstances that lower court judges could consider as legitimate reasons for delays in desegregation on the part of school officials. The eventual result of *Brown II* was, then, to give reluctant officials more breathing room and time to avoid implementing the mandates of *Brown I*.

If the original decision may cause confusion, so too may the communication process by which the message is transmitted from the Supreme Court to the implementing agencies. Officials in the implementing agencies rarely read the full opinion of the Court; instead they rely on interpretations of the opinion by others, on an excerpt of the opinion distributed by someone inside or outside of the agency, or on summary information supplied by coworkers or the news media. The communication of criminal justice decisions, for example, appears to be a haphazard, multistage process, which according to some critics inadequately informs police officers of judicial decisions and expectations. Stephen Wasby found that police officers learn of judicial decisions from a variety of sources, including personal friends, the general media, training sessions, and bulletins from law enforcement agencies. He notes that although the local prosecutor is another source of information, the degree to which prosecutors actually inform the police of current due process standards is open to some question. Wasby reports that local prosecuting attorneys were the dominant source of information for the police officers he interviewed in Illinois and Massachusetts, yet the police often felt the prosecutors gave them too little information.[14]

In his study of many parts of the criminal justice system in a middle-sized Illinois city he called Prairie City, David Neubauer notes that the prosecutor's office rarely sent memos to or attempted any other communication with the police and that informal contacts, where information could also be conveyed, were limited.[15] As a last example, Milner reports that the sources and levels of information varied among the four Wisconsin communities he studied, with the most professional department depending on other law enforcement agencies such as the FBI as a source of information.[16] Thus, sources and levels of information vary from individual to individual and from department to department. However, whether these sources are related to different responses generally remains an open question because no scholars have shown any direct links between variations in information and variations in responses.

The Policy Setting

Members of the implementing population must consider the impact of the judicial policies they carry out, including how their own operations are affected. The police, for example, are interested in and concerned about the outcomes of Supreme Court decisions that limit or expand their powers to make arrests, conduct searches, or deter crime. School officials are frequently anxious about court announcements on desegregation, student rights, school prayer, and a variety of other topics affecting the day-to-day operation of their schools. Similarly, others in a community who are affected by a judicial decision may be concerned about its impact, and they may communicate their concern to relevant members of the implementing population. For example, parents are sometimes upset if their children are bused, and may protest vigorously; welfare families are worried if judicial decisions such as *Wyman v. James* (1971) threaten the continuation of welfare payments, and they and their advocates may fight implementation of the decision.

Generally, the political and social environment into which a decision is announced as well as the reactions of affected individuals constitute what we call the *policy setting* for the implementation of a judicial decision. At times, the policy setting of a court decision influences the responses of implementing groups, regardless of how the decision is communicated or how the implementing groups are affected. Three aspects of the policy setting are most often examined by judicial impact researchers: the community's policy preferences, based on prevailing norms or traditions; the pressure from external forces to make changes or to retain the status quo; and the levels of coercion from the judiciary faced by the implementing group.

Policy Preferences. It stands to reason that a community's policy preferences, which are based on existing norms and traditions, will have a direct effect on how a judicial decision is received. And one might expect the anticipated community reaction to the implementation of a judicial decision to be an important factor in the response of an implementing agency. If the policy preference is reinforced by a judicial decision, the community is likely to react positively; if a judicial policy runs counter to a community's traditional preferences, reactions will be negative. While a relationship between preference and acceptance would seem obvious, not all empirical studies find that one exists.

Some researchers have noted that the policy area of school prayer illustrates the importance of community traditions. Several analyses suggest that local traditions regarding school prayers heavily influenced the levels of change after the Supreme Court decisions banning school prayers. The data reported from a survey by John H. Laubauch reveal that changes in behavior and policies were minimal in the South, where religion and education were traditionally mixed. Areas of the country that did not have such a tradition underwent more dramatic change after the prayer decisions.[17] Donald Reich's study compared religious practices in Ohio, where schoolhouse religion was common, and Minnesota, where it was not; he found little policy change in Ohio and widespread approval of the decision in Minnesota. Reich suggests that the particular histories of these two states account for differences in the responses of local school boards.[18]

The prevailing community opinions and preferences on a particular issue may also be important. Of course, whether there is a community consensus on an issue may be difficult to ascertain, and whether community opinions are perceived correctly by implementing groups is also open to question. While there may often be a relationship between community pressure and implementing group response in such policy areas as school desegregation in the 1950s, the evidence on the whole is mixed. Bradley C. Canon's study of police compliance with *Mapp* in 19 cities suggests that the attitudes of a city's political leadership toward a police department's professionalism may be as critical as community sentiment.[19] In another issue area, Birkby's study of the responses of Tennessee school districts to the school prayer decisions showed that two measures of community sentiment, religious pluralism and the degree of opposition to public prayers, were *uncorrelated* with local board policies.[20]

Whereas community norms rarely have the effect of forcing changes, the community frequently acts as a constraint on organizational changes. The constraint imposed by the community may be overriden by other factors, as we will show, but the initial effect of community preferences effectively maintains the status quo in many systems. Dolbeare and Hammond's study of five communities in Indiana underscores the constraints of community preferences. Officials in these communities essentially did nothing in response to the *Schempp* decision—they did not announce a new policy, call for changes in behavior, or comment on the decision at any length. Most officials believed that making program changes would raise the ire of the community, thus jeopardizing other school district projects. The threat or fear of community retaliation was sufficient to deter compliance with the Supreme Court's order. Interestingly, although school board officials believed that the community was heavily committed to certain religious practices in the local schools, Dolbeare and Hammond found little evidence that such a commitment existed or that retaliation for compliance with the Supreme Court's decisions would have been likely.[21] Nonetheless, even if community preferences are more perception than reality, they can be effective constraints on implementing groups.

Local Support for or Opposition to Change. Another critical feature of the policy setting is whether other groups or affected individuals oppose or support changes resulting from a judicial decision. If, for example, local groups oppose a judicial policy and those groups are particularly influential or important to an implementing organization, then one might expect changes to be less likely than if there are no relevant groups or if such groups support the judicial policy. The impact of external groups has been documented in studies about several policy areas, but perhaps the best illustrations come from the studies of the implementation of school desegregation decisions by southern school boards.

Resistance to desegregation was both widespread and intense. While some cities in border areas, such as Baltimore and St. Louis, moved to desegregate swiftly—at least in policy if not in practice[22]— the Deep South simply refused to consider changing. There was little pressure to desegregate from the U.S. Supreme Court and from local courts, while influential leaders in southern communities provided considerable guidance and incentives to continue with segregationist policies. Legislatures in many states passed laws that would overrule the school boards or close the schools in the state if segregation should be abandoned. In Texas, for example, state funds were to be withheld from school systems where desegregation was planned unless approval for desegregation was obtained in a popular referendum.[23] And in New Orleans, after the school board prepared to abide by court-ordered integration, it had to fight to retain control of the school system, a fight it lost temporarily to the state legislature and governor.[24] In another nationally known case of opposition, local officials controlling funds in Prince Edward County, Virginia, forced the closing of public schools, over the school administrators' objections, rather than allowing desegregation.[25]

Another source of support for the status quo came from the "Southern Manifesto" —a document signed in 1957 by 96 U.S. senators and representatives from the South, which says, in part:

> We pledge ourselves to use all lawful means to bring about a reversal of this decision [*Brown v. Board of Education*] which is contrary to the Constitution and to prevent the use of force in its implementation.
>
> In this trying period, as we seek to right this wrong, we appeal to our people not to be provoked by the agitators and trouble makers invading our states and to scrupulously refain from disorder and lawlessness.[26]

Many southern officials had focused a good deal of attention on the possibility of reversing the desegregation decision or of blocking its implementation, so for many of them the Southern Manifesto legitimized opposition to the *Brown* decision. Wasby, D'Amato, and Metrailer suggest that the Manifesto "was probably the single most influential document defying desegregation in the South. It provided important approval of and support for the plan of 'massive resistance' and made such resistance 'socially acceptable' by giving [it] the blessing of the Southern Establishment." [27]

The first decade after *Brown* did not see a great deal of change in policies or behavior. However, the rate of desegregation increased dramatically in the mid-1960s. By then the pressures on southern school boards from external forces had changed from overwhelming support for segregation to substantial support for desegregation. The U.S. Supreme Court abandoned its hands-off policy and required local boards to take positive steps to desegregate. Many lower federal courts followed suit. But perhaps more important was the passage of the 1964 Civil Rights Act, which ushered in what Harrell Rodgers and Charles Bullock call the "Administrative-Judicial Era" of the civil rights movement.[28] Title VI of the act provided that the Department of Health, Education and Welfare (HEW) could terminate funds to public schools that practiced racial discrimination. With this provision the slow, case-by-case approach using the courts was

replaced by administrative guidelines establishing particular requirements for school districts in progressing toward desegregation. Also,
the law required that the districts report their progress to HEW, thus
placing them in the position of defending the current racial distributions of the schools under their jurisdiction. Soon after the passage of
the law, HEW moved to terminate funding in several districts, and a
small number were subjected to a cutoff of federal funds in 1967. The
net effect of these measures was to increase coercive pressures to
desegregate on reluctant school systems. By and large, the increased
levels of coercion worked to bring about an end to dual school systems
in the South by the mid-1970s.

Pressures from significant others in the community may be
another important factor in accounting for responses of implementors
to judicial decisions. Local school boards considering desegregation
moves, for example, were reportedly influenced by the civic elites in
the communities. The U.S. Commission on Civil Rights found that
the support or lack of support for desegregation among the community elite was very important in accounting for school board responses
to the *Brown* decision. The commission reported, for example, that
"even where political leaders have actually opposed the specifics of a
court order, . . . if they take a position of 'obedience to the law,' the
result is a positive contribution to the desegregation process." Similar
comments were made by the commission about the effect of the
business community on the implementation of desegregation plans in
several northern as well as southern communities.[29]

Coercion to Produce Change. The level of coercion used by the
courts to force changes in policies or behavior is the third feature of
the policy setting that affects implementation. Of course, as we noted
earlier in this chapter, courts cannot initiate review of an implementing agency's responsiveness to a judicial policy; they must instead
await a suit that charges violation of the policy. However, once a case
is brought to court, a judge may bring pressure to bear on implementing agencies to change their policies or behavior, thus overriding the
effects of community traditions or organizational concerns. Coercive
actions available to the judiciary include judges' private persuasive
efforts, court hearings on the implementing agency's progress in
implementing a judicial policy, citations for contempt of court, fines
against agencies or officials for noncompliance, and the assumption of
the administrative powers of the agency itself. The last alternative
allows the judge to implement the policy from the courthouse.

The likelihood of a court's becoming involved in forcing an
implementing group to make programmatic changes depends on a

variety of factors, some of which we will discuss later. At this point we will consider an agency's reactions when levels of coercion vary from low to high. There is substantial evidence that as levels of coercion increase, the probability that program adjustments will be made also increases.[30] As an example of low levels of coercion leading to few changes, consider the aftermath of the Supreme Court's school prayer decisions. Few school boards were pressured by local groups or courts to conform with the decisions. The absence of lawsuits allowed many school boards to do as they pleased—which often meant that they continued school prayers. Sometimes boards engaged in cosmetic compliance by repealing formal policies requiring prayers, but not prohibiting principals or teachers from initiating their own prayer activities. Under such circumstances the coercive power of the courts is particularly limited because there is no visible policy to serve as a target. Of course, courts sometimes did compel changes in school policies and practices, but only infrequently.[31]

The element of coercion is much greater for police groups, on the other hand, because the probability that courts will review that implementing group's actions is much higher. Of course, the courts do not review every police encounter to ensure the protection of the rights of the criminal suspect; but the likelihood that police behavior will be reviewed is reasonably high, especially if there is an arrest. The more likely departmental superiors or judicial officials are to review an officer's behavior, the more likely the officer will be to comply with due process standards.[32]

Many judicial officers are in a position to review and supervise the implementation of criminal justice decisions. In theory, prosecutors may monitor police activity and refuse to prosecute a suspect if they believe that the police have not conducted their investigation and made the arrest according to the requirements set down in various court decisions. Similarly, judges are in a position to rule certain evidence inadmissible if they believe the defendant's rights have been violated during earlier stages of the legal process. However, prosecutors' and judges' tolerance for police misbehavior has been widely reported.[33] In addition, some observers report that the police are unconcerned about the possibility of undercutting an investigation by violating a suspect's rights, except when the "bust" is considered a large or an important one.[34]

If prosecutors and judges do not ensure some measure of compliance with criminal justice decisions by the police, defense attorneys may be effective. Neubauer's study of the criminal justice system in "Prairie City" indicated that "specialized defense attorneys" occasionally charged that rights had been violated by the police.[35] Milner found that one of the four Wisconsin cities he examined had a criminal lawyer who specialized in making constitutional challenges to the arrest procedures of local police.[36] While the success rate for these claims usually is not high, police in jurisdictions with such attorneys tend to keep in line with judicial policies on criminal justice to a greater extent than do police where vigilant attorneys are not around.

Internal Dynamics of Responding Organizations

Forces within the implementing group may also compel program changes. We loosely refer to these forces as *internal dynamics*. A simple, straightforward relationship is often observed by students of judicial impact: barring other constraints or pressures, groups that support a judicial policy will implement the policy faithfully; those who do not will either ignore it or resist its implementation, wherever and whenever possible. An agency's approval or disapproval of a judicial policy may be rooted in several factors. One of these factors is the cost of the policy or program changes to the agency. Assuming that the decision is not generally beneficial to the agency and that the costs of implementation are not insurmountable, three other factors affect implementation: whether the policy conflicts with an agency's goals or mission, whether the policy conflicts with preferences of key agency personnel, and whether the agency can effectively resist judicial pressure to implement a policy.

Cost of Change. The cost factors include the amount of time required to implement program changes and the loss of money and skills invested in the existing program. Sometimes the costs of compliance may be substantial. For example, the police commissioner of New York City reported that a great deal of money was spent in retraining police officers after the Supreme Court announced several decisions, such as *Mapp v. Ohio,* regarding the rights of criminal defendants.[37] Similarly, the costs of some school desegregation programs can be very high. The funds required to bus students or to build new schools to achieve a desegregated school system may be so great that the entire system and the community strain to pay the costs.

Other changes may require very little change at minimal cost to an agency. For example, one of the immediate responses of many police organizations to the *Miranda* decision was to change department policies by issuing "*Miranda* cards" from which a police officer had to read criminal suspects their rights. Relatively speaking, such a change was not very costly, compared with massive retraining or major capital expenditures. Resistance in cases that incur major costs is more prevalent than it is in those cases where compliance is inexpensive.

In addition to considering the liabilities of adopting a program, the agency may also evaluate the benefits. Benefits might include an increase in resources (for example, funding or staff), various social or political rewards (for example, more power or authority), or the enhanced ability to attain agency goals (for example, court approval for agency activities). Police departments often use *Mapp* or *Miranda* as a justification for increased funding—or as an explanation for their failure to keep crime rates down. And prison bureaus, while resentful of judicial decisions calling for improvements in prison conditions, have sometimes found a silver lining in such decisions as states increase their prison appropriations to meet court orders. Such decisions are not likely to be viewed as totally adverse; they result in a mixture of costs and benefits.

Court approval of an agency's program in a particular policy area usually encourages the agency to implement judicial policy fully. Martin Shapiro documents how, during the 1950s, the Federal Power Commission slowly and continuously developed its ability to regulate natural gas prices beyond the letter of the law. When the Supreme Court approved the FPC's policies, the agency abandoned its caution and engaged in open and vigorous price regulation.[38]

Organizational Norms and Individual Attitudes. In many instances, the organizational goals or mission may be the sum of the attitudes and preferences of agency personnel; but with some organizations the pervasive nature of an organizational ethos or set of norms overrides or reshapes individual attitudes. To examine the impact of organizational norms and goals on the implementation of judicial decisions, we will turn once again to the field of criminal justice. Police as individuals did not readily accept the Supreme Court's criminal justice decisions imposing stricter due process standards. Jerome Skolnick's classic study of police behavior in the 1960s summarizes police attitudes toward *Mapp* and the exclusionary rule:

> [Most officers believe] the impact of the exclusionary rule . . . has not been to guarantee greater protection of the freedom of "decent citizens" from unreasonable police zeal, but rather to complicate unnecessarily the task of detecting and apprehending criminals. From the pragmatic perspective of the police, the right to conduct exploratory investigations and searches ought largely to be a matter of police-supervisory discretion.[39]

Almost a decade later, Wasby found that attitudes had changed somewhat. His study of police officers in small communities in Illinois and Massachusetts reveals that officers still reported being "irritated when judges granted motions to suppress evidence" but generally seemed willing to "live within the new search rules." Wasby also reports that officers were more willing than they had been to follow judicial policies concerning a suspect's right to legal assistance early in the arrest process.[40]

Many researchers have noted the "crime control orientation" of police officers in general. In this orientation—which pervades many police organizations—the police view themselves as professional crime fighters who solve crimes and whose judgments ought not to be seriously challenged by the courts. A. T. Quick, for example, argues that while police officers spend on the average about one-fifth of their training time on due process subjects, the effects of such training are frequently offset by peer pressure or supervisory expectations that encourage crime control attitudes. The pressure to capture criminals and gather evidence results in a "general hostility toward concepts of procedural due process and those institutions that are identified with securing individual rights." [41]

While many of the Warren Court criminal justice decisions ran counter to the prevailing organizational norms of the police, it appears that *Miranda* achieved widespread compliance. Studies in the District of Columbia, New Haven, and a few other communities indicate that by and large the police read suspects their rights and offered legal counsel.[42] While the courts still get cases involving absent or incomplete *Miranda* warnings, no judicial evidence or social science research has indicated open noncompliance with the decision.

In the face of this evidence of compliance with *Miranda,* one might conclude that relevant judicial decisions affect behavior in spite of organizational norms that do not support change. However, some scholars suggest that these measures of compliance with *Miranda* are incomplete; compliance with the letter of the law—as when a *Miranda* card is read—can easily be measured, but compliance with the spirit of the law is much harder to evaluate. For example, Wald et al., studying police behavior in New Haven after *Miranda,* found that many times the warnings were read in a "formalized, bureaucratic tone to indicate that his [the police officer's] remarks were simply a routine, meaningless legalism." Moreover, if a suspect expressed an interest in finding an attorney, the police frequently "offered him a telephone book without further comment, and that response was enough to deter him from calling a lawyer." [43] In a technical sense, the officer who reads a suspect his or her *Miranda* rights in a formalized tone of voice or who does not aid a suspect in securing an attorney is not disobeying *Miranda*. Nevertheless, as we shall see in

Chapter 4, such behavior could effectively dissuade a suspect from using his or her constitutional rights.

In addition to implementing judicial decisions passively, many police officers adjusted their behavior so as to avoid the impact or consequences of due process policies. In these instances, police behavior consisted of actions that were not easily reviewed by superiors or judges. For example, a study of narcotics division activity in New York City a few years after *Mapp* revealed that some officers had developed aggressive policies of searching the homes or clothing of minor drug dealers or users. Sometimes there were arrests, but seldom with any real attempt to prosecute. The narcotics officers were just harassing suspected drug dealers and "avoiding the frustrations of following *Mapp*" by keeping the case out of court.[44]

Similarly, Wald et al. observed several instances of aggressive interrogations by the New Haven police; these frequently resulted in confessions or useful incriminating evidence.[45] Unlike the narcotics searches, the aggressive interrogations were marginally within the law—suspects were read their rights—but whether the aggressiveness bordered on coercion could not easily be subject to review or challenge before a judge. If the prosecutor refused to press charges against a suspect who had been subject to an aggressive interrogation or who had been stopped and searched without probable cause, then police behavior in violation of *Mapp, Miranda,* and other due process decisions would not be subject to court review. In such an instance, a suspect may press charges against the police officer in a civil suit claiming violation of his or her civil rights, or the police officer may be subject to disciplinary proceedings within the department; however, these courses of action are rarely followed.[46]

Police resistance to judicial decisions may have a variety of causes, but one study after another suggests that the organizational expectations of police officers account for many of their responses in implementing (or not implementing) judicial policies concerning the rights of criminal suspects. In general, most police departments are insulated from community pressures, and they tend to develop a culture of their own; such an environment is likely to intensify the impact of organizational expectations.[47]

Attitudes and Preferences of Key Agency Personnel. Another important factor in accounting for an organization's responses to judicial policies is the collective attitude of key agency personnel. Of course, the attitudes of key agency personnel may on occasion differ from the prevailing attitudes among rank and file personnel within an organization. Nevertheless, some of the research regarding the reactions of school systems to judicial policies suggests that the preferences of top officials can be responsible for changing the policies and practices of the entire organization. The impact of organizational leadership is most clearly demonstrated when new leaders take over an organization. In their study of Georgia school systems Rodgers and Bullock noted that many superintendents were committed to segregation during the late 1950s and early 1960s; indeed, some were actually leaders of local segregationist forces. However, counties that changed superintendents were more likely to desegregate under the new leadership, since the new superintendents were less committed to segregation than their predecessors and also "felt no need to continue resistance for the purpose of defending past recalcitrance." [48] David Morgan and Robert England, in their study of school desegregation, found that the presence of a new superintendent was positively related to desegregation in the 52 big-city school systems they studied.[49] Similarly, in his case study on the reaction of a small Illinois community to the *Schempp* decision, Richard Johnson discovered that the coming of a new school superintendent who was committed to the Court's decision led to the eventual adoption of a policy banning prayers in school.[50] In his classic study of police departments, James Q. Wilson has shown that the appointment of new police chiefs dedicated to by-the-book professional values has altered older norms which all but ignored procedural due process for suspects.[51]

Commitments to make changes in policy by the governing board or the policy makers within an agency are also important, even if the changes run counter to organizational routines or norms. Again, the responses of school systems to judicial policies regarding desegregation serve as good examples. The U.S. Commission on Civil Rights reported in 1976 that school boards that supported *Brown* were the most likely to desegregate voluntarily and that boards that opposed *Brown* were the most likely to require some type of external pressure to desegregate.[52] Robert Crain's study of school desegregation in the first decade after *Brown* found that when a school board opposed desegregation it made no moves to change either policies or practices.[53] Studying desegregation during more recent times, Morgan and England still report a positive correlation between board support for desegregation and changes in levels of segregation in their sample of 52 metropolitan school districts.[54]

In the absence of clear acceptance or rejection of judicial policies by key members of an implementing organization, the influence of the attitudes and preferences of others in the organization increases substantially. That is, if boards or high-level administrators take no action or make unclear agency policies, lower level persons are likely to gain discretionary power; this diffusion of decision making complicates the implementation of judicial policies. A good illustration of this point comes from the research of Dolbeare and Hammond, who report on the implementation of the Supreme Court school prayer decision in five Indiana communities. None of the leading school officials in any of the communities took any action regarding the Supreme Court's decision; as a result, there was a wide variety of practices within each of the school systems. The inaction allowed many teachers to construct their own interpretation of the decision and to make their own informal policy regarding what they should do in their classrooms. An example of the degree to which some of the teachers misunderstood the requirements of the Court decision comes from an interview with an elementary school teacher by Dolbeare and Hammond. This teacher discontinued saying the prayer in the morning and now said only the pledge. However, while accepting that part of the policy, she continued a series of religious activities, which included posting charts of Sunday school attendance, telling Christmas and Easter stories, making nativity scenes during Christmas, and having students make oral reports on what they learned in Sunday school. Her room's bulletin boards were also adorned with religious themes. Her closing remark to Dolbeare and Hammond was, "I'm not able to be at church any more but feel I compensate by what I do in school." [55] Dolbeare and Hammond found that the failure of the school system leadership to adopt precise policies allowed many teachers to construct an interpretation of the decision that was highly consistent with their own attitudes about schoolhouse religion and to behave accordingly.

Internal Capacity to Resist External Pressures. We pointed out earlier that on occasion environmental pressures concerning the implementation of desegregation policies and school prayer policies shaped the responses of many school boards to judicial policies in those areas. Thus, while the prevailing attitudes or norms of an implementing organization substantially affect responses to judicial policies, most organizations must also be sensitive to external pressures to respond positively or negatively to judicial decisions. In some circumstances, implementing agencies are able to avoid environmental pressures and follow their own preferences in responding to judicial actions. In those situations, the agency may be politically isolated from the community, as is the case for local offices of federal agencies, or it may be psychologically separate from the community, as sometimes happens in universities and other institutions staffed with highly trained persons from outside the area. This separation does much to allow the agency to respond as it wishes, consistent with organizational goals and preferences, and not as others would have it respond.

An implementing agency may take steps to insulate itself from external pressures. Insulation may be accomplished by limiting the methods by which agency personnel are selected (for example, appointment rather than election) and limiting mechanisms for public input to the agency's decision making (for example, closed rather than open meetings). In the area of school desegregation, the insulation of a school board through the number of officials on the board, the term of the officials, and the number of public meetings per month was correlated with changes in levels of desegregation in the 52-city study by Morgan and England.[56] Similarly, protections for civil service appointees and tenure for educators shield personnel in many agencies from external pressures.

Resisting external pressures through insulating the agency does not work in all instances, so an agency may turn to another strategy. That strategy consists of using organizational resources to protect or promote agency interests—regardless of whether those interests are to evade or to implement a judicial policy. Administrative agencies possess a variety of resources. One is the agency's legal staff. If the legal division of the agency is large, and if it devotes time to develop alternatives to a court decision, then agency-controlled responses are possible. An effective legal staff can also develop new justifications for continuing the original policy threatened by the court decision, or it can defend an agency from external pressure to change after a judicial decision. All important federal agencies have battalions of attorneys who can, if the matter is important enough, engage in delaying tactics and formulate alternatives that require only minor adjustments. At the local level, the use of legal support to forestall the impact of a judicial order was used widely in the South after *Brown.* In New Orleans, for example, the school board retained an attorney who busily filed appeals from the first court order to desegregate in 1956 to the final order in 1960.[57] That case eventually reached the Supreme Court six times before the desegregation order was final, all at the direction of the segregationist school board and the expense of the taxpayers.

Less tangible resources include an agency's prestige, political support, and expertise. Good relations with the legislative or executive branches or with influential interest groups can be translated into support for an agency's program, whether it is evasive of or compliant with the Court's decision. Again, we can turn to the desegregation of public schools to illustrate the role political support from outside forces may play in implementing judicial policy. An analysis of desegregation in 92 northern cities by David Kirby, Robert Harris, and Robert Crain suggests that mayors often played an important role in the desegregation of school systems. Usually the mayors were a liberal force, pressing the school board to desegregate and to avoid conflict. Most of the actions were moves "to clarify the situation, to encourage meetings, to reassure groups, to discourage the civil rights movement from demonstrating." [58] How frequently school boards actually called upon the mayor or other officials to support their decisions is not generally known. However, the prestige of the mayoral office may serve to protect the school board from forces opposed to its desegregation moves or to push the school board to do whatever is necessary to maintain peace in the community.

A school board examined by Richard Johnson decided to comply with the Supreme Court's school prayer decisions and called on "influentials" in the community to support compliance. These influentials for the most part included the leading citizens in the community, including some elected officials. The influentials' calm acceptance of the school board's action was important in obtaining the community's acquiescence. Moreover, the influentials furthered implementation in several ways: by communicating information about the decision to others in the community, by interpreting the information for others, and by encouraging public compliance.[59]

Implementing agencies may also develop a norm of professional expertise that enables their personnel to respond in a particular way. As we have already seen, professionalism is particularly prevalent among police officers. It is also found among physicians, educators, and welfare agencies. Indeed, hardly any implementing agency is without some sense of professionalism these days. An argument in favor of the professional handling of a policy may be used to limit external pressures: "Why not let the police (or the schools or the military) handle it? They're the experts!" While the issue of compliance with judicial policy usually extends well beyond questions of professional judgment, agencies with strong public images of professional expertise nonetheless can substantially reduce outside pressures on their behavior. Research by Charles Johnson and Jon Bond revealed that after *Roe v. Wade* (1973) hospitals were not responsive to community demands for the availability of abortion services or to religious or right-to-life group demands to limit abortions. The authors conclude that "there is little that individuals or groups in the community can do to influence hospital policy, even on a highly salient, non-technical issue such as abortion." [60]

JUDICIAL POLICIES: IMPLEMENTATION AND IMPACT

SUMMARY

Like all public policies, judicial policies are rarely implemented by the policy's originators. Presidents, legislators, and judges rely on others in the political and social system to put their policies into action. The implementing population for judicial policies is varied and may at times include private individuals or institutions. However, the most visible members of the implementing population are those who are part of government agencies that provide public services or public protection. Most of the research on this population concerns two subpopulations—educators and police officers.

Implementing agencies usually follow through on judicial policies independent of direct judicial supervision. A court may not initiate a review of whether and how an agency is implementing a judicial policy; instead, the court must wait until a consumer challenges the agency on the issue of implementation. Moreover, while courts have an array of powers to deal with noncompliance, they do not have the power of the purse in most cases, especially to order the expenditure of money an agency does not have. Courts usually have few supervisory or oversight powers and cannot supervise day-to-day agency operations. Courts' powers are largely punitive and thus are not usually employed unless it is absolutely necessary.

Most members of the implementing population are organizations and most, therefore, follow a similar pattern when confronted by an applicable judicial decision. The agency must first interpret the decision to determine what the court says the agency ought to be doing or whether changes might be required. This interpretation stage tends to be guided by the policy preferences of agencies in that an adverse decision is interpreted more narrowly than one expanding the powers or authority of the agency. Then, if the decision requires some response, the agency will initiate a search for alternative courses of action. Finally, if it is necessary, the organization will change some of its policies or behavior.

Three factors account for the extent to which implementing organizations change their policies or behavior in response to a policy-making court's desires. First, the communication of the decision to relevant implementing groups may be distorted and thus may occasionally activate agencies to do more or less than is expected of them by the court. Second, the environmental setting of the agency may be influential. If, for example, community traditions are inconsistent with a judicial policy or if relevant interest groups are opposed to it, then little change can be expected. The opposite is true if the policy reinforces existing traditions or if it is supported by interest groups.

Another environmental factor is the level of coercion to compel change by an agency. As coercion increases, the benefits of noncompliance decline and greater adjustments in policy and behavior can be expected. Third, organizational characteristics—such as commitments to existing policies and the attitudes of organizational personnel—influence an agency's responses. These forces operate from within an organization much like environmental forces operate from outside. In addition, the resources of an organization may affect its responses to a judicial policy, regardless of the organization's acceptance of the policy itself.

NOTES

1. Micheal Giles, "HEW versus the Federal Courts: A Comparison of School Desegregation Enforcement," *American Politics Quarterly* 3 (January 1975): 81-90.
2. Lawrence Baum, "The Influence of Legislatures and Appellate Courts over the Policy Implementation Process," *Policy Studies Journal* 8 (special issue no. 2, 1980): 561.
3. This discussion of organizational responses to judicial decisions is drawn from Charles A. Johnson, "Judicial Decisions and Organizational Change: A Theory," *Administration and Society* 11 (May 1979): 27-51.
4. James March and Herbert Simon, *Organizations* (New York: Wiley, 1958); Anthony Downs, *Inside Bureaucracy* (Boston: Little, Brown, 1968).
5. Kenneth Dolbeare and Phillip Hammond, *The School Prayer Decisions: From Court Policy to Local Practice* (Chicago: University of Chicago Press, 1971), 90.
6. William Muir, *Prayer in the Public Schools: Law and Attitude Change* (Chicago: University of Chicago Press, 1967).
7. Richard Johnson, *The Dynamics of Compliance* (Evanston, Ill.: Northwestern University Press, 1967); Robert Birkby, "The Supreme Court and the Bible Belt: Tennessee Reaction to the *Schempp* Decision," *Midwest Journal of Political Science* 10 (August 1966): 304-319.
8. Downs, *Inside Bureaucracy,* 169-170.
9. Neal Milner, *The Court and Local Law Enforcement: The Impact of* Miranda (Beverly Hills: Sage, 1971), ch. 5-8.
10. Michael S. Wald et al., "Interrogations in New Haven: The Impact of *Miranda,*" *Yale Law Journal* 76 (July 1967): 1519-1648.
11. Michael J. Murphy, "The Problem of Compliance by Police Departments," *Texas Law Review* 44 (April 1966): 945.
12. Stephen Wasby, Anthony D'Amato, and Rosemary Metrailer, *Desegregation from* Brown *to* Alexander (Carbondale, Ill.: Southern Illinois University Press, 1977), 122.
13. Ibid., 123-126.

14. Stephen Wasby, *Small Town Police and the Supreme Court: Hearing the Word* (Lexington, Mass.: Lexington Books, 1976), 120-122.
15. David Neubauer, *Criminal Justice in Middle America* (Morristown, N.J.: General Learning Press, 1974), 183-186.
16. Milner, *The Court and Local Law Enforcement,* 171-184.
17. John H. Laubauch, *School Prayers: Congress, the Courts, and the Public* (Washington: Public Affairs Press, 1969), 138.
18. Donald Reich, "The Impact of Judicial Decision-Making: The School Prayer Cases," in *The Supreme Court as Policy-Maker: Three Studies on the Impact of Judicial Decisions,* ed. David Everson (Carbondale, Ill.: Public Affairs Research Bureau, Southern Illinois University, 1968).
19. Bradley C. Canon, "Testing the Effectiveness of Civil Liberties Policies at the State and Federal Levels: The Case of the Exclusionary Rule," *American Politics Quarterly* 5 (January 1977): 71.
20. Birkby, "The Supreme Court and the Bible Belt," 310.
21. Dolbeare and Hammond, *The School Prayer Decisions,* 95-128.
22. Robert Crain, *The Politics of School Desegregation* (Chicago: Aldine, 1968), ch. 2 and 7.
23. Harrell Rodgers and Charles Bullock III, *Law and Social Change: Civil Rights Laws and Their Consequences* (New York: McGraw-Hill, 1972), 72.
24. Crain, *Politics of School Desegregation,* ch. 15-16.
25. Bob Smith, *They Closed Their Schools* (Chapel Hill: University of North Carolina Press, 1965).
26. "Text of 96 Congressmen's Declaration on Integration," *New York Times,* March 12, 1956, 19.
27. Wasby, D'Amato, and Metrailer, *Desegregation from* Brown *to* Alexander, 168.
28. Rodgers and Bullock, *Law and Social Change,* 81-88.
29. U.S. Commission on Civil Rights, *Fulfilling the Letter and Spirit of the Law: Desegregation of the Nation's Public Schools* (Washington, D.C.: U.S. Government Printing Office, 1976), 180, 174.
30. Harrell Rodgers and Charles Bullock III, *Coercion to Compliance* (Lexington, Mass.: Lexington Books, 1976).
31. Laubauch, *School Prayers,* 104-111.
32. Jerome Skolnick, *Justice without Trial* (New York: Wiley, 1966), ch. 10.
33. Neubauer, *Criminal Justice,* 180-182; and Comment, "Effect of *Mapp v. Ohio* on Police Search-and-Seizure Practices in Narcotics Cases," *Columbia Journal of Law and Social Problems* 4 (March 1968), 101.
34. Skolnick, *Justice without Trial,* 155-162.
35. Neubauer, *Criminal Justice,* 173-174.
36. Milner, *The Court and Local Law Enforcement,* 111-113. See also Neubauer, *Criminal Justice,* 177-179.
37. Murphy, "The Problem of Compliance by Police Departments."
38. Martin Shapiro, *The Supreme Court and Administrative Agencies* (New York: Free Press, 1968), ch. 4.
39. Skolnick, *Justice without Trial,* 227.
40. Wasby, *Small Town Police and the Supreme Court,* 217-218.

41. A. T. Quick, "Attitudinal Aspects of Police Compliance with Procedural Due Process," *American Journal of Criminal Due Process* 6 (January 1978): 26.
42. Richard Medalie, Leonard Zeitz, and Paul Alexander, "Custodial Police Interrogation in Our Nation's Capital: The Attempt to Implement *Miranda,*" *Michigan Law Review* 66 (May 1968): 1347-1422; Wald et al., "Interrogations in New Haven."
43. Wald et al., "Interrogations in New Haven," 1552.
44. Comment, "Effect of *Mapp v. Ohio,*" 100.
45. Wald et al., "Interrogations in New Haven," 1562.
46. Skolnick, *Justice without Trial,* 221-223.
47. Ibid., 219-225.
48. Rodgers and Bullock, *Law and Social Change,* 44.
49. David Morgan and Robert England, *Assessing the Progress of Large City School Desegregation: A Case Survey Approach* (Norman: Bureau of Government Research, University of Oklahoma, 1981), 68.
50. Johnson, *The Dynamics of Compliance,* 106-108.
51. James Q. Wilson, *Varieties of Police Behavior* (Cambridge, Mass.: Harvard University Press, 1969).
52. U.S. Commission on Civil Rights, *Fulfilling the Letter and Spirit of the Law,* 126, 128.
53. Crain, *Politics of School Desegregation.*
54. Morgan and England, *Assessing the Progress of Desegregation,* 67.
55. Dolbeare and Hammond, *The School Prayer Decisions,* 77.
56. Morgan and England, *Assessing the Progress of Desegregation,* 67.
57. Crain, *Politics of School Desegregation,* 245.
58. David J. Kirby, T. Robert Harris, and Robert L. Crain, *Political Strategies in Northern School Desegregation* (Lexington, Mass.: Lexington Books, 1973), 107-108.
59. Johnson, *The Dynamics of Compliance,* 113-114.
60. Charles A. Johnson and Jon Bond, "Policy Implementation and Responsiveness in Nongovernmental Institutions: Hospital Abortion Services after *Roe v. Wade,*" *Western Political Quarterly* 35 (September 1982): 403.

CHAPTER FOUR

The Consumer Population

The concept of consumers is familiar to all of us. To the question, "Who buys and uses American products and services?" the answer is, "We all do." The entire population is a consumer population. We can expand the concept of a consumer population beyond the use of products and services; we can think in terms of consuming judicial policies. Everybody is a consumer of judicial policies.

Of course, the consumer population varies for specific products. Laundry detergent, for example, has a fairly universal consumer population, whereas electrical generators are used by a small, specialized group of people. Court decisions likewise have different consumer populations. The school prayer decision affects all public school children, while a decision relating to the patentability of new life forms has very limited applicability.

Thus, while we can talk about the people of the United States as consumers of judicial policies in general, only persons who are affected by a particular decision constitute the consumer population for that decision. Consequently, our discussion of the consumer population will include a greater variety of actors than did previous chapters.

CHARACTERISTICS OF CONSUMERS AND CONSUMPTION

As we have seen in Chapters 2 and 3, scholars have done considerable research about the interpreting and implementing populations and the variables that affect their reactions to judicial decisions. Such research is to be expected, of course, as those populations are involved in the first steps of the process of implementing court decisions. In contrast, social scientists have paid little attention to the consumers of judicial decisions. Indeed, the idea of consumption of judicial decisions and policies is not nearly as well articulated as are those of interpretation and implementation. This failure is unfortunate because knowledge about consumption is crucial to understanding ultimate judicial impact; in some ways it is analogous to consider the business executive who, while knowing how a product is manufactured and advertised, still must ask the bottom-line question, "How well does it sell?" The paucity of attention to consumption means we are lacking in empirical knowledge about this population as well as a conceptual framework with which we may describe who the population is and what it does. Thus, at the outset of this chapter, we must make a few conceptual distinctions about the consumption of judicial policies. First, we distinguish the consumer population from the implementing and secondary populations, which may be in some instances related or similar. Second, we discuss the nature of judicial policies, whom they benefit, and under what circumstances. Having set some of this groundwork, the remaining sections of this chapter discuss the responses of consumers to judicial policies.

Distinguishing the Consumer Population

Persons who use judicial policies—that is, who actually engage in acceptance and adjustment behavior (or who may have it forced upon them in the case of disadvantageous policies)—constitute the core of the consumer population. But often people are *potential* rather than actual users of a judicial policy: it is available to them but they choose not to use it. For example, many pregnant women decide to have babies although they could choose abortion, and many adults never see X-rated movies although such movies are readily available. Nonetheless, such persons must be considered as part of the consumer population for decisions such as *Roe v. Wade* (1973) and *Miller v. California* (1973), respectively. The judicial policies have given them the choice; the availability of the choice in an area that affects them places them in the consumer population.

A more difficult problem in identifying the consumer population occurs when the use of judicial policies is contingent upon some prior happening. For example, a woman has to conceive before she can use the abortion decision. Do all fertile women constitute that decision's consumer population? After all, the availability of abortions might affect various aspects of such women's sexual behavior. In regard to another decision, one has to undergo police questioning in order to use *Miranda v. Arizona* (1966). Anyone might be arrested and questioned at some time in the future. Does that make all of us part of *Miranda*'s consumer population?

By and large, we will treat such persons as part of the secondary population, not the consumer population, in the absence of the contingency that makes the judicial policy available to them. However, we recognize that there are gradations of potential consumption and will not be dogmatic here. Clearly, large numbers of women will become pregnant at some time in their lives, whereas only a minuscule proportion of the general public will ever be subject to police interrogation. Generally, the more likely a contingency is to occur, the more reasonable it is to include a large number of people in at least the outer dimensions of the consumer population.

Consumers and Implementors. The consumer population differs from the implementing population. In one sense, implementors are often consumers. The police may be as disadvantaged by *Miranda* as suspects are advantaged by it. A busing order may inconvenience school administrators almost as much as it does the children who dislike being bused across town. But the implementors are affected in their official capacity and so remain in the implementing population for the policy. This distinction may be somewhat artificial, but we will maintain it in order to keep the concepts of the implementing and consumer populations separate.

It is not always easy, of course, to make the distinction. Are physicians implementors or consumers of the abortion decision? Are teachers implementors or consumers of a decision allowing scientific theories of evolution to be taught (*Epperson v. Arkansas,* 1968)? We recognize that there is a gray area between the two populations, and we will not always try to place borderline groups definitively in one or the other category. Speaking generally, however, government officials, particularly policy makers and administrators, fall into the implementing population while private persons and corporations are generally in the consumer population. Government officials may make up the consumer population in those infrequent instances when court decisions affect the power of one governmental entity in relation to another and neither is representing a discrete constituency of private citizens; for example, a president and Congress could be considered the consumers of the Supreme Court's ruling that the legislative veto (provisions in legislation allowing Congress to nullify executive agency decisions or regulations) was unconstitutional (*Immigration and Naturalization Service v. Chadha,* 1983).

Consumers and Secondary Groups. It is similarly useful to distinguish the consumer population from the secondary population. Members of the latter group are not personally affected by a judicial policy. They receive or can claim no real benefits, and no real disadvantages are imposed upon them. Of course, they may be interested in the policy—at times more intensely than those actually affected. But their interest is motivated by ideological or religious values or perhaps simply by sympathy toward friends who are actually affected by the policy. It is not an interest based upon a sense of gain or loss to one's own life. For example, a Catholic priest will never consume the Court's abortion policy personally, although he may well be vitally interested in it and perhaps become engaged in extensive feedback behavior.

Once again, a neat separation of populations is not always possible. For instance, it is difficult to specify in which population the parents of a woman considering an abortion could be placed. Obviously, the possibility of a (or another) grandchild is of more immediate concern to them than it is to their priest. Generally, however, the impact of the woman's decision will not be nearly as great on her parents' lives as it will be on that of the father—to say nothing of the woman herself. Here, also, a gray area exists; we will explore it as well as we can, keeping in mind that the degree to which a judicial policy affects a person's life directly is the crucial element distinguishing the consumer from the secondary population.

For some judicial policies, everyone is a consumer and there is no secondary population. The Supreme Court's reapportionment decisions of the 1960s provide a prime example. While the Court's orders were directed to state legislators, the true consumers were the voters whom the legislators represented. Urban and suburban residents gained political power; rural voters lost it. Roger Hanson and Robert Crew have demonstrated that during the 1960s expenditures for education, welfare, and highways increased more rapidly in states with reapportioned legislatures than in those with malapportioned legislatures; suburbs were bigger winners than were central cities.[1]

Similarly, judicial decisions that impose economic gains or losses on nearly everyone can have an all-encompassing consumer population, as did, for example, the New Jersey Supreme Court decision virtually establishing a state income tax (*Robinson v. Cahill,* 1975) or the 1982 federal district court ruling breaking up the Bell Telephone System, which increased the cost of local telephone service and decreased the cost of long-distance service.

At times, however, the temptation to say that society as a whole constitutes the consumer population must be resisted. Politicians sometimes argue, for instance, that everyone is adversely affected by *Mapp v. Ohio* (1961) because fewer criminals can be brought to justice when illegally seized—but nonetheless incriminating—evidence is excluded from the trial. But this linkage is too remote and speculative to justify putting the whole public into *Mapp*'s consumer population. However, if clear evidence were to emerge that the decision had significantly affected the crime rate, it would be fair to include the public in *Mapp*'s consumer population.

In the remainder of this chapter, we will consider the acceptance and adjustment behavior of the consumer population. We will focus on the degree to which individuals and organizations accept relevant policies and alter their thinking and patterns of behavior or institutional arrangements to accommodate them. Since the reactions of consumers to judicial policies that are advantageous to them are likely to be quite different from the reactions of consumers to policies that are disadvantageous, we will consider the acceptance and adjustment behavior for each circumstance separately.

It is worth noting again that social scientists have paid less attention to the reactions of the consumer population to judicial policies than they have to the reactions of any other population. The consumer population has been neglected primarily because its members are both more amorphous and less visible than are members of the interpreting, the implementing, and some segments of the secondary populations. Consequently, researchers have more difficulty probing the behavior of consumers. Much of the discussion in this chapter is therefore speculative or inferential rather than research-based. However, we will report on two areas where significant social science investigation into consumer population reactions to judicial policies has occurred—the *Miranda* warnings and court-ordered busing to achieve racial integration.

Types of Consumption

Advantageous and Disadvantageous Consumption. We normally think of economic consumption as a beneficial activity. We don't buy an item unless we believe that it will make a contribution to our well-being. In classical economic theory there are no losers in such transactions (except in the face of the occasional misjudgment or poor quality product); everyone benefits.

The consumption of judicial policies, however, can be disadvantageous as well as advantageous. Lawsuits are adversarial by their nature and thus require losers as well as winners. Of course, in some suits both sides are not members of the consumer population; one party may be in the implementing population. Cases in which the government or one of its agencies is a party often pit the interests of an implementing population against those of a relevant group of consumers. *Miranda,* for instance, broadened the rights of criminal suspects (the consumers) by limiting the discretion of the police (an implementing agency). By contrast, in *Zurcher v. The Stanford Daily* (1978) the Supreme Court ruled that the First Amendment did not protect newspaper editorial offices from a police search (with a warrant), thus broadening the discretion of the police at the expense of journalists. In these cases, members of the affected consumer population either universally benefited from a judicial policy or universally suffered disadvantages from it.

At times, however, consumers similarly affected by a decision can feel quite differently about it. Children who were gratified by saying prayers in school would see *Abington School District v. Schempp* (1963) as a disadvantageous judicial policy, while those who were embarrassed or bothered about saying prayers would see it as advantageous.

When members of the consumer population are direct adversaries in a lawsuit, one will gain what the other loses. This is known as a *zero-sum-game situation;* within the consumer population as a whole, gains and losses balance out and equal zero. The zero sum game describes the traditional suit where both plaintiff and defendant are private parties and there usually is no precise implementing population. For example, in the 1960s many state supreme courts began limiting the ancient maxim of property law, *caveat emptor* ("let the buyer beware"), to make builders of new homes liable to purchasers for defective or unsafe construction (see *Carpenter v. Donohue,* 1964; and *Humber v. Morton,* 1967). Here one segment of the consumer population, families buying new homes, had gained legal rights at the expense of another segment of the consumer population, the home construction industry.

Sometimes when a government agency is a party to a court case, the agency is not so much implementor as it is a representative of one element of the consumer population. Here, too, the zero-sum-game situation prevails. Good examples of such representation can be found in regulatory agencies, which often try to protect the interests of the industry they supervise. When the Supreme Court struck down the Virginia Board of Pharmacy's rule prohibiting pharmacists from advertising drug prices (*Virginia State Board of Pharmacy v. Virginia Citizens Consumer Council,* 1976), the real losers were pharmacists and the pharmaceutical industry. The main purpose of the rule had been to discourage competitive pricing and thus keep pharmacy profits up. Also, when a government agency functions to regulate disputes between various parts of the American economy, it will represent one economic interest or another depending on the nature of its decision. The National Labor Relations Board is a good example. In the 1930s and 1940s, in such cases as *National Labor Relations Board v. Jones & Laughlin Steel Co.* (1937), judicial decisions in favor of the board enabled labor unions to organize workers in basic industries over the employers' opposition. By the 1950s the unions were often going to court to challenge board decisions that had put limits on labor's organizing tactics.

More recently, many state and federal agencies have pushed affirmative action programs for minorities. In the *Bakke* case, a medical school's policy of setting aside 16 percent of the entering seats for minority applicants was advantageous to would-be minority medical students and disadvantageous to nonminority applicants whose scores on admission criteria were higher than were those of minority admittees. The Supreme Court struck down the strict quota, but said that race was a factor that could be considered in the admission process (*Regents of University of California v. Bakke,* 1978; see Chapter 2, p. 50). Sometimes government agencies are on the other side of the affirmative action picture. In *Personnel Administrator of Massachusetts v. Feeney* (1979), Massachusetts successfully defended its policy of giving preference to veterans in filling state jobs. The veterans' preference had been challenged as discriminatory by women's groups because so few women had been in the military service.

In fact, there are occasions when two government agencies, each representing a segment of the consumer population, clash in court. When this occurs, one agency is likely to be at the federal level and the other at the state or local level. *Federal Energy Regulatory Commission v. Mississippi* (1982) is a good example. Mississippi's state utility regulatory commission, acting in the interest of large electric power companies, challenged the validity of the Public Utilities Regulatory Policies Act of 1978, which required state utility commissions to follow certain procedures benefiting smaller utilities and users of electric power. The Supreme Court held that the 1978 Act did not violate the Tenth Amendment.

Direct and Indirect Consumption. Returning to our products and services analogy, we can see that there may be more than one level of consumption. Most of us, for instance, often purchase laundry detergents but almost never buy electric generators. The latter are purchased by utility companies. But the quality and capacity of the generators will affect all of us in terms of frequency of power outages and increases in electricity rates. Thus a larger set of consumers may be *indirectly* affected by the choices of a smaller population that consumes more directly.

Some judicial policies have both direct and indirect consumer populations. For example, as we noted above, in the *Virginia Board of Pharmacy* case, the Supreme Court permitted pharmacists to advertise the prices of their products; later the Court ruled that lawyers could advertise their legal services (*Bates v. Arizona State Bar,* 1977). Presumably, competitive advertising benefits the public generally, but it appears that only a few pharmacies and an even smaller proportion of lawyers have actually chosen to advertise their prices. In choosing not to advertise, they have minimized the advantages of these policies for persons who need prescriptions filled or legal advice, the indirect consumer populations.

The indirect consumer population need not be the general public or even a large group. The families of criminal suspects who are released due to violations of their constitutional rights are indirect consumers. Their lives are obviously affected by the consumption of such judicial decisions as *Mapp* or *Miranda,* but they do not make the decision to consume the policies, nor do they bear the immediate consequences of consumption.

Disadvantageous judicial policies may also have an indirect consumer population. For example, in *Thor Power Tool Co. v. Commissioner of Internal Revenue* (1979) the Supreme Court upheld an Internal Revenue Service tax accounting policy that made it costly for manufacturers to keep unsold products in stock. Soon thereafter, many book publishers began destroying their remaining stock of a particular book after its sales declined. The book-buying public suffered more than did the publishers. (Beyond this, the *Thor Power Tool* case is a good illustration of a judicial policy developed with respect to one part of the consumer population [in this case, tool manufacturers and their stocking of spare parts] that has an unexpected adverse impact on another segment of the consumer population [namely, book publishers].)

RESPONSES TO BENEFICIAL DECISIONS

The responses of consumer populations may depend heavily on whether particular judicial decisions are seen as beneficial or as adverse. Some decisions improve the lives of members of their consumer population; others are in some way detrimental. In our discussions of each type of decision, we make an important distinction between those situations where consumers need not take any action to receive the advantages or disadvantages of the judicial decision and those where some action is required in order to secure the benefits or avoid the implications of the decision.

Automatic Consumption

Often benefits accrue to consumers automatically. No action—that is, no acceptance decision or behavior—on the part of the consumer is necessary. All necessary adjustments are performed by the implementing population. Put another way, there is no choice about being a consumer; everyone in the affected population consumes the policy.

One type of automatic consumption occurs when a court decision requires a government official or agency to follow or expand due process guarantees in certain situations. For instance, the Supreme Court has recently held that benefits to persons on welfare cannot be terminated and public school students cannot be suspended or expelled without a hearing (*Goldberg v. Kelly,* 1970; *Goss v. Lopez,* 1975). Thus in the absence of ignorance or willful noncompliance on the part of implementors, persons suspected of cheating on welfare and students accused of violating school regulations automatically obtained the benefits of these decisions. Similarly, *Gideon v. Wainwright* (1963) required that indigent defendants in felony cases be represented by counsel at their trial. Today, virtually all indigents charged with felonies are assigned attorneys.

Another type of automatic consumption occurs when a decision restrains someone, usually a government official, from acting to the detriment of members of the consumer population. In *Mapp* (1961) the police were discouraged from conducting illegal searches. As we noted in Chapter 3 (pp. 93-97), there is some controversy about the degree of police compliance with *Mapp.* Of course, the real benefits of *Mapp* will vary. Most people are less likely to be subjects of an illegal search than are those suspected of involvement in criminal activities or, perhaps, unpopular political behavior. A more tangible benefit automatically came to a consumer population in 1973, when the Supreme Court prevented Congress from depriving some college students and residents of communes of the right to obtain food stamps (*U.S. Department of Agriculture v. Moreno*).

Another benefit accrues automatically when a court decision confers economic advantages on a group of people in the form of lower prices or higher quality goods and services. Sometimes these benefits are given to indirect consumers at the discretion of the direct consumer population. For example, in 1975 the Supreme Court held that bar association minimum fee schedules violated the Sherman Antitrust Act (*Goldfarb v. Virginia State Bar*). Similarly, in 1980 the Court held that so-called fair trade laws establishing minimum prices for liquor were illegal (*California Liquor Dealers v. Midcal Aluminum*). Presumably, these cases led some attorneys and liquor stores to charge lower prices, although we do not know how many. At other times, automatic economic benefits can accrue to direct consumers, with little or no discretion left to others. The *Norris* decision equalizing pensions will give additional money to female state employees without any action on their part (*Arizona Governing Committee v. Norris,* 1983). State courts sometimes void or reduce utility rate hikes, which benefits the general population automatically. In some instances, consumers of automatic benefits may be few in number. The Arizona Supreme Court, for example, ruled that for bankers to draw up documents such as trust agreements and for realtors to draw up deeds constituted the unauthorized practice of law (*State Bar of Arizona v. Arizona Land Title and Trust Co.,* 1961). This policy automatically enhanced the economic fortunes of a small group of lawyers.

Consumption by Choice

Quite often judicial policies are structured so that members of the consumer population have to act in order to take advantage of them. That is, the consumer is given an option or choice that previously did not exist or that was much more difficult to exercise. However, the direct benefits of the policy are gained only when the person makes the newly available choice. In contrast to the automatic consumption of actual benefits, these policies create only a *potential* consumer population. Potential consumers must become actual consumers on their own volition.

It may be that most members of the potential consumer population are not interested in taking advantage of a particular judicial policy. This is particularly true when the policy addresses behavior that has little direct or personal benefit. Supreme Court decisions expanding the meaning of the First Amendment's freedom of speech and press clauses are a good example. Not many of us take our soapbox down to a city park, even though courts have held that the city officials cannot stop us from speaking freely there. And millions of people will never see an X-rated movie or enter an adult bookstore, even though the Court has held that the First Amendment protects such material.

Potential consumers often do not become actual consumers for several reasons. Some may reject a policy, believing it to be harmful or immoral rather than beneficial. For instance, following a series of liberal Supreme Court decisions a survey of bookstore proprietors by James P. Levine revealed that many refused to stock salacious material because of personal objections to it or for fear of offending their customers.[2]

Other people may make no acceptance decision at all. Such persons, while not necessarily objecting to the existence of such theaters or bookstores, simply have no interest in visiting them. Or a potential consumer may passively accept such policies, believing them just or useful, but he or she may have no reason to take personal advantage of them. A person may lack the motivation or temperament for making a public speech; he or she may feel that a cause can be better advanced through letters to the editor or through door-to-door canvassing.

Even when a judicial policy offers a choice impinging directly upon the lives of the affected population, many will not accept it. Many women who are unhappy at finding themselves pregnant will reject the abortion alternative due to their strongly held religious or ethical beliefs. Even when a pregnant woman is not morally opposed to abortion, reasons of cost, absence of local facilities, family or community pressure, or the availability of alternative arrangements may induce her not to obtain one. Indeed, the whole purpose behind laws that restrict access to abortion by such means as refusing Medicaid funds or requiring parental permission (see pp. 8-11) is to discourage the potential consumer population from exercising the choice established by the Supreme Court.

Of course, many people do actually consume the benefits conferred on the public by broad-scope decisions. Adult bookstores and X-rated movies do attract customers, and some of today's R-rated films (which 20 years ago would have been banned as obscene in most communities) are nationwide hits with millions of viewers. And many persons do make public speeches, take part in parades or picketing, and so on, on behalf of political, social, or economic causes. Moreover, such activity can draw attention to societal grievances and become a cutting edge of change—as happened with the civil rights and anti-Vietnam War demonstrations of the 1960s. As for abortions, over one million occur each year in the U.S.[3] This means that from 20 to 25 percent of all pregnancies in this country terminate in abortion. Obviously, many women are taking advantage of the Court's policy here. And the Court, of course, never intended or believed that all pregnant women would choose abortion; it only intended that they not be denied the choice.

Nevertheless, at times, real impediments can make seemingly advantageous options hollow. For example, in the decade following the Supreme Court's decision that segregation was unconstitutional (*Brown v. Board of Education,* 1954), not many blacks tried to enroll their children in previously all-white schools. One reason is that many blacks believed that the personal disadvantages of taking such action outweighed its benefits. Disadvantages might include the probable loss of employment or income, the disruption of existing relationships with the white community (and perhaps part of the black community also), the harassment of their children in school, and the possibility of injury or death—to say nothing of the cost in time, energy, and perhaps money of litigating a desegregation suit for several years. (It must also be recognized that some blacks were so steeped in the culture of segregation that they could not accept *Brown*'s legitimacy. Ingrained behavior patterns, even disadvantageous and humiliating ones, do not disappear overnight.)

It was, in fact, the inability or disinclination of all but a handful of blacks to seek desegregation actively that led Congress (in the 1964 Civil Rights Act) to empower the Justice Department to file integration suits itself; a year later Congress mandated that the Department of Health, Education and Welfare require local school boards to adopt desegregation plans as a condition for receiving federal aid. And when it became clear that segregated housing patterns were an impediment to school integration, some federal courts mandated busing to integrate the schools. Thus, instead of being largely potential consumers who had had to exercise a difficult option in order to receive *Brown*'s benefits, blacks became actual consumers by virtue of an automatic conferral of benefits.

Of course, shifts of consumer categories or other alleviation of impediments do not always happen. The Supreme Court has held that subdivision developers or proprietors of private schools cannot discriminate on the basis of race (*Jones v. Alfred H. Mayer Co.,* 1968; *Runyon v. McCrary,* 1976). But blacks generally make less money than whites, and no programs exist to assist them in meeting the costs of purchasing a home or making tuition payments. While no systematic research exists, it seems safe to conclude that economic impediments have precluded most blacks from being consumers of these judicial policies.

Even decisions that seem to bring a direct economic advantage may not always be accepted by consumers. In 1977 the Supreme Court overturned an ancient and rigid professional rule by holding that lawyers had a First Amendment right to advertise their services (*Bates v. Arizona State Bar*). A look at your local newspaper or phone directory will show that only a comparative handful actually do so. Presumably, most lawyers have refused to accept the legitimacy of professional advertising, have found it easier to stick with old habits, or perhaps have decided that the probable returns from advertising are not sufficient to justify the energy and expense. Of course, *Bates* is a recent decision. Over time lawyers may become less inhibited about advertising. It is also worth noting that the indirect consumers—members of the public who need legal services—were probably the intended beneficiaries of the Court's policy; but their benefits will be quite curtailed if the direct consumer population refuses to use the policy.

Consumer Reaction to a Beneficial Decision: *Miranda v. Arizona*

The *Miranda* decision is one judicial policy that has been the subject of some fairly systematic research. In *Miranda* the Supreme Court required that suspects undergoing in-custody questioning by the police be informed that they have the right to remain silent, that anything they say can be used against them in court, that they may have an attorney present during the questioning, and, if they cannot afford one, that an attorney will be furnished to them before questioning begins. The object of *Miranda*, according to the Court, was to make the Fifth Amendment guarantee against self-incrimination more meaningful by giving the suspect sufficient information and flexibility to be able to make rational decisions about acting in his or her own best interest. It was also clear that the Court believed that usually the most rational course a suspect would or could pursue was to remain silent, at least until he or she could consult with a lawyer.[4]

Following the decision several researchers observed police interrogations, interviewed suspects, or examined interrogation records in five American cities: Washington, D.C., New Haven, Denver, Pittsburgh, and Los Angeles.[5] Leaving aside police noncompliance—which, while considerable at first in some cities, declined over time[6]—it was found that a large proportion of the suspects readily answered

Table 4.1 Police Interrogation Success in Five Cities

City	(1) Pre-*Miranda* incriminating statements	(2) Post-*Miranda* incriminating statements	(3) Post-*Miranda* nonincriminating statements	(4) Post-*Miranda* refusals to talk	(5) Post-*Miranda*: no incriminating statements[a]
Washington	47%	40%	—	—	60%
New Haven	—	51	29%	20%	49
Denver	—	50	17	33	50
Los Angeles	40	47	—	—	53
Pittsburgh	54	38	—	—	62

[a] For the New Haven and Denver studies category (5) represents the sum of categories (3) and (4). The other studies did not differentiate between nonincriminating statements and refusals to talk.

Note: Figures represent percentage of suspects that fell into each category. Dashes indicate that no data for the category were collected in the study.

Sources: Medalie et al., "Custodial Police Interrogation in Our Nation's Capital," 1363; Wald et al., "Interrogations in New Haven," 1565-1566; Leiken, "Police Interrogation in Colorado," 17; Younger, "Effect of the *Miranda* Decision upon the Prosecution of Felony Cases [Los Angeles]," 35-36; and Seeburger and Wettick, "*Miranda* in Pittsburgh," 11. (Full citations may be found in note 5, p. 136.) In some cases reanalysis of the data was necessary for comparisons.

questions and did not request to have a lawyer present. Moreover, a good number of those who initially asked for counsel effectively negated their own request by answering police questions before the lawyer arrived.

Summary data taken from the five studies are shown in Table 4.1. For three of the cities comparisons were made with pre-*Miranda* interrogation data; it is interesting to note that suspects' willingness to make incriminating statements actually increased in Los Angeles after *Miranda* (though in the other two cities, as one might expect, it declined somewhat). In all five cities, however, a substantial proportion of the suspects—from 40 to 50 percent—gave incriminating statements to the police despite the *Miranda* warnings. Moreover, of those who did not give incriminating statements, a sizable proportion were nonetheless willing to talk with police.

The observations and interviews done in Washington and New Haven revealed several reasons why so many suspects failed to take advantage of their *Miranda* rights. For perhaps as many as 25 percent it was a communication problem—the suspects simply did not understand the meaning of the warning. The following are typical of the misinterpretations made by suspects regarding their right to have a lawyer present:

> "The police had some lawyer of their own who was working with them."
> "It means that I would have to pay for a lawyer."
> "They planned to appoint someone at court."

Similarly, the right to silence was misunderstood:

> "If I . . . like tried to bribe them they would use it against me in court."
> "I should . . . say something so they could use it in evidence in court." [7]

Even when the warnings were adequately understood, there was often no acceptance decision. Some suspects simply refused to take the warnings at face value. They cynically believed that the warnings were only a formality, a card read by the police because they had to, and that the police would not really forgo interrogation or allow an attorney to be present. For these suspects no meaningful choice existed.

But the largest group of suspects who failed to take advantage of *Miranda* rejected it not out of cynicism but because they believed it was better to cooperate with the police. They accepted the legitimacy of the warnings, but decided that their best interests were served by not adjusting to the options *Miranda* offered. There are several reasons why suspects might come to such a decision. One, of course, might be conscience: "I did it and I'm sorry." Or a suspect might perceive that he or she couldn't hide guilt anyway—witnesses might testify or damning evidence might already be available—and might as well get it over with. Closely related to this might be a suspect's calculation that he or she risks more—perhaps a longer sentence—by defiance than by cooperation.

Most suspects quite naturally believed that refusing to talk or insisting upon the presence of an attorney would be a tacit admission of guilt. It follows that such behavior would only intensify police suspicion and investigation. The best course, then, would be to deflect suspicion from oneself by appearing to be cooperative. So in order to avoid detection and punishment, some suspects take the risk of lying or telling less than the whole truth.

Then there are the suspects who believe that the warnings are for use only by criminals. Those with this perspective may be innocent, or they may think their actions were justified, as do some people who have killed an unfaithful spouse. They reject their *Miranda* options because they do not see that any harm can result from their choice. Often they are right. But sometimes they misperceive the situation, believing that they have not committed a crime, when what may seem to be acceptable behavior in a suspect's mind is not justified in the eyes of the law. For instance, murdering an adulterous mate is just as serious a crime as murdering anyone else.

Despite the evidence regarding the actual behavior of suspects, one might believe—and apparently several Supreme Court justices did believe—that the most rational course for a suspect regardless of circumstances is to remain silent and request an attorney. After all, he or she can always cooperate later if, after talking it over with the attorney, cooperation seems to be the best course of action. Little would be sacrificed by delay, and an irrevocable, damaging admission might be avoided. However, those studying the impact of *Miranda* remind us that the interrogation atmosphere is not conducive to rationality. As the New Haven researchers put it:

> The suspect arrested and brought downtown for questioning is in a crisis-laden situation. The stakes for him are high—often his freedom for a few or many years—and his prospects hinge on decisions that must be made quickly: To cooperate and hope for lenience, to try and talk his way out, to stand adamantly on his rights . . . the likely consequences of the alternatives open to him are unclear—how much lenience cooperation may earn, how likely fast talk is to succeed, how much a steadfast refusal to talk may contribute to a decision by the police, prosecutor or judge to "throw the book" at him.[8]

In such situations many people can't act rationally. "My mind wasn't functioning," is typical of suspects' reactions.[9] Thus, they do what many of us do when we find ourselves alone in a strange situation:

they take the path of least resistance, which under the circumstances means cooperating with the police.

Added to the general confusion is the natural tendency of people to be responsive and even polite—to talk with people and answer their questions. This tendency is exacerbated by the suspect's lack of freedom. The police are, temporarily at least, the captors. The suspect cannot call home or use the bathroom without permission, let alone leave the building. The police will determine how long the questioning lasts, and they may have some influence on setting bail. Most of us are friendly and perhaps even ingratiating to those who have power over us, and the suspect is normally no exception.

The tendency to cooperate also affects suspects who are well educated and are questioned in their own homes or offices. In 1967, the FBI interviewed over 20 Yale graduate students and faculty members in connection with the destruction of their draft cards, a crime punishable by up to five years in jail. Although most were independently aware of their *Miranda* rights and virtually all were given the warnings, almost all of them waived their rights. Based upon this incident as well as the earlier New Haven study, law professors John Griffiths and Richard Ayres concluded that despite *Miranda*, "The psychological interaction between the interrogator and the suspect in an interrogation is extremely subtle and the interrogator has most of the advantages." [10]

Of course we cannot lose sight of the fact that many suspects did choose to exercise their *Miranda* rights (see Table 4.1). The various researchers made little effort to obtain the suspects' own reasons for their acceptance and consumption of *Miranda*'s benefits, presumably because using their rights was the rational thing to do. But given both the direct and the subtle pressures on suspects to cooperate with the police, a direct investigation of why suspects did claim their rights might prove illuminating. In fact, Robert Roper has noted an *inverse* relationship between police pressure or intimidation and suspects' exercise of their rights. [11] This relationship, of course, comports with rationality (after all, if the interrogation atmosphere is already extremely hostile, the suspect risks little by asserting his or her rights), but it also indicates that the police may affect suspects' perceptions of rationality by controlling the emotional structure of the interrogation.

Moreover, available research tells us little about the consequences of exercising *Miranda* rights. How many suspects, after consulting with an attorney, decide to undergo police questioning? How many, despite their silence, are charged anyway? How many are convicted? There have been no direct investigations of such questions.

The conclusion of the Washington, D.C., researchers was that the consumer population's indifference to its *Miranda* benefits meant that "the odds against even beginning to approach the model established by the Court [are] exceedingly high." [12] But we must note that virtually all the research about suspects' acceptance or rejection of *Miranda* took place in the first few years following the decision.[13] It is not clear to what extent the researchers' findings are applicable in the 1980s. With the widespread publicity, it may be that rights granted by the decision are more routinely accepted by those suspected of crimes and are thus exercised with less trepidation. Unfortunately, scholars have a tendency to rush into impact research in the wake of dramatic policy changes, and then ignore the area once the policy has matured.

RESPONSES TO ADVERSE DECISIONS

The consequences of judicial policies that are disadvantageous to members of the consumer population are conceptually rather similar to those of advantageous policies. Of course, disadvantageous decisions tend to be imposed much more automatically upon the consumers; one rarely chooses to accept and adjust to a detrimental situation. Usually there is no way for the consumer to avoid the imposition of an undesirable policy. But at times at least some members of the consumer population have a choice. They can choose whether to accept and adjust to the adverse decision or whether to engage in some type of alternative behavior, which presumably would have fewer disadvantageous consequences.

Automatic Imposition

For some disadvantageous judicial policies, acceptance behavior is simply an irrelevant concept, in much the same way as it is irrelevant to raises in social security taxes (which are withheld from your paycheck, so that even defiance is not a viable option). If your social security taxes are raised, it follows that you will adjust by spending less money on other items. An example of a judicial policy producing automatic consumption can be found in the numerous state supreme court decisions during the 1960s and 1970s that required property to be assessed at full market value. For most people property taxes went up dramatically, and the property owner had no choice but to pay the tax or sell the property. In these situations the acceptance decision is irrelevant and the adjustment behavior is forced. (Of course, forced adjustments do not constrain feedback behavior where consumers bring pressures upon the court to reverse itself or upon other government agencies to mitigate the court's policy. For example, legislative and judicial decisions in California requiring full market value assessment of real property prompted voters to put a proposition to limit real estate taxes on the ballot in 1978 [known as Proposition 13]. Overwhelming voter approval of Proposition 13 largely negated the disadvantageous consequences of the full market value assessment decisions for property owners.)

Private (usually Catholic) schools and their pupils provide an important example of how disadvantageous judicial policies leave a consumer population without much choice. In the 1960s states with sizable Catholic populations, such as Pennsylvania, New York, and Rhode Island, sought to alleviate the financial pressures on parochial schools by such devices as paying the salaries of teachers of nonreligious subjects, providing the maintenance and repair of school buildings, and giving parents of parochial school students tax credits or tuition grants. The Supreme Court declared all these programs unconstitutional (*Lemon v. Kurtzman,* 1971; *Committee for Public Education and Religious Liberty v. Nyquist,* 1973). With state officials enjoined from making such payments, there was little the Catholic schools or parents could do in the immediate sense but live with the situation. Of course, they generated political pressure in the hope of ultimately changing the Court's policy—and were partly successful 10 years later when the Court upheld a Minnesota law allowing state income tax deductions for parents paying private school tuition (*Mueller v. Allen,* 1983).

Some judicial policies will leave disadvantaged members of the consumer population no option when they give advantages to other members of the consumer population. This is particularly true in zero-sum-game disputes. For instance, in the classic cases of *Lochner v. New York* (1905) and *Adkins v. Children's Hospital* (1923), where the Supreme Court struck down maximum hours and minimum wage legislation, it was imposing a considerable economic disadvantage on large groups of workers. While a rare worker might have quit as a result of one of these decisions, in the aggregate the workers had no choice but to suffer the consequences of employers' policies of long hours and low wages. The same holds true for the Court's negation of laws regulating child labor (*Hammer v. Dagenhart,* 1918; *Bailey v. Drexel Furniture Co.,* 1922). When the court reversed its policies concerning regulation of the economy in 1941 (*United States v. Darby Lumber Co.*), it imposed an automatic disadvantage on those companies that were profiting from child labor, low wages, and long working hours (although the losses might be reduced by passing on the higher cost to their customers to the extent that competition would allow).

Another way the courts can impose automatic economic disadvantages on individuals or groups is by denying or limiting legal redress for injuries. In one of the earliest major judicial intrusions into economic policy making, American state courts in the middle of the nineteenth century developed three common law doctrines designed to limit the ability of industrial employees to recover for injury or death suffered on the job. The *fellow servant doctrine* denied recovery if the accident was caused by another employee's negligence. The *contributory negligence doctrine* forbade all recovery if the employee had at all added to the possibility of being injured, and the *assumption of risk doctrine* denied recovery if the injury stemmed from a common hazard that the employee knew existed when he or she took the job. The courts said, in effect, that if any of these three situations was applicable to a worker's injuries, there was little point in his or her going to court. Capital won and labor lost. Nascent American industries, such as railroads and steelmaking, were thus able to accumulate considerable money that otherwise might have gone to compensate for employee injuries or deaths. The acquisition of such capital permitted existing industries to expand rapidly and encouraged others to invest in industrial enterprises. Thus because of the courts' policies, many of the costs of industrial expansion were borne bodily and economically by the workers. The adherence of courts to these doctrines into the twentieth century finally led to the passage of federal and state workmen's compensation laws, which established administrative agencies to compensate employees' injuries, regardless of who was at fault.[14]

Since the New Deal of the 1930s, the courts have generally abandoned such dramatic intrusions into the making of economic policy. With only a few exceptions courts now uphold laws and administrative regulations governing the economy. Still, by their very nature, the courts cannot avoid developing some important economic policies, especially when private lawsuits between adverse economic interests are involved. Types of disputes that often fall into the zero-sum-game model are labor-management disputes and smaller businesses' antitrust suits against larger businesses.

At times the broad public—consumers of certain products and services—constitutes the direct consumer population for such zero-sum-game situations. Tort law provides good examples. In the 1960s and 1970s, the great majority of state supreme courts abandoned manufacturers' negligence as the standard for liability for faulty products harmful to their purchasers and adopted strict liability instead (if the product, properly used, caused harm, the manufacturer is liable even if it used all diligent care in the course of production). Thus, while the public opportunity for monetary recovery was enhanced, the manufacturers' potential liability, and presumably their insurance costs, unavoidably went up (they could, of course, avoid them by going out of business, but this was not a real option). Conversely, the public lost in 1977 when the Supreme Court interpreted an antitrust statute to mean that consumers (or state attorneys general on their behalf) could not recover damages from manufacturers who had conspired to fix prices, unless they had bought directly from such a manufacturer and not through a retailer (*Illinois Brick Company v. Illinois*). As most products are purchased through retailers, this decision effectively gutted the antitrust law's provisions for consumer redress and significantly lessened constraints on price fixing.

In the past decade the courts have frequently been called on to settle disputes between environmentalists and growth-oriented businesses. Victories for the former often have considerable adverse economic consequences for the business community, while decisions favoring the latter may have a less quantitative but no less important detrimental impact upon many persons' quality of life. Often, however, these clashes turn legally on statutory interpretation or points of administrative law rather than on the substantive policy at issue. In such cases, when Congress feels strongly that the outcome is not good public policy, it can reverse the Court's action, as it did in the Alaska pipeline and the Tennessee snail darter cases (*Wilderness Society v. Aleyeska Pipeline Company,* 1973; *Tennessee Valley Authority v. Hill,* 1978).

Choosing Alternative Adjustment Behavior

When a disadvantageous judicial policy is not automatically imposed upon its consumer population, persons in that population choose to accept or reject the policy in accordance with their assessment of the situation. One form of acceptance occurs when people come to believe that the policy, though personally disadvantageous, is a legitimate one: the policy may serve the overall public interest; it may be required by the Constitution; or it may for some other reason transcend individual interests. Many people slowly and perhaps subconsciously change their attitudes in the face of authoritative pronouncements or seemingly unavoidable conditions. Political scientists have found that such adjustments occur particularly when the Supreme Court has unequivocally mandated certain policies.[15]

But people can also accept a disadvantageous policy without coming to believe in its legitimacy. They accept it in the sense that they decide that their best option is simply to live with the policy and adjust their behavior accordingly. (However, even as they live with it, people may engage in feedback behavior designed to modify or overturn such a policy.) Most people do in fact live with most policies, judicial or otherwise, that they perceive as disadvantageous; if this were not so, we would not live in an ordered society.

At times, however, members of the consumer population will decide not to accept a judicial policy. In such situations they have essentially two choices: they can refuse to alter their behavior, thereby defying the policy; or they can adjust their behavior so as to avoid the policy's impact without being defiant.

Defiance. As is the case with the interpreting and implementing populations, deliberate defiance on the part of the consumer population is infrequent but not unknown. More frequent is a failure to adjust behavior because the policy is not clear or its nature is misperceived or because no one insists on a change of behavior. Kenneth Dolbeare and Phillip Hammond's study of the impact of the school prayer decision in Indiana illustrates the latter situation.[16] The primary implementing population—the school administrators—abandoned all requirements for prayer and by omission left the choice up to the teachers (who could be viewed as a consuming population in this situation). Many teachers as well as parents believed that prayers were permissible as long as they were voluntary. But even among those more fully aware of what the Court had held, the tendency was to continue the prayers until someone forced them to do otherwise. It seems likely that similar reactions occurred in many rural areas of the country, although perhaps not everywhere.[17]

As with *Miranda*, many scholars investigated the impact of the school prayer situation in the half dozen or so years after it was promulgated, but none have done so recently. However, it is not too likely that the picture here has changed significantly over time. Following the Supreme Court's rejection of Kentucky's attempt to post the Ten Commandments in classrooms (*Stone v. Graham,* 1980), strong pressures arose in rural areas of the state against removing the plaques. In fact, students in some areas began coming to school wearing T-shirts printed with the Ten Commandments.[18] Those who engage in prayer often feel strongly about its rightness. No one wants to put teachers or schoolchildren in jail, and if defiance is widespread, it is virtually impossible to enforce judicial decisions in this policy area.

Most situations are less conducive to the consumer population's ignoring or defying a judicial policy. Nonetheless, a defiant refusal to change behavior is not uncommon to a few decisions. Such defiance is evident in the wake of *Branzburg v. Hayes* (1972), in which the Supreme Court held that the First Amendment gave journalists no right to refuse to answer court or grand jury questions about the sources of their news reports. (Put otherwise, journalists have no rights as witnesses not held by the public at large.) This policy is disadvantageous to journalists (and presumably to the public, the policy's indirect consumer), as it is likely to make persons who want anonymity unwilling to talk to them. Since *Branzburg,* a good number of journalists have defied the policy, refusing to answer court or grand jury questions about their news sources. The most spectacular instance occurred when *New York Times* reporter Myron Farber spent over two months in jail for refusing to give his notes to the presiding judge in the New Jersey murder trial of Dr. Mario Jascalevich. In addition, the *Times* was fined $250,000. Farber's investigative stories in the *Times* had been the catalyst for authorities to bring charges against Dr. Jascalevich. Farber avoided a longer stay in jail only because the doctor's acquittal mooted Farber's contempt sentence.

Generally, reporters like Farber do not expect to avoid the consequences of their defiant behavior. They engage in it anyway because they refuse to accept the legitimacy of the Court's interpretation of the First Amendment in *Branzburg* or because they feel that a commitment to preserve an interviewee's confidentiality is a matter of honor.

Avoidance.   Often a disadvantageous judicial policy is of such a nature that members of its consumer population can avoid the full force of its impact. This can be done by engaging in adjustment behavior that significantly minimizes or evades the policy's consequences. Of course, such adjustment behavior usually incurs a cost. Sometimes the cost is not very problematic. For instance, when the Supreme Court struck down the so-called released time programs whereby churches provided religious instruction in the public schools (*Illinois ex rel. McCullom v. Board of Education,* 1948), many churches simply shifted their instruction to off-campus locations (a strategy the Court upheld in *Zorach v. Clausen,* 1952). Similarly, after the school prayer case, some teachers or pupils began spontaneous oral prayer or silent meditation.

Usually, however, the costs are not so nominal. Pregnant women on welfare seeking an abortion might have to pay $200 or $300 for it following the Supreme Court's 1980 *Harris v. McRae* decision upholding Congress's cutoff of Medicaid payments for this purpose (the Hyde Amendment). This is a considerable but perhaps not impossible sum for a poor woman. Cancer patients who sought laetrile treatment had to travel to Mexico to obtain it after the Court upheld the Food and Drug Administration's ban on the substance in 1979 (*United States v. Rutherford*).

The cutoff of abortion funds and the banning of laetrile are examples of prohibitive judicial policies. These policies tell consumers that they cannot do something they want to do or have been doing, or at least that they cannot do it in the most convenient and effective manner. For the most part, judicial decisions are prohibitive; their message is, "Thou shalt not." After all, most legal controversies simply do not call for remedies that require a sizable consumer population to begin engaging in behavior that it finds disadvantageous or offensive. Moreover, the courts are reluctant to make "thou shalt" policies because they are difficult to enforce and they generate a high degree of resentment. However, the courts have had to impose "thou shalt" commands in developing desegregation policies that a large number of whites perceive as being to their disadvantage. In *Brown* and other early decisions that ordered the desegregation of such facilities as parks, buses, restaurants, and hotels, the courts did not require any changes in behavior on the part of resistant whites. They could continue to use such facilities as they had in the past, but blacks would now share in their use. The problem was that in the mores of the white South in that era, sharing facilities with blacks constituted a degree of social acceptance. Whites who refused to accept desegregation decisions viewed themselves as being forced into social behavior patterns they did not want.

This led to numerous acts of avoidance behavior. In a typical response, Jackson, Mississippi, closed its swimming pools rather than integrate them. This measure, of course, was carried out by the implementing population (city council), but seems to have been mandated by the white consumer population. (The Supreme Court upheld such an avoidance strategy in *Palmer v. Thompson* [1971], deciding that while the Fourteenth Amendment required public pools to be integrated, it did not require their existence.) Such avoidance behavior may seem like "cutting off your nose to spite your face," but it illustrates the fact that on some occasions members of the consumer population will feel so strongly about a policy that they will choose avoidance without regard to convenience or economic calculations. Members of the consumer population did engage in much direct avoidance behavior. Some restaurants closed. Others made blacks unwelcome (usually in ways somewhat less blatant than Georgia restaurant owner, and later governor, Lester Maddox, who chased them out with an ax handle). Some parents sent their children to private schools; in South Carolina, which repealed the compulsory school attendance laws, some parents did not send their children to school at all. This sort of avoidance behavior continues to this day, although as integration has won more widespread acceptance, it is not generally as frequent or egregious as in the past.

Consumer Reaction to Adverse Decisions: Busing

In contrast to passive acceptance, a few desegregation policies require active changes in behavior on the part of whites, for example, busing, fair housing, and equal opportunity employment. Here we will focus on white reactions to busing because it is an area where a fair amount of systematic social science research has occurred. Busing as a means of achieving racial integration in a school district means that thousands of white children, often in elementary schools, will be transported to classes some miles away rather than being assigned to the nearest school. This is disadvantageous to white pupils and their parents, at least in terms of inconvenience. (Many blacks were also inconvenienced by busing, but generally blacks felt that busing was more advantageous than disadvantageous to them. While some whites approved of busing, on the whole they have been more critical about it and have seen themselves as losing more than they gained from court-ordered busing.) Many whites perceive a disadvantage in attending formerly all-black inner-city schools, which they may feel are intellectually and physically inferior to the predominantly white schools in their own neighborhoods. And many may for several reasons want to avoid schools in which blacks constitute a majority or a large minority.

Avoidance is possible and legal. One method of evading busing is for parents to place their children in a private school. Another is for the family to move to a different area, perhaps in the suburbs, that is unaffected by the busing order. (In some situations the scope of the busing order may be so broad geographically that this option is not available.) These two forms of avoidance behavior are often termed *white flight.* (The phenomenon known as white flight includes behavior that may not be motivated by school desegregation, but we will limit our use of the term here to movement to the suburbs or to enrolling children in private schools.) Obviously, there are considerable costs in money and inconvenience to white flight. Tuition at a private school is expensive, and the school may be inconveniently located. A house in the suburbs may be high priced and may not be convenient to the parents' jobs. Still, as we noted earlier, avoidance can be motivated by emotion at least as much as by calculation.

Several social scientists have investigated the extent to which busing has produced white flight. Some have found that a causal relationship exists, while others have found virtually none. This disparity in findings has been accompanied by much controversy between the researchers, reflecting in part different data bases and focuses and in part the researchers' own opinions about the wisdom of busing. It is one of the few social science controversies that has reached the front pages of the newspapers.

The controversy began in 1975, when sociologist James Coleman published research reporting a strong link between school desegregation and white flight from big cities.[19] His conclusion was drawn from an analysis of enrollment data in 20 large metropolitan and 46 mid-size school districts. Coleman was studying the effects of integration per se, and many of the districts he examined were desegregating through means other than court-ordered busing. Nonetheless, he felt justified in concluding:

> The extremely strong reactions of individual whites in moving their children out of large districts engaged in massive and rapid desegregation suggests that in the long run the policies that have been pursued will defeat the purpose of increasing overall contact among the races in the schools. . . . Thus a major policy implication of this analysis is that in an area such as school desegregation, which has important consequences for individuals and in which individuals retain control of some actions that can, in the end, defeat the policy, the courts are probably the worst instrument of social policy.[20]

(Coleman had changed his mind since 1966, when he published the results of a well-publicized study offering considerable evidence that school desegregation was educationally beneficial to both blacks and whites.)[21]

Coleman's 1975 findings were attacked by other social scientists on two grounds: first, that he was too selective with regard to which school districts he examined and second, that white flight from the central cities is a long-term phenomenon predating desegregation and occurring even in cities that are not undergoing rapid desegregation.[22] Political scientist Christine Rossell not only criticized Coleman's conclusion, but conducted her own analysis based upon data from 86 school districts.[23] She found that only two of them (Pasadena, California, and Pontiac, Michigan) showed significant white flight above and beyond normal out-migration patterns and that even in these two cities it was "minimal and temporary." Desegregation, she concluded, was not substantially related to white flight. Rossell, herself, however, was charged with using statistical methods that minimized the appearance of white flight; one commentator pointed out that her figures showed that busing in Boston—which was accompanied by violence, boycotts, and eventually a complete judicial takeover of the school system—produced no white flight, even though white enrollment dropped four times as much in the six years following the court-ordered busing as it had in the six preceding years.[24]

Coleman and Rossell based their findings on inferences drawn from changes in school enrollment data. Three political scientists at Florida Atlantic University, Micheal Giles, Douglas Gatlin, and Everett Cataldo, used another approach: interviewing parents about their attitudes and behavior.[25] Their study was done in seven Florida counties subject to court-ordered busing. They found that large numbers of the parents did not accept the busing order. Eight of the parents' reasons brought out in the interviews are shown in column 1 of Table 4.2.

The question arises, Did these nonaccepting parents become part of white flight? Only a relatively small proportion—perhaps 15 percent—actually sent their children to private schools. (Since the entire county was included in the busing order, moving out of town was not an avoidance option for most respondents. Further, less than 1 percent of the white parents claimed to have moved to avoid busing.)[26] Most interesting is, as column 2 of Table 4.2 shows, only one of these eight factors influenced actual avoidance behavior: percentage of blacks in the new school. The other seven factors, although related to the acceptance decision, did not induce an avoidance form of adjustment behavior. Indeed, two factors (racism and perception of busing as being illegitimate) were negatively related to avoidance. The reason for this is clear when we note that income, which was not at all related to the acceptance decision, is highly related to avoidance behavior. Racism and perceptions of busing as illegitimate were most prevalent among lower income whites who could not afford private schools. Higher income parents, while less racist and less bothered by busing per se, often avoided the busing policy because they had the capacity to do so.

The findings suggest that attitudes have a far greater effect on acceptance decisions than upon adjustment behavior. The latter is more affected by the magnitude of the inconvenience and the consumer's capacity to avoid it. Of course, this may not be true for all disadvantageous judicial policies. However, the Florida Atlantic findings do comport with ones by David Sears from his study of reactions to energy conservation policies which indicated that self-

Table 4.2 Factors Significantly Related to Acceptance and Avoidance Decision by Persons Subject to Court-Ordered Busing

Factor	Significant difference between acceptors and nonacceptors[a]	Significant difference between avoiders and nonavoiders[a]
Policy factors		
Percent black at new school	X	X
Previous racial status of new school	X	
Distance to new school	X	
Busing per se	X	
Attitudinal factors		
Racism	X	*
Class prejudice	X	
Perceptual factors		
Legitimacy of busing	X	*
Community leaders' support for busing		
Sense of personal efficiency	X	
Capacity factor		
Income		X

[a] X = positive relationship, * = negative relationship.

Source: Adapted from Micheal Giles and Douglas Gatlin, "Mass Level Compliance with Public Policy: The Case of School Desegregation," *Journal of Politics* 42 (August 1980): 722-746, with permission of the publisher.

interest and avoidance capacity were more important predictors of noncompliance with energy conservation policies than were attitudes toward the policies.[27]

Existing research gives no precise answer about the degree to which busing—or other forms of court-ordered desegregation—causes white flight. But it is clear that a significant number of parents do engage in avoidance behavior. Private, virtually all-white schools have proliferated throughout the South. And court-ordered busing has certainly been one of several factors that have induced families to move to the suburbs.

SUMMARY

The consumer population is probably the most variable of all the populations. For some cases it can consist of the general public while for others it will consist of only a handful of persons, depending on the subject matter of the judicial policy involved.

Consumption is advantageous when affected persons perceive themselves as benefiting from the judicial decision. Consumption is disadvantageous to persons who believe they are adversely affected by a policy. Moreover, consumption can be direct or indirect. Individuals who are directly affected by a policy take part in direct consumption. Those who receive benefits or disadvantages depending upon consumption choices made by another group are indirect consumers.

Some judicial policies are consumed automatically: benefits or disabilities accrue to people without any action on their part. This occurs when a court constrains an implementing agency from granting an advantage or imposing a disadvantage upon a group, or, conversely, when the court requires such a response of the agency. Judicial decisions requiring tax assessors to raise or lower property values, for example, give the affected individuals no choice but to adjust to the decisions. Automatic consumption also is in effect when a judicial policy leads to an increase or decrease in the price of goods or services or when it affects the quality of persons' lives, as does a decision regarding safety conditions in the workplace.

Other judicial decisions are consumed by choice. Decisions to consume beneficial policies are affected by such things as a person's temperament, interest, beliefs, or knowledge; the availability of opportunities; and the monetary and social costs involved. For combinations of these reasons, many people do not take advantage of judicial policies such as those that have made sexually explicit literature more widely available; many arrested persons do not exercise their *Miranda* rights; and many blacks do not buy homes in the suburbs.

When disadvantageous consumption is not automatic, members of the consumer population have the choice of accepting the disabilities imposed or of engaging in alternative adjustment behavior. The choice depends upon two main variables: their perception of the legitimacy of the judicial policy and their assessment of the monetary and psychic costs of abiding by it versus not abiding by it. One alternative form of adjustment behavior is defiance, which is not too common and is usually followed as a matter of principle. Another is avoidance, which is more common, occurring when people take steps to get away from or avoid the situation covered by the judicial policy. Sometimes this can be done simply; at other times it can be costly, as when parents send their children to private schools in order to avoid a busing order.

NOTES

1. Roger A. Hanson and Robert E. Crew, Jr., "The Policy Impact of Reapportionment," *Law and Society Review* 8 (Fall 1973): 69-94. But see Eric Uslaner, "Comparative State Policy Formation, Interparty Competition and Malapportionment," *Journal of Politics* 40 (May 1978): 409-432, for skepticism that reapportionment had a major impact on legislative policies.
2. James P. Levine, "Constitutional Law and Obscene Literature: An Investigation of Bookseller Censorship Practices," in *The Impact of Supreme Court Decisions*, 2d ed., ed. Theodore L. Becker and Malcolm Feeley (New York: Oxford University Press, 1973), 119-138.
3. Susan B. Hansen, "State Implementation of Supreme Court Decisions: Abortion Rates since *Roe v. Wade,*" *Journal of Politics* 42 (May 1980): 375.
4. *Miranda v. Arizona*, 384 U.S. 436 (1966) at 468-473.
5. See Richard J. Medalie et al., "Custodial Police Interrogation in Our Nation's Capital: An Attempt to Implement *Miranda,*" *Michigan Law Review* 66 (May 1968): 1347-1421; Michael Wald et al., "Interrogations in New Haven: The Impact of *Miranda,*" *Yale Law Journal* 76 (July 1967): 1521-1648; Lawrence S. Leiken, "Police Interrogation in Colorado: The Implementation of *Miranda,*" *Denver Law Journal* 47 (1970): 1-47; Richard H. Seeburger and Stanton Wettick, Jr., "*Miranda* in Pittsburgh: A Statistical Study," *University of Pittsburgh Law Review* 29 (October 1967): 1-26; and Evelle J. Younger, "Results of a Survey Conducted by the District Attorney's Office of Los Angeles County Regarding the Effect of the *Miranda* Decision upon the Prosecution of Felony Cases," *American Criminal Law Quarterly* 5 (Fall 1966): 32-39.
6. Medalie et al., "Custodial Police Interrogation."
7. Ibid., 1375, 1378.
8. Wald et al., "Interrogations in New Haven," 1613-1614.
9. Medalie et al., "Custodial Police Interrogation," 1375.
10. John Griffiths and Richard Ayres, "A Postscript to the *Miranda* Project: Interrogation of Draft Protesters," *Yale Law Journal* 77 (December 1967): 318.
11. Robert T. Roper, "Miranda behind Bars: Prisoners Evaluate Their Invocation of Constitutional Guarantees" (Paper delivered at the 34th Annual Meeting of the Midwest Political Science Association, Chicago, Ill., 1976), 25-26.
12. Medalie et al., "Custodial Police Interrogation," 1379.
13. Roper, "Miranda behind Bars" is the only exception.
14. See Lawrence Friedman and Jack Ladinsky, "Social Change and the Law of Industrial Accidents," *Columbia Law Review* 67 (January 1967): 50-82.

15. See Kenneth Dolbeare, "The Supreme Court and the States: From Abstract Doctrine to Local Conformity," in *The Impact of Supreme Court Decisions*, 2d ed., ed. Theodore L. Becker and Malcolm Feeley (New York: Oxford University Press, 1973), 202-220; and William K. Muir, Jr., *Prayer in the Public Schools: Law and Attitude Change* (Chicago: University of Chicago Press, 1971).

16. Kenneth M. Dolbeare and Phillip E. Hammond, *The School Prayer Decisions: From Court Policy to Local Practice* (Chicago: University of Chicago Press, 1971).

17. See H. Frank Way, Jr., "Survey Research on Judicial Decisions: The Prayer and Bible Reading Cases," *Western Political Quarterly* 21 (June 1968): 189-205; Robert Birkby, "The Supreme Court and the Bible Belt: Tennessee Reaction to the *Schempp* Decision," *Midwest Journal of Political Science* 10 (August 1966): 304-319; and Ellis Katz, "Patterns of Compliance with the *Schempp* Decision," *Journal of Public Law* 14 (Fall 1965): 396-408.

18. "Opinion on Ten Commandments Has Its Ups and Downs for School Officials," *Louisville Courier-Journal*, January 25, 1981, 1.

19. James S. Coleman, Sara D. Kelly, and John Moore, "Recent Trends in School Desegregation" (Paper delivered at the meeting of the American Educational Research Association, Washington, D.C., April 1975); rev. version, Washington, D.C.: Urban Institute, 1975.

20. Ibid., 21-22.

21. James S. Coleman et al., *Equality of Educational Opportunity* (Washington, D.C.: Government Printing Office, 1966).

22. See Thomas Pettigrew and Robert L. Green, "School Desegregation in Large Cities: A Critique of the Coleman 'White Flight' Thesis," *Harvard Educational Review* 46 (February 1976): 1-53.

23. Christine H. Rossell, "School Desegregation and White Flight," *Political Science Quarterly* 90 (Winter 1975-76): 675-695.

24. Diane Ravitch, "The 'White Flight' Controversy," *The Public Interest* 51 (Spring 1978): 135-149.

25. Micheal Giles, Douglas Gatlin, and Everett Cataldo, "White Flight and Percent Black: The Tipping Point Reexamined," *Social Science Quarterly* 56 (June 1976): 85-92; Douglas Gatlin, Micheal Giles, and Everett Cataldo, "Policy Support within a Target Group: The Case of School Desegregation," *American Political Science Review* 72 (September 1978): 985-995; and Micheal Giles and Douglas Gatlin, "Mass Level Compliance with Public Policy: The Case of School Desegregation," *Journal of Politics* 42 (August 1980): 722-746.

26. Gatlin, Giles, and Cataldo, "White Flight and Percent Black," 86.

27. David O. Sears et al., "Political System Support and Public Response to the Energy Crisis," *American Journal of Political Science* 22 (February 1978): 56-82.

CHAPTER FIVE

The Secondary Population

I n this chapter we examine how the secondary population reacts to judicial policies. The secondary population is a residual category; it is composed of those who are not in the other populations. As we discussed briefly in Chapter 4, the distinctions between the secondary population and other populations, especially the consumer population, are not always sharply drawn; indeed, some policies with universal impact (for example, those relating to income taxes) may have virtually no secondary population. But in regard to most judicial policies there are numerous individuals whose lives are not directly affected. Many such persons, of course, could care less about these policies; but many others do react to judicial policies that do not directly concern them. For instance, many members of the clergy and persons beyond childbearing age are vitally concerned with the abortion decision, and many persons without children in public schools have reacted vigorously to the school prayer decision. There is nothing wrong with this concern. It is part of the ethos of democracy that citizens should be interested in public policies beyond ones that may directly affect them.

For our discussion we will divide the secondary population into four categories. First we consider public officeholders such as members of Congress, the president, and state legislators. For some judicial policies, of course, officeholders may be implementors or consumers and not members of the secondary population. Beyond that, some officials, such as budget makers and legislators, can influence the course of implementation through the appropriation process. But more often than not, officeholders fall within the secondary population, and as such we will focus on them in this chapter. Officeholders form a particular kind of secondary population. They are the public's elected representatives in government, and it is through them that the public voices its reactions to judicial policies. Officeholders are part of institutions that can bring pressure, both on the courts to maintain or change their policies and on the interpreting and implementing populations to reinforce or constrain the impact of judicial policies. These officials are a major conduit by which the consumer population and other members of the secondary population send feedback to the courts.

Second we discuss interest groups that are not composed of members of the consumer population. On many occasions interest groups are responsible for bringing cases to the judiciary; we will review how interest groups react to favorable and to adverse decisions of the judiciary. In some instances, these groups may effectively influence either follow-up decisions by the judiciary or implementation decisions by government agencies. These groups may, therefore, be potent forces that affect the aftermath of a judicial decision.

Third we briefly consider the impact of the media on judicial policies. We have occasionally mentioned aspects of communications in discussing how other populations react to judicial decisions, and we will discuss communications theory more extensively in Chapter 6. In this chapter we review some of the research on the attention given the judicial policies by the media as well as the impact of that attention on efforts to implement judicial policies.

Fourth, as the last section of this chapter, we discuss the reactions of the other members of the secondary population. We shall label these members as the public at large and divide them into two categories, the attentive public and the mass public. (We noted in Chapter 4 that distinguishing the general public from the consumer population is not always easy.) Much of our discussion centers on how well informed these groups are: who knows what about judicial policies? We also discuss what impact these publics have on efforts to implement judicial policies. Unfortunately, research in this area is scattered, and our remarks are largely speculative.

PUBLIC OFFICIALS AND JUDICIAL POLICIES

Congress

More than any other public agency, Congress tends to be the focal point for public reaction to judicial policies. As a political body, Congress cannot ignore any sizable or prominent group of constituents. Some groups become especially agitated when they are unhappy with some judicial decision or doctrine, and they make their dissatisfaction known to members of Congress. If the pressure is great enough and is not counterbalanced by pressure from groups that support the judicial policy, Congress will, if feasible, take action. At the very least, numerous members of Congress will score political points by showing righteous indignation on behalf of the disaffected groups.

Moreover, on some issues the legislators may feel an institutional involvement that extends well beyond their need to respond to constituents. Just as an author or a playwright may feel personally affronted when his or her work receives a devastating review, so may legislators feel personally involved when the courts strike down or limit the laws they have written. This is especially the case if the laws have only recently been enacted.

While Congress usually relates to the courts as a member of the secondary population, such is not always the case. From time to time a dispute over the powers of Congress ends up before the courts; on those occasions Congress is a direct consumer of judicial decisions. Congress directly consumed a judicial decision in 1969, when the Supreme Court ordered it to restore Rep. Adam Clayton Powell, Jr.'s seat to him following the refusal of the House of Representatives to seat him in 1967, in part because of a state court's criminal contempt judgment against him (*Powell v. McCormack*). Other examples are found in cases involving how much power legislative committees have to gather information from private citizens (a frequently litigated issue in the heyday of the House Un-American Activities Committee in the 1950s), and in the clashes between legislative and executive authority that the courts must sometimes settle. A dramatic example of the latter is the 1983 legislative veto case (*Immigration and Naturalization Service v. Chadha;* see Chapter 4, p. 110). Here the Court nullified a convenient method of controlling administrative policy making that Congress had used for over half a century. Congress will now have to devote considerable time and energy to find alternative and presumably less satisfactory means of accomplishing this function. Although, strictly speaking, congressional reactions to such decisions belong in our discussion of the consumer population, we will consider some of them in order to make our discussion of relations between Congress and the judiciary more complete.

Clashes between Congress and the courts are virtually as old as the two branches. *Marbury v. Madison* (1803) was a political finesse of a hostile Congress by the Supreme Court. Constitutional crises have been provoked by such decisions as *Dred Scott* (*Scott v. Sandford,* 1857) and several anti-New Deal decisions in the 1930s. Strained relationships just short of crises have developed from numerous other decisions. Of course, not all differences between the courts and Congress are emotionally charged. Often they involve differences over such mundane issues as bankruptcy or admiralty law. Either way, hardly a session of Congress goes by without that body's reacting in some way to several judicial decisions. Usually these decisions are made by the Supreme Court, but occasionally Congress reacts to a lower court ruling. The 1982 federal district court decision breaking up the Bell Telephone System generated congressional reaction, for example.

Two matters are worth examining at this point. First, what can Congress do in reaction to a Supreme Court decision? Second, what factors influence Congress's choices of action? Several scholars have investigated these questions, particularly the second one, as they relate to the post-World War II era; we will use their findings in our discussion.

Options in Statutory Interpretation Situations. What Congress can do in reaction to a Court decision, of course, depends upon the situation. If the decision involves a statutory interpretation, Congress can "reverse" the Court by rewriting the statute. Sometimes, in fact, the Court virtually requests such action if it feels that the law is poorly worded, ambiguous, or out of date. In other situations, Congress may feel that the Court has misinterpreted the statute by ignoring the meaning of the language or the policy intentions of the statute's drafters. In still other situations, the statute at issue is one establishing a major congressional policy, such as the Sherman Antitrust Act (1890), the National Labor Relations Act (1935), and the Civil Rights Act of 1964. Such laws often lack details about the scope of their coverage, and the courts are continually having to make decisions about the applicability of the laws. Indeed, many such decisions have a greater impact than those interpreting provisions of the Constitution. Finally, Congress may reverse the Court when it wants to make a particular exception to a generally approved statutory interpretation. The very first congressional reversal was of this type: Congress passed a law to save a bridge over the Ohio River after the Court had ruled that the bridge violated an earlier law (*Pennsylvania v. Wheeling and Belmont Bridge Co.,* 1852). More recently, Congress has approved exceptions to judicial interpretations of the Environmental Protection Act and the Endangered Species Act to facilitate construction of the Alaska pipeline and save a nearly completed dam in Tennessee.

Congress can reverse the Court on nonstatutory matters, also. These involve questions about traditional understandings, common law, and administrative policies regarding such areas as federal-state relations, federal land, navigable waters, and Indian tribes. When the Court has to make a decision concerning a nonstatutory issue, but it is not a constitutional law decision, Congress may want to do things differently. For example, in the Tidelands Oil controversy, in 1953 Congress said that the coastal states held title to offshore mineral rights, even though the Supreme Court had ruled six years earlier (*United States v. California,* 1947) that title resided with the federal government. The Supreme Court later accepted Congress's right to transfer title (*Alabama v. Texas,* 1954).

Congress does not often reverse statutory interpretations. Because the legislative process is cumbersome, interest groups benefiting from the Court's interpretation are often successful in preventing congressional action. At times Congress may adopt deliberately ambiguous language to pass the buck to the courts and thus avoid responsibility for displeasing some group of constituents. Questions of whether the provisions of the 1964 Civil Rights Act or the 1972 Educational Amendments Act prohibit compensatory advancement for minorities or protect university employees (as opposed to students) from discrimination fall into this category. Notably, there has been no real congressional movement to reverse the Court's interpretations on these questions (*Kaiser Aluminum & Chemical Corp. v. Weber,* 1979; *North Haven Board of Education v. Bell,* 1982). Even when there is no great opposition in Congress to changing a low-profile statutory interpretation, efforts to do so will often get bogged down, wither, and die. Beth Henschen reports that of 222 Supreme Court statutory interpretations in the antitrust and labor relations areas between 1950 and 1972, only 27 (or 12 percent) were subject to reversal attempts in Congress, and in only 9 (or 4 percent) did a reversal bill actually pass.[1] A study of congressional roll calls reversing Supreme Court decisions over a 24-year period by John Schmidhauser and his colleagues showed that while 114 roll calls occurred, they involved only 30 court policies.[2] A less quantitative study of statutory reversals concluded that

> Nearly all [successful reversals] ... involved a return to a "common understanding" which had been disrupted by the Court's decision, that nearly all enjoyed the unanimous support of the politically articulate groups affected by the Court's decision. The few exceptions ... occurred either at a time of major legislative reassessment in the area of the decision, or through the efforts of a political group powerful enough to maintain an intense nationwide lobbying campaign.[3]

An exception to this generalization occurred in the internal security area during the 1950s. Congress quickly passed notable reversals of two Supreme Court decisions that had made it more difficult to prosecute suspected subversives and to deport suspected alien subversives (*Jencks v. United States*, 1957; *Wong Yang Sung v. McGrath*, 1950). However, even in this area, reversal was not the norm. Bills reversing decisions such as *Yates v. United States* (1957), which virtually gutted the Smith Act; *Kent v. Dulles* (1958), which prohibited the denial of passports to political radicals; and *Greene v. McElroy* (1959), which in effect required a hearing before the security clearance of an employee of a defense contractor could be revoked, passed only one house of Congress.[4]

Congressional reversals do not always accomplish their purpose. Occasionally, the Court will ignore the reversal or work its way around it. A dramatic example occurred during the Vietnam War when the Court held in *United States v. Seeger* (1965) that the Selective Service Act's exemption from military service "by reason of religious training or belief" applied to those persons whose objections to military service stemmed from moral or philosophical beliefs unconnected with a belief in a supreme being. Congress quickly rewrote the Act to make it clear that the religious exemption was to be given only to those whose religious beliefs were conventionally related to a supreme being. Nonetheless, the Court interpreted the revised statute in virtually the same way as it had the original wording in *Seeger* (*Welsh v. United States*, 1970). Such Court reversals of a congressional reversal are, however, quite infrequent.

Options in Judicial Procedure Situations. Congress also has the power under Article III of the Constitution to change Supreme Court decisions that establish nonconstitutional rules of judicial procedure and evidence. Usually Congress leaves such rules alone in deference to judicial expertise. But Congress is full of lawyers who are not unknowledgeable about the judicial process, and occasionally it will alter the rules, especially rules that provoke considerable opposition. One such instance occurred in 1980. After the Court held that law enforcement officers could obtain search warrants to search newsrooms (*Zurcher v. The Stanford Daily,* 1978), Congress passed legislation requiring that evidence from newsrooms be obtained by subpoena. (The *Zurcher* reversal is also noteworthy because it is one of the few times in recent years that Congress has substituted a pro-civil liberties policy for a conservative judicial decision.)

Options in Constitutional Law Situations. The situation is different when the judicial decision involves constitutional law rather than statutory interpretation. Constitutional decisions generally involve matters likely to arouse widespread public attention, whereas statutory interpretations tend to be of more concern to special interests such as business, labor, or environmental groups. Constitutional law decisions, such as those involving school prayer or abortion, can arouse tremendous emotions; statutory interpretations seldom do. We have discussed how Congress as part of the secondary population for decisions interpreting statutes can modify or change such decisions. However, Congress cannot ordinarily reverse the Court in constitutional matters—it must find other ways to react. Congress has two avenues of reaction: members can address the disliked policy and attempt to circumvent it or have it altered; or they can retaliate by attacking the courts (particularly the Supreme Court) directly.

One obvious way of overcoming a constitutional law decision is to pass a constitutional amendment changing it. It is just as obvious that changes in the Constitution are not easily accomplished. A constitutional amendment requires a two-thirds vote in each house of Congress, followed by ratification by three-quarters of the states. Only four Supreme Court decisions in U.S. history have been overruled by constitutional amendment.[5] However, members of Congress have shown no reluctance to introduce constitutional amendments to overturn Supreme Court decisions. For example, in the 18 months after the school prayer decision, 146 different amendments to modify or overturn this decision were filed in Congress.[6] In the last quarter century, Congress has considered proposed amendments that would negate or severely modify the Court's decisions in such areas as reapportionment, abortion, busing to achieve racial balance, and school prayers. A couple of proposals have been approved by one house or the other, but despite repeated attempts and the unpopularity of some of the Court's decisions, no amendment has been submitted to the states. The amendment route can be used to overcome a Supreme Court interpretation of the Constitution only when there is a general consensus that the policy inherent in the Court's decision ought to be altered. The Twenty-sixth Amendment, which was passed in 1971 and lowered the voting age in all elections to 18, resulted from a widespread belief that the Court's decision in *Oregon v. Mitchell* (1970), which would have lowered the voting age to 18 in federal but not state elections, was both unwise and unworkable.

Occasionally Congress will try to negate a Court decision through ordinary but contradictory legislation. Following *Miranda v. Arizona* (1966), Congress inserted a section in the Crime Control Act of 1968 permitting federal courts to receive in evidence the in-custody testimony of suspects obtained without the *Miranda* warnings if the judge believed that the "totality of circumstances" was such that the testimony was given voluntarily. However, federal judges have rarely cited this section, and it is for all legal purposes a dead issue. Congress was in effect letting off steam and was not seriously trying to reverse *Miranda*. Nonetheless, such efforts are not totally without effect: they serve as warnings to the Court not to go further, and they encourage the interpreting population to give only minimal scope to the decision.

Even in making symbolic gestures, Congress sometimes needs to proceed carefully. When it appeared unlikely in 1981-1982 that there were sufficient votes to pass a constitutional amendment outlawing abortion, many congressional opponents of abortion switched to the ordinary law strategy. They pushed for a statute declaring that life begins at conception, in contrast to the Court's opinion that there was no certainty about when life began. Such a law was not adopted in good part because of fears that if taken seriously it would lead to a major constitutional confrontation between Congress and the judiciary. If not taken seriously it would be unenforceable and simply expose Congress's impotence.

In 1964 many lawmakers, led by Sen. Everett Dirksen, R-Ill., tried another limiting strategic tack. Dirksen proposed a bill that would suspend the operation of the Supreme Court's reapportionment decisions (particularly *Reynolds v. Sims,* 1964) for two years. While the constitutionality of such a law was dubious, it did not on its face seem like an unreasonable invasion of the judicial prerogative. Dirksen's real goal, however, was to give Congress and the unreapportioned state legislatures sufficient time to pass a constitutional amendment modifying or nullifying the reapportionment decisions. When Dirksen and his supporters were unable to break a six-week liberal filibuster, the Senate settled for a face-saving resolution (not a law) asking the courts to give legislatures six months to adjust to the reapportionment decisions.[7]

Sometimes Congress can pass legislation that minimizes the impact of undesired court decisions. We noted in Chapter 1 (pp. 8-

11) that following the abortion decision Congress passed the Hyde Amendment and other laws restricting the use of federal funds for elective and therapeutic abortions. In fact, Congress's most potent weapon for blunting judicial policies is the power of the purse. On one occasion, for example, the House of Representatives came within one vote of refusing to appropriate money to provide back pay for a government official who had won a Supreme Court decision (*United States v. Lovett,* 1946) entitling him to the money.[8] In reaction to busing decisions, Congress considered several proposals to withhold federal funds from school systems involved in busing to achieve racial integration; but the only such proposal adopted made an exception for court-ordered busing. In 1980 President Jimmy Carter vetoed the Justice Department appropriations bill because it contained a rider prohibiting funds from being spent on efforts to obtain court decisions favoring busing. Still, the fiscal weapon is a limited one. Many of the Supreme Court's policies regarded most negatively by Congress involve civil liberties issues where no appropriations are involved.

Finally, and most drastically, Congress in theory has the authority to withdraw the Supreme Court's jurisdiction to hear certain types of cases. (Article III of the Constitution gives the Supreme Court appellate jurisdiction "with such Exceptions and under such Regulations as the Congress shall make.") This power has been exercised substantively only once. In the Reconstruction period, Congress, in anticipation of a possible Court ruling that statutes imposing military rule on the South would be held unconstitutional, withdrew the high Court's appellate jurisdiction of habeas corpus from military detention. Post-World War II proposals to withdraw the Court's jurisdiction in such areas as reapportionment, school prayers, interrogation of suspects, busing, and abortion have all been defeated in Congress, although bills in the first two areas did pass in one house (reapportionment in the House, 1964; prayer in the Senate, 1979).

Several proposals to strip the Supreme Court's jurisdiction over various aspects of internal security matters came close to passage in 1958. There was a highly negative reaction to several internal security decisions handed down in 1956 and 1957, most notably *Slochower v. Board of Higher Education of New York City, Watkins v. United States,* and *Konigsberg v. State Bar of California.* Bills to strip the Court's jurisdiction passed easily in the House, but were either blocked or defeated in the Senate, the closest (the Jenner-Butler bill) by a 41-40 vote.

In fact, while the Court did acquiesce in the Reconstruction withdrawal (*Ex parte McCardle,* 1869) we mentioned, there is some reason to believe that the modern Court would find such a narrow and retaliatory curbing of its jurisdiction unconstitutional. Even if it were to be found constitutional, a withdrawal of jurisdiction would not overrule the Court's previous decision. The decision would remain valid, but its interpretive future would be entirely in the hands of lower federal and state appellate judges. Without a final authority, confusion would reign.

General Retaliation. Congress can also respond negatively to judicial policies through general punitive actions or through actions designed to change decision rules or judicial personnel. Punitive actions are basically symbolic and usually involve the refusal of Congress to appropriate sufficient funds for the Supreme Court. For instance, Congress has not seen fit to appropriate funds for an automobile to take the Supreme Court's associate justices to and from work or on other official business, despite the fact that every federal district judge is provided such a vehicle. One southern senator responded to the justices' request for automobiles, by proposing, "Couldn't we get a bus to bus the judges? I learned about busing from reading the *Swann* case." [9] Congressional punishment of the Court is nothing new: in 1816 Congress refused to appropriate one thousand dollars for a court reporter because of its displeasure with the decision in *Martin v. Hunter's Lessee* (1816).[10]

Another retaliatory tactic involves the judges' salaries. Article III prohibits Congress from reducing judges' salaries; it was intended to prevent fiscal punishment for unpopular decisions. In an inflationary era, however, the failure to increase salaries is tantamount to a reduction. In 1964 Congress raised the salaries of all federal judges except those on the Supreme Court by $7,000; the justices received only a $4,500 raise. In debating the issue, several members of Congress made it clear that dissatisfaction with the Supreme Court's decisions motivated their action. Republican Representative (later Senator) Robert Dole of Kansas was quite blunt about the connection, virtually to the point of suggesting blackmail. He said:

> Whenever thinking of the Supreme Court I think of last June 15, 1964, and reapportionment decisions handed down in *Reynolds against Simms* [sic] and the related cases. It has been suggested that perhaps Section 2 of the Bill might be amended whereby the effective date of the pay increase if adopted by this House, would be the date the Supreme Court reverses the decision in *Reynolds against Simms* [sic].[11]

While it is unlikely that the justices can be "bought" for $2,500, such congressional actions, in conjunction with other forms of pressure, may have a long-term influence on the Court.

Another approach is for Congress to initiate a constitutional amendment making changes in the Supreme Court's decision-making rules. In the early part of the twentieth century, Progressives, angered at the conservative Court's frequent negation of laws regulating labor conditions, proposed two amendments: one that would require two-thirds of the justices to concur before a federal law could be declared unconstitutional and one that would permit Congress by a two-thirds vote to overrule the Court and reenact a statute held unconstitutional. Neither amendment was adopted by Congress, but the tactic surfaced again in the 1950s, when similar amendments were proposed by conservatives angered at the Warren Court's liberal rulings in the internal security and criminal justice areas.

Congressional actions to change court personnel occur more regularly; when pursued vigorously over time, these efforts can be successful in altering judicial policies. At times Congress has acted to change the number of justices on the Supreme Court. In the nineteenth century the number of justices on the court was increased several times; one increase was considered to be directly responsible for reversing the Court's position in the *Legal Tender* cases in the 1870s (*Hepburn v. Griswold,* 1870; *Knox v. Lee,* 1871). The tactic was tried only once in the twentieth century, when President Franklin D. Roosevelt asked Congress to enlarge the Court from 9 to as many as 15 justices (the proposal would allow a new justice to be named for each one over 70 who did not retire, with a maximum of 6 new justices). Although Congress eventually defeated the proposal, the Court evidently got the message and, in what one wag described as "the switch in time that saved nine," never again declared a piece of New Deal legislation unconstitutional. Congress has also created or refused to create new lower federal judgeships depending on who was president and the probable political ideology of the judges he would appoint.[12]

In a related tactic, the legislators have proposed laws that would require Supreme Court justices to have a certain number of years— usually five or ten—of prior judicial service. The assumption behind such proposals is that the requirement would prevent the appointment of liberal justices in the mode of William O. Douglas, Hugo L. Black, and Earl Warren, all of whom had no judicial experience before coming to the Supreme Court. The strategy would hardly be fool-proof, however, as liberal justices such as William J. Brennan, Jr., and Thurgood Marshall did have previous experience on the bench. For that matter, conservative justice William Rehnquist never served as a judge before coming to the Supreme Court. While such proposals were frequently offered in the 1950s, they never received serious consideration, and there is substantial doubt that Congress could make such a restriction without a constitutional amendment.

The Senate, in particular, can also influence the composition of the courts through its confirmation powers. Even when the Senate approves a nominee, the hearings, debate, and vote can be used as a vehicle for senators to express their displeasure with current judicial policies. In fact, nearly one-fifth (26 of 140) of the nominees to the Supreme Court have been rejected by the Senate. Of course, failure to confirm is largely a reaction to a nominee's political or legal perspective. But if the nominee's views are similar to those prevailing on the Court, it is also a warning to the Court and a message to the president to choose a different kind of appointee. Sometimes direct retaliation plays a part in the Senate rejection. The defeat of Herbert Hoover's nomination of John J. Parker in 1931, and to a lesser extent of Richard Nixon's nominations of Clement Haynsworth, Jr., and G. Harrold Carswell in 1969 and 1970, came partly in response to several highly conservative decisions these men had made as court of appeals judges. Even more dramatically, when President Lyndon B. Johnson nominated sitting justice Abe Fortas to the chief justiceship in 1968, the nomination was defeated by a filibuster motivated largely by Fortas's liberal votes and opinions as an associate justice.

The Senate pays much less attention to the ideology of appointees to lower federal judgeships. Even here, however, a nomination will occasionally be defeated or sidetracked for policy reasons, especially if the opposition is strong in the nominee's home state or geographical area.

Finally, Congress can impeach a federal judge, but the process is cumbersome and time-consuming. In 1804 the Jeffersonian House of Representatives impeached Supreme Court Justice Samuel Chase, a blatant Federalist partisan both on and off the bench, but failed to secure a conviction in the Senate. Since then, the House has impeached judges only in cases of severe malfeasance in office. In 1970, however, then house minority leader Gerald Ford tried to initiate impeachment proceedings against the Supreme Court's most liberal justice, William O. Douglas, for what were clearly political reasons. The attempt was rejected by the House Judiciary Committee.[13]

Factors Affecting Congressional Reaction. It is largely Congress's position in the secondary population—its representative role—that produces its occasionally severe negative reactions to judicial policies. When Congress was itself the consumer population for displeasing decisions, as when Representative Powell was ordered reinstated and when congressional immunity from libel suits was narrowed (*Hutchinson v. Proxmire,* 1979), there was virtually no protest or resistance in Congress. The public was not deeply involved in these issues. (There were attempts to counteract the Court's 1957 *Watkins* decision limiting congressional investigative powers, but this decision came in the context of worry about internal security and attempts to reverse several other court decisions in the same area.)

In other words, most clashes between Congress and the Supreme Court, especially on matters of constitutional interpretation, are stimulated by a widespread public reaction. Polls show, for instance, that a large majority of the general public favors school prayers, opposes busing, and believes criminal suspects have too many rights. The intensity of public feelings is also important. In the relatively tolerant 1960s, Court decisions that accorded members of the the Communist Party greater due process rights (for example, *Aptheker v. Secretary of State,* 1964; *United States v. Robel,* 1967) drew much less intense negative congressional reaction than had similar but less sweeping decisions made during the politically orthodox 1950s. Moreover, intensity can be even more important than majority support. Over the years, polls have consistently shown that a majority of the public supports a woman's right to obtain an abortion under some circumstances; yet the opponents of abortion are so active and concerned that many use the question as the major, or even the sole, determinant of their vote in congressional elections. By contrast, few proponents feel as strongly about the issue. Consequently, Congress has reacted against the abortion decision.

When a Court decision evenly divides the public or when emotions run high on both sides, there may be little reaction from Congress. While southern members of Congress denounced *Brown v. Board of Education,* many of the northern members approved of it; as a body, Congress largely ignored the desegregation issue in the decade following *Brown.* More recently, Congress has all but ignored such decisions as *Regents of University of California v. Bakke* (1978) and *Weber* (1979), which involved so-called reverse discrimination practices. Although feelings may be strong on these issues, Congress is not unified; in fact, many members from divided constituencies would probably rather avoid being put on the spot and let the judiciary handle the matter.

Congressional reactions are usually based more upon ideology than upon strict party affiliation. In the 1900-1930 era, progressive Republicans were often the Supreme Court's most vociferous critics and conservative Republicans its most stalwart defenders. In the 1950s and 1960s southern Democrats joined more often with the Court's Republican critics than with its liberal Democratic defenders.

This ideological split is illustrated in Table 5.1, which is based upon John Schmidhauser's and Larry Berg's research on roll call votes from 1947 to 1968 in relation to legislation to limit the Court's power.[14]

Several comments about Table 5.1 are in order. First, southern members of Congress demonstrated little support for the Court, even though not one of these bills was related to desegregation or race relations. Second, the ideological division persisted even for statutory reversals. (Of course, some statutory reversals not included here passed without roll calls or upon nearly unanimous votes.) Third, Senate Republicans and Senate Democrats tended to be about twice as supportive of the Court as their House counterparts were. The reasons for the difference in houses are largely structural: senators do not have to seek reelection as often, and Senate rules are more conducive to minority obstruction of action. Were it not for these factors, the Court would have been reversed and even humiliated on several major issues, including *Miranda,* reapportionment, and several rulings in the area of subversive activity. Indeed, in 1957-1959 the House passed six bills to reverse Court decisions regarding

Table 5.1   Party and Regional Differences in Roll Call Votes on Bills to Curb or Reverse the Supreme Court, 1947-1968

Type of Issue	Percentage Supporting the Court		
	Republicans	Northern Democrats	Southern Democrats
Constitutional Issues/ Curbing Bills			
House	19.2	82.3	7.1
Senate	37.3	83.0	15.2
Statutory Issues/ Reversing Bills			
House	13.0	65.3	16.5
Senate	24.2	72.3	33.5

Source: John Schmidhauser and Larry Berg, *The Supreme Court and Congress: Conflict and Interaction, 1945-68* (New York: Free Press, 1972), Tables 7-2, 7-4, 7-5, and 7-7.

internal security. All but one were defeated or blocked in the Senate, often with the assistance of then majority leader Lyndon Johnson.

C. Herman Pritchett and Walter Murphy have independently advanced what might be termed the *sacrosanctity theory* to explain the failure of Congress to use its most potent weapons against the Court in their disagreements over constitutional interpretation.[15] This argument, in brief, holds that the public will not tolerate a congressional invasion of the Supreme Court's territory of constitutional interpretion. Similarly, many congressional opponents of the Court's decisions ultimately respect the Court's authority to make such decisions. Pritchett, explaining the failure of attempts in Congress to reverse the Court after its decisions liberalizing internal security procedures, writes:

> Basically, the Court was protected by the respect which is so widely felt for the judicial institution in the United States. This attitude is often rather inchoate and not based on a well formulated understanding of the judicial function. It may grow in part out of unsophisticated assumptions about the "non-political" character of the Supreme Court's role, which are fundamentally in error. But, whether for the right reasons or for the wrong reasons, a great part of opinion in the United States holds that the Supreme Court should be let alone, or rather that it should be subject to influence only in the accepted manner, namely by the use of the appointing power when vacancies occur. This sense of fitness of things was outraged when Franklin Roosevelt proposed to lay hands on an economically conservative Court in 1937 and, in spite of some changing of sides due to the different direction from which complaints against the Court came, the same feelings protected the Court in 1957.[16]

At bottom, the argument goes, one must respect the doctrine of separation of powers and view the judges as necessary and, one hopes, impartial interpreters of the law. To undermine the Supreme Court's authority is to undermine the sanctity of the Constitution, which is the enduring symbol of our unique nationhood. "The Supreme Court as symbol goes hand in hand with the Constitution as symbol," argued Max Lerner in 1937.[17] The two are inextricably linked in the public mind. And so, one might say that Congress may bark at the Court but it must not bite it.

There is some truth to the sacrosanctity argument. Many congressional supporters of the New Deal opposed President Roosevelt's "Court packing" plan in 1937, even before it became apparent that the Court was going to back off from its opposition to the president. Likewise, several conservatives were opposed in 1958 to passage of the Jenner-Butler Bill, which would have substantially diluted the Supreme Court's appellate jurisdiction in the area of internal security procedures. Certainly some people have come to believe that a quick and drastic legislative cure may be worse than the judicial disease.

Still, as Harry Stumpf argues, there is not much empirical support for the existence of such a belief.[18] His studies of congressional roll calls relating to the Supreme Court show little relationship between the invocation in debate of symbols of Supreme Court authority or legitimacy and the defeat of anti-Court measures.[19] (Nonetheless, Stumpf and to a lesser extent, Schmidhauser and Berg,[20] are unwilling to dismiss the sacrosanctity hypothesis completely.) Moreover, recent poll data, which we discuss in Chapter 6, do not indicate much public support for the legitimacy of several major Supreme Court interpretations of the Constitution. It must be recognized that making a rigorous test of the sacrosanctity theory is difficult. Further, no particularly appealing alternative theory has been set forth to explain why Congress has not actively exercised its considerable powers more frequently against a Supreme Court that has made many highly unpopular decisions during the twentieth century.

Court Responses. How has the Court responded to congressional manifestations of displeasure? In the long run, as we will discuss in Chapter 7, the Court cannot stand against Congress when it is determined to enact a general legislative policy, especially when Congress is allied with the president. Here we will discuss some short-run responses.

Sometimes the Court treads gingerly after arousing congressional displeasure. On the volatile internal security issues of the 1950s, the Court seemed to take one step backward for every two forward. Its imposition of due process requirements on the removal of allegedly subversive teachers in its 1956 *Slochower* decision was largely undermined two years later (*Beilan v. Board of Public Education, School District of Philadelphia,* 1958). Similarly, the Court's 1957 *Watkins* decision limiting legislative investigation into political activities was largely negated two years later in *Barenblatt v. United States* (1959). It does not seem unreasonable to believe that some justices were influenced in the intervening years by the passage in Congress of one law reversing the Court in this area and the pendency or narrow defeat of several other reversal proposals.

A similar but less dramatic change in the Court's attitude occurred with respect to the *Miranda* decision. The Court has in cases such as *Harris v. New York* (1971), *Michigan v. Tucker* (1974), and *Rhode Island v. Innis* (1980) limited *Miranda*'s applicability without overruling it. More directly, several Court decisions in the 1970s undercut *United States v. Wade* (1967), which required the presence of counsel at a lineup. Of course, four Nixon justices were appointed to the Court in 1969-1971; so the Court's response was less one of fearful treading than one of genuine change in beliefs about correct judicial policy in this area.

The Court is not always intimidated by congressional opposition. Despite repeated measures passed by Congress to signify its intense displeasure with the Court's busing policies, the Court has refused to backtrack on this issue. Similarly, after 10 years of congressional hostility to the abortion decision, the Court in 1983 forcefully reiterated its basic position (*Akron v. Akron Center for Reproductive Health*).

Congressional Cooperation. So far we have focused on Congress's negative reactions to judicial decisions. Such reactions often provoke conflict and drama and naturally receive attention disproportionate to their number. Congress reacts strongly against only a very small number of judicial decisions. More often, there have been instances in which Congress has reacted positively to and cooperated with court decisions. Congress sometimes ratifies the Supreme Court's statutory interpretations by incorporating the decisions into statutory revisions. *Silent ratification*—where Congress does nothing to alter the Court's interpretation or to indicate that it is erroneous— is quite common. Also, the lawmakers will at times offer praise for a judicial decision on the floor of the House or Senate. More important, Congress will quietly accommodate itself to most decisions and appropriate money or adjust the machinery of government as necessary. For example, following *Gideon v. Wainwright* (1963), holding that indigent defendants in felony trials were entitled to be represented by a lawyer, Congress passed legislation establishing a system for providing attorneys at federal expense for impoverished persons charged with a federal crime.

State Legislatures

Although researchers have directed extensive attention to Congress, they have seldom examined how state legislatures react to judicial policies. Therefore our discussion is necessarily brief, and we focus for the most part on general propositions. Since state legislatures relate to state supreme courts in much the same way as Congress does to the U.S. Supreme Court, much of what we have said about congressional reactions is also applicable to state legislatures. Of course, state legislatures can and do react to Supreme Court and other federal court decisions as well as to state court decisions. (Congress, by contrast, is seldom concerned with the decisions of state courts.)

Reactions to State Supreme Courts. State legislatures have several powers similar to those of Congress, including the power to reverse statutory interpretations, initiate constitutional amendments, and impeach judges. Legislatures also have the power of the purse and can, through constitutional amendment or statute, affect the general nature of a state's judicial system. However, most state legislatures lack two of the powers that Congress has to thwart or reverse court decisions: control over appellate jurisdiction and approval of the appointment of judges. Since most state constitutions do not give the legislature the power to control the state supreme court's appellate jurisdiction, there is no threat of an *Ex parte McCardle* or a Jenner-Butler Bill at the state level. Also, unlike the U.S. Senate, most state legislatures have no power over the selection or confirmation of judges. Most commonly, judges either are elected or are selected by the governor from a judicial nominating commission's list without confirmation by the legislature. (Of course, the fact that judges are subject to reelection may, as noted in Chapter 2, make them politically quite sensitive, and thus their decisions may give the legislature less cause for displeasure.) It is also likely that to the extent the sacrosanctity theory is true, it is less applicable to state constitutions and state supreme courts. If so, one might expect to find less protection from legislative reprisal for state supreme courts.

In a few states, however, such as Virginia and South Carolina, the legislature has the direct power to appoint and remove judges. It may not be a coincidence that the supreme courts of these states have a reputation for conservatism. In the nineteenth century many legislatures had more control over the selection of judges and the structure of the courts. In the 1820s the Kentucky legislature exercised its power to an extreme extent. When the state supreme court adopted some unpopular doctrines relating to disputed land claims, the legislature abolished the court and appointed a new one. The first court refused to go out of existence, however, and for several years Kentucky had two supreme courts, reminiscent of the medieval episode when the Catholic church had two popes.

Modern state supreme court decisions seldom arouse the interest or emotion that U.S. Supreme Court decisions do; so regardless of such a court's powers, legislative reactions are rarely intense. Legislatures occasionally reverse statutory interpretations or adopt new statutes in response to common law decisions. Most legislatures, however, meet for limited time periods and have small staffs, so their ability to oversee, modify, or reverse court decisions is limited. State courts for their part tend to be deferential to legislatures on matters of any political importance. The New Jersey Supreme Court's decision requiring the state legislature to levy an income tax to support a badly underfunded public school system (*Robinson v. Cahill,* 1975) and the California Supreme Court's decision requiring equal funding for school districts regardless of local resources (*Serrano v. Priest,* 1971) are noteworthy because of their rare boldness; the courts were willing to virtually bulldoze the legislatures into major policy changes.[21]

State Legislatures' Reactions to the U.S. Supreme Court. The U.S. Supreme Court strikes down state laws far more often than it does federal laws, but state legislatures have a much more limited ability than Congress to express displeasure meaningfully. The states' impotence here, of course, is inherent in the nature of the Union. Justice Oliver Wendell Holmes once said, "I do not think the United States would come to an end if we lost our power to declare an act of Congress unconstitutional. I do think the Union would be imperiled if we could not make that declaration as to the laws of the several states."[22] Nonetheless, state legislatures are not reluctant to try to thwart the impact of a U.S. Supreme Court decision when they feel strongly about it. Desegregation provides the most notable examples. Adopting a "massive resistance" program, Virginia's legislature required the closing of public schools in any district subject to an integration order, while the South Carolina and Mississippi legislatures repealed their compulsory education laws. When a federal judge ordered integration in New Orleans in 1960, the Louisiana legislature was repeatedly convened in special session to pass a series of laws in a last-ditch effort to forestall the order. All southern legislative resistance proved unsuccessful. (Actually, the response of southern legislatures to *Brown* was temperate in comparison with the response of the Georgia House of Representatives to *Chisholm v. Georgia* [1793]; that body passed a bill providing for death by hanging for any federal marshal who attempted to serve writs in accordance with the case.)

More often, state legislatures try to minimize the impact of a decision. We have already discussed in Chapter 1 the legislative attempts, following *Roe v. Wade* (1973), to limit the circumstances when a woman could obtain an abortion. Similarly, several states have recently adopted laws requiring a minute of silence for meditation at the beginning of each school day. Others have tried to limit busing. The success of such minimization attempts usually depends

157

upon the degree to which the new law does not seem to explicitly contradict the Court's policy. In the abortion area, most laws that required third party consent, called for a waiting period, or limited physicians' discretion were struck down by federal courts, but state laws severely limiting the circumstances under which the state would pay the cost of an abortion for women on welfare were upheld (*Maher v. Roe*, 1977; *Williams v. Zbraz*, 1980).

Indeed, widespread reaction to a decision by state legislatures can influence the Court's development of policy. Following *Furman v. Georgia* (1972), which left uncertain the constitutional status of the death penalty, 37 legislatures repassed death penalty statutes—a phenomenon that did not go unnoticed by the Court when it eventually held the death penalty constitutional (*Gregg v. Georgia*, 1976).

Again, it should be noted that attempts by state legislatures to block or minimize U.S. Supreme Court decisions are the exception and not the rule. Most commonly when a decision finds a state law unconstitutional, the legislature either does nothing in reaction or it revises its legislation in accordance with the Court's opinion. In reaction to obscenity decisions, for instance, many legislatures have simply ignored the decision and let the state courts handle things; others have redrafted their laws. However, in Iowa the legislature got so fed up with the U.S. Supreme Court's continual imprecision and shifting of obscenity standards that it simply repealed all its laws against obscenity insofar as adults were concerned. Indeed, even in the reapportionment area, where the legislatures were consumers rather than part of the secondary population, the lawmakers often complied, albeit unhappily, with the Supreme Court's mandates.

While state legislatures are largely powerless when it comes to having a direct influence on federal judicial policy, they can complain loudly about such matters. Before the Civil War legislatures in several states, in both North and South, passed resolutions either denying the authority of the Supreme Court to settle certain types of cases or proposing that Congress alter the Supreme Court's authority. In the 1950s the Georgia legislature forwarded a resolution to the state's congressional delegation demanding the impeachment of six Supreme Court justices. Moreover, state legislatures do have one weapon to use against judicial policies. Under Article V of the Constitution, if two-thirds of the state legislatures propose a specific constitutional amendment, Congress must call a national constitutional convention to consider that amendment. In the 1960s, 32 legislatures of the required 34 proposed an amendment that would have reversed the Court's *Reynolds v. Sims* (1964) decision requiring both houses of state legislatures to be apportioned according to population. More recently, a large number of state legislatures have proposed a constitutional amendment that would reverse *Roe v. Wade,* although not all of these have agreed on what shape such an amendment should take.

The President

Like Congress, the president can stand in any of several relationships to judicial policies. As chief executive and the person charged by the Constitution to "take care that the laws be faithfully executed," he is an important part of the implementing population, insofar as federal courts are concerned. In a constitutional system that emphasizes limited authority and separation of powers, the actions of the president and of his subordinates on his behalf are often subject to challenge; therefore he is frequently a consumer of judicial policies. And, of course, as a politician, national leader, and head of state, he must have a keen interest in judicial policies that may not affect him directly. In such cases, he is in the secondary population. Because of our focus in this chapter we will treat the president primarily as a member of the secondary population.

Enforcement and Influence. The president's roles are not always easily differentiated. In modern times, federal executive agencies constitute the implementing population for a large number of court decisions. Ultimately, courts may even have to call upon the president himself to enforce their policies. At different times, the president can be both an interested bystander and an actual participant in the shaping of the impact of a particular judicial policy. Usually, of course, the president implements judicial decisions, even those with which he disagrees. But recall that we opened this book with President Andrew Jackson's famous (though perhaps apocryphal) remark, "John Marshall has made his decision, now let him enforce it." (This was said to follow *Worcester v. Georgia* [1832], a decision denying Georgia courts jurisdiction over crimes committed on Indian lands within the state.) President Abraham Lincoln actually did order his military commanders on occasion to refuse obedience to several writs of habeas corpus, including one from Chief Justice Roger Taney, during the Civil War. Even in the Carter administration, Attorney General Griffin Bell was held in contempt of court for refusing to turn over a list of informers to a court in the course of a Socialist Workers Party civil rights suit. (The contempt citation was later overturned.) Even when a president does not defy a decision, his reluctance to enforce it may encourage others in

159

defiance. President Dwight D. Eisenhower was not enthusiastic about *Brown v. Board of Education,* and his unwillingness to condemn southern resistance in more than a pro forma fashion encouraged Arkansas Governor Orval Faubus to block integration of Little Rock Central High School in 1957. Eventually Eisenhower had to dispatch a U.S. Army division to the city to enforce a federal district court's integration order.

Even when enforcement is not in question, the president can have an influence on the impact of a judicial policy. The president, more than anyone else, has access to the public; his words and deeds, even subtle or casual ones, can do much to encourage people to cooperate with or to resist judicial policies. President Franklin D. Roosevelt used some of his famous "fireside chats" to label the justices as the "nine old men" and inform the public how their anti-New Deal decisions were impeding economic recovery. Similarly, Richard Nixon blamed the Supreme Court for aiding the "criminal element" at the expense of the "peace forces," and he frequently called for strict construction of the Constitution. John F. Kennedy's attitude toward the school prayer decision provides an illustrative contrast with Ronald Reagan's. Kennedy obliquely supported the decision by remarking that perhaps we should emphasize religion more in the church and home; Reagan, on the other hand, has repeatedly said he believes the decision was in error and that there ought to be prayer in the public schools.

The president's powers can be used more specifically. Modern presidents are major sources of legislative proposals, and most of the powers that Congress has to reverse judicial decisions and to retaliate against the Courts can be initiated, encouraged, or discouraged by the president. When the Supreme Court found New Deal laws unconstitutional, President Roosevelt asked Congress to pass new laws of a similar nature. He would not accept the Court's decisions. Certainly, Congress would not likely have considered "packing" the Court in 1937 had Roosevelt not asked it to. The Twenty-sixth Amendment, which reversed the Court's action striking down a law that gave 18-to-20-year-olds the right to vote in state elections, had President Nixon's active support. Presidents Nixon and Reagan both vigorously advocated federal tax credit for tuition for religious schools, though the Supreme Court had decided that such aid was unconstitutional (*Committee for Public Education and Religious Liberty v. Nyquist,* 1973). Unsuccessful attempts in 1982 to pass constitutional amendments overturning the school prayer and the abortion decisions were supported by President Reagan (although some conservatives complained that the measures failed because the president did not twist enough arms). Of course, the president is not always able or willing to control Congress. The Jenner-Butler bill of 1957-1958 was considered without much active involvement by President Eisenhower. Sometimes, in fact, the president finds himself at odds with Congress over judicial policy. President Jimmy Carter had to veto a congressional appropriation measure that would have limited federal participation in busing litigation.

The Appointment Power. As we noted earlier, the president shares the power of appointing federal judges with the Senate. However, the president's power is predominant, particularly for the courts of appeals and the Supreme Court. The Senate can reject a presidential nominee, but twentieth-century custom is to accept nominees, even when they are politically distasteful, unless some reason (for example, a poor legal record or improper behavior) can be found to justify rejection. Thus, Justice Rehnquist was approved by many liberal senators who had voted against President Nixon's nominations of Haynsworth and Carswell.

The importance of the appointing power is enormous—especially to the Supreme Court. Obviously, major judicial policies cannot survive the appointment of justices dedicated to different policies. The long-run implications of the appointment power will be part of our look at the overall impact of the courts in Chapter 7. In the short run and on narrower issues, the ability of a president to affect judicial decisions through appointments depends on factors such as the division of the Court and the number of vacancies that he gets to fill. When President Nixon was able to name four justices within three years, the Court's five- or six-member majority bloc of liberals in the area of defendants' rights (Brennan, Marshall, Douglas, Fortas, Warren, and sometimes Black) was reduced to a minority of three (Brennan, Marshall, and Douglas). By contrast, Jimmy Carter was the first president in American history to serve a full term and not be faced with a single Supreme Court vacancy.

Some presidents think quite seriously about the implications of their appointments on current judicial policies. Here is a part of a letter from President Theodore Roosevelt to Sen. Henry Cabot Lodge, R.-Mass., about appointing Oliver Wendell Holmes to the Supreme Court:

> The majority of the present Court who have, although without satisfactory unanimity, upheld the policies of President McKinley and the Republican Party in Congress, have rendered a great service to mankind and to this nation. The minority—a minority so large as to lack but one vote from being a majority—have stood for such reactionary folly as would have

161

hampered well-nigh helplessly this people in doing efficient and honorable work for the national welfare, and for the welfare of the islands themselves in Porto Rico and the Philippines. . . . Now I should like to know that Judge Holmes was in entire sympathy with our views, that is with your views and mine . . . before I would feel justified in appointing him.[23]

Roosevelt was later enraged when Holmes voted contrary to his expectations in an important antitrust case (*Northern Securities Co. v. United States,* 1904). Roosevelt's successor, William Howard Taft, believed the Supreme Court was the most important policy maker in government and chose his appointees with great care. But not all presidents have been as concerned about judicial policy. Harry Truman appointed some of his friends from his Senate days to the Court, and Dwight Eisenhower's five appointees certainly had a mixture of ideological approaches.

The Justice Department. Through the Department of Justice the president has a unique ability to influence the courts—particularly the Supreme Court. The department has the power to initiate criminal prosecutions and civil suits; thus it can advance novel legal propositions that are likely to go to the Supreme Court for final adjudication. In other words, the department has some ability to shape the federal judiciary's agenda of policy issues. This has been particularly true in the area of civil rights cases: for over 40 years the Justice Department has in such exemplary cases as *United States v. Classic* (1941) and *United States v. Guest* (1966) urged—usually successfully—the Supreme Court to expand statutory and constitutional interpretations to give minorities greater federal protection from local abuse and repression. Of course, not all novel propositions advanced by the Justice Department win acceptance. The occasional failure was dramatically illustrated in the Pentagon Papers case (*New York Times Co. v. United States,* 1971), when the Court rejected government claims that the president had an inherent power to prohibit the publication of secret documents. However, the government is more often victorious than not before the high Court. Robert Scigliano, in his study of the performance of the Department of Justice, indicates that the department has consistently won from 62 to 64 percent of the cases it has brought before the Supreme Court in every decade since 1800.[24]

In cases where the government is not a party, the Justice Department can file an *amicus curiae* ("friend of the court") brief with the Supreme Court. Of course, almost any interested group can file such a brief, but briefs filed by the solicitor general (the department's chief lawyer) are usually quite well prepared and traditionally the Court accords them great weight. Indeed, on occasion, the Court invites the solicitor general to submit a brief and at times permits him to participate in oral argument in a case where the government is not a party. Through the amicus brief, the administration can communicate directly with the Court, advancing viewpoints, warnings, and encouragements. Moreover, the government generally fares even better in cases where it submits an amicus brief than in cases where it is a party. Its winning percentage for amicus briefs in 1945 through 1970 was nearly 80 percent.[25]

Most Justice Department actions are taken with little or no direct consultation with the president. Nonetheless, his views are usually known or sought. When President Reagan made his view that a tax exemption for private schools that racially discriminate was still legal, the Justice Department withdrew from the *Bob Jones* case (*Bob Jones University v. United States*, 1983). And President Carter himself took part in the meetings to determine the Department of Justice's position in the *Bakke* case.

INTEREST GROUPS AND JUDICIAL DECISIONS

The role of interest groups in judicial policy making has been researched for a number of years. The basic view of the relationship was set forth by David Truman: he has argued that interest groups could "lobby" the courts when they lost in other political arenas.[26] Indeed, the pluralist theory of American politics holds that the judiciary is only one of many forums for organized interests. Most recent research considers the effects of interest groups on judicial policies *before* the decisions are rendered by the courts. There has been little research about the role and influence of interest groups on the implementation and impact of judicial policies once the courts reach a decision. Nonetheless, we can offer several observations, based on a few case studies, about postdecision involvement by interest groups.

Under some circumstances, judicial victories or defeats for interest groups are important because they have a symbolic impact. However, in most instances decisions are not self-executing and the degree to which they are implemented can be quite important to interest groups. We are interested in whether an interest group trying to influence a judicial policy follows through with its efforts either to implement or refine a policy that is considered favorable or to overturn or block a policy that adversely affects its client groups.

Of course, not all interest groups are part of the secondary population. Many are consumers of judicial policies. In some instances, the interest groups may directly benefit from a court decision. Political action committees (PACs), for example, directly benefited from the Supreme Court's decision in *Buckley v. Valeo* (1976), which allowed corporations to organize PACs to contribute to political campaigns. While other interest groups may have participated in this case by arguing against such a ruling, all interest groups were willing or unwilling consumers of this decision. Even when an interest group itself is not directly affected by a court decision, the group often represents individuals who consume judicial policies. The National Association for the Advancement of Colored People (NAACP) or the National Education Association, for example, represent clearly identifiable segments of the consumer population that often directly receive advantages or disadvantages from judicial decisions.

There are many interest groups, however, whose members are not directly affected by particular judicial policies in which the group has an interest. Civil liberties, environmental, and right to life groups are illustrative. As we noted in Chapter 4, many ardent right to life advocates are not personally affected by the Supreme Court's abortion policies. Also, interest groups may be in the consumer population for some judicial policies and in the secondary population for others. For instance, groups such as the U.S. Chamber of Commerce and the Fraternal Order of Police urged the Supreme Court in the *Bakke* case to find a fixed quota of minority seats for admission to medical school unconstitutional, while groups such as the American Bar Association and the United Auto Workers argued for this quota's constitutionality. In this chapter we are less interested in cases for which interest groups are direct consumers; we are interested here in their actions as members of the secondary population.

The most important role of interest groups as members of the secondary population is to help or hinder the implementation and use of judicial policies once they have been announced by a court. In this role, interest groups will often return to the judiciary for a broad or narrow interpretation of the policy, or to see if implementation can be delayed, applied more broadly, or made more effective. In addition, interest groups will often turn to other branches of the government in order to enhance or block the implementation or use of a judicial policy. We will examine the responses of interest groups from three perspectives: first, how they are activated or organized in response to a judicial decision; second, how these groups are able to enhance or obstruct the implementation of judicial policies; and third, how interest groups on the whole affect the impact of judicial policies.

Activation of Interest Groups
in Response to Judicial Decisions

Stuart Scheingold suggests that judicial decisions often create rights that are best understood as "political resources" and that are "best viewed as the beginning of a political process. . . ." Thus, Scheingold asserts that in our political system the victory gained by interest groups that have tried for a favorable judicial decision actually results only in additional support for their policy demands; with a favorable judicial decision, eventually they may be able to "alter the balance of power" in the government.[27] Ultimately, then, a court decision merely serves as another tool for persuading others to behave as certain interests want.

Judicial decisions frequently fulfill the function of motivating their proponents and opponents to take political action. Scheingold refers to this function as "a dual process of activating a quiescent citizenry and organizing groups into effective political units." Scheingold's theory is that "perceptions of entitlement" are associated with rights and that these perceptions serve to activate and organize interests in the political system. Thus, "insofar as court decisions can legitimate claims and cue expectations, litigation can contribute to both activation and organization; to the building of new coalitions; and, in the long run, to a realignment of forces within the political arena." [28]

Scheingold, in observing that rights may activate interest groups, assumes that the groups *winning* new rights will respond. However, *losing* rights or some government benefit or services may provoke similar activities. The Supreme Court's decision in *Roe v. Wade,* for example, prompted considerable efforts by pro- and, especially, antiabortion interest groups. While proabortion advocates were active prior to the Court's decision, their activities were basically aimed at state legislatures. And the prolife groups such as the National Right to Life Committee did not exist as a national, viable interest group until the Court's decision in *Roe.* Similarly, after the *Brown* decision, many groups composed of white liberals allied themselves with the NAACP and began paying attention to the implementation of desegregation. In both instances, the objectives were to use the Court's decision as a lever to win benefits for a new class of consumers or to oppose the implementation of the decision in order to maintain the status quo.

While winning a judicial decision frequently serves to activate organizations, there are a few notable exceptions. Some organizations appear to be more content with winning judicial decisions than with following through with the implementation of the newly won rights. The American Civil Liberties Union (ACLU), for example, is a frequent user of the courts to win new rights or to defend against government abuse of established rights. But as some researchers have noted, the ACLU has not inititiated the follow-up cases necessary to implement judicial policies nationwide. Karen O'Connor, for example, finds that cases are accepted by the Women's Rights Project of the ACLU only if they meet such criteria as being "novel and nationally important," being likely to end in victory if handled correctly, taking the law to its next logical step, benefiting a large number of women, and having no other attorney available to the client.[29] The law production orientation of the ACLU is also discussed by Stephen Halpern, who found that a sizable percentage of the cases brought to the local chapters of the ACLU in his study were enforcement cases; but these chapters rarely took action on such cases. In fact, most cases were either rejected, referred elsewhere, or deferred. Halpern concludes that "by emphasizing test cases, the ACLU has overvalued achieving official, public declarations of changes in policy and minimized the value of monitoring whether and how rights are enforced." [30]

Enhancing the Implementation of Judicial Decisions

Because judicial decisions are not self-implementing and because many agencies fail to implement judicial policies fully and faithfully, interest groups often find that they are largely responsible for pressing for the implementation of judicial policies. Groups may engage in several activities to enhance the impact of a favorable decision, thereby increasing the probability that the intended consumers actually benefit. Among these activities are returning to the courts for clarification, extension, or enforcement of the decision; finding and supporting consumers who will benefit from the policy; and enlisting the aid of other groups and institutions.

Interest groups may return to the courts with two objectives in mind. By returning to the original policy-making court, an interest group may try to influence the nature and scope of subsequent clarifications and interpretations of a judicial policy. At the same time, in lower courts, the interest group may seek enforcement of a judicial policy by filing or sponsoring suits on behalf of the consumer population. A fairly standard procedure in the civil rights movement, for example, was for civil rights groups to file suits to force desegregation of schools after the *Brown* decision. Such actions were difficult, since they required extensive efforts by these groups on a district-by-district basis. Nevertheless, such suits are at least the beginning of interpretation and implementation. The key factor in predicting success for such moves is the longevity of the interest group. Citing several studies of the success of the NAACP in the civil rights field, O'Connor notes, "Interest group longevity appears to be critical if an organization sets upon a course of litigious activity that calls for it to systematically whittle away adverse precedent to attain its goals." [31] Such longevity is also necessary for a group to realize those goals if changes are required in government policies or private practices.

Kenneth Dolbeare and Phillip Hammond, moreover, report that potentially helpful interest groups were largely ineffective in pressing for the implementation of the Court's school prayer decisions because "they were not well established, they seriously lacked legitimacy and influence, and their memberships were pitifully small and isolated." [32] This lack of resources, plus their discouraging prior experiences with unpopular causes, can lead these groups to assume a less than aggressive stance for implementing the Court's decisions. Whether aggressiveness or persistence could have affected local policies is an open question, but Dolbeare and Hammond suggest that such activities would have broken the quiescence with which the Supreme Court's prayer decisions were received.

Interest groups may also enhance implemention by finding and supporting consumers of the policy. Indeed, interest groups are often invaluable in informing potential consumers of their rights and opportunities. Joel Handler points out that national civil rights groups were instrumental in alerting the local black population to registration opportunities after passage in 1965 of the Voting Rights Act and subsequent litigation. The litigation, Handler argues, was especially useful because it was "consciousness raising . . . [and] good press." [33]

Finally, interest groups may enhance the implementation of judicial policies by turning to other groups or institutions for assistance. As we have noted in previous chapters, for judicial policies to have full effect, they often require the cooperation of legislative or executive bodies not directly involved in the implementation process. Legislatures, for example, may have to appropriate money to fund the implementation of a judicial policy. Here, too, civil rights groups provide a good example of occasions where they have convinced other branches of government to become involved in the enforcement of judicial policies. And real success in the implementation of the Supreme Court's school desegregation policy did not come about until enforcement responsibilities were assumed by the Department of Justice and the Department of Health, Education and Welfare. In this instance, convincing Congress to give such authority to these departments relieved the pressures and strains on the resources of civil rights groups that had been involved in district-by-district litigation.[34]

Restricting the Implementation of Judicial Decisions

On many occasions, certain interest groups can be as intent on blocking or minimizing the implementation of judicial decisions as others are on implementing them. To some extent, groups promoting restrictions on a policy use similar strategies as groups promoting compliance with it. For example, a group that has lost its bid for a particular decision may return to the courts in hopes of obtaining either a limited interpretation or a policy reversal based on a different principle. While interest groups may recognize that having lost in a court means that the likelihood of their winning in the same court is low, they may be more successful in another court. Interest groups favoring change in the way school systems are financed, for example, lost in the U.S. Supreme Court (see *San Antonio Independent School District v. Rodriguez,* 1973), but many carried on their fight in state courts, making arguments based on state constitutions. In California and New Jersey the state supreme courts accepted their arguments and ordered changes in the financing of schools (*Serrano v. Priest,* 1971; *Robinson v. Cahill,* 1975).[35]

Interest groups that oppose a particular policy may also generate information about how a decision might be narrowly applied or interpreted. In the criminal justice area, for example, national law enforcement associations are pictured by Neal Milner and by Stephen Wasby as being a source of information and advice for local police departments.[36] Milner reports that the major source of information for the police departments he studied passed along information about how *Miranda* could be minimized. Similarly, the FBI offered lectures and workshops that presented "relatively straightforward" accounts of the requirements of *Miranda.* Milner notes, however, that parts of the lectures manifested "a definite unwillingness to accept what lawyers would call the 'spirit' of the decision." For example, there were discussions about situations where warnings were probably not required and about how the police should make every effort to keep any interrogation session "noncustodial," thus avoiding the need to read warnings to suspects.[37]

Groups opposed to a court decision may also try to convince government officials or agencies to help block or limit the impact of the decision. As we have noted, Congress, the president, and state governments may substantially affect the implementation of a judicial decision—either positively or negatively. Thus it is not unusual for an interest group that loses in the Supreme Court to head straight for the lobby of Congress. For example, as we discussed in Chapter 1, antiabortion groups were effective in lobbying Congress to limit drastically the federal funding of abortions for poor women. The adoption of the Hyde Amendment in the mid-1970s and its acceptance by the Supreme Court constituted a major victory for the antiabortion forces (*Harris v. McRae,* 1980). Similarly, antiabortion groups have pressured state governments to pass numerous statutes limiting the Court's abortion decision. While some of these laws have been overturned, many are still on the books and limit the local availablity of abortions to some women who want them.

The Impact of Interest Groups on Implementation

The degree to which interest groups actually affect the implementation of judicial policies is not easily assessed. An interest group's influence depends on the situation, on who is doing the implementing, and on the group's resources. So far, researchers have not identified the conditions under which particular groups are likely to be successful or unsuccessful. Obviously, when a group's cause is politically popular, the group's ability to ensure compliance or to restrict or block implementation is enhanced. The prestige or reputation of an interest group is also an important factor affecting its success. The ACLU is unpopular in some areas of the country, and many public officials will not readily cooperate with it.[38] Environmental groups such as the Audubon Society are usually more highly regarded, and their efforts may receive more respectful consideration by various state and federal agencies. The size of secondary interest groups is a less determinative factor because most of them tend to have relatively few members. Occasionally a large interest group, such as a labor union, whose main purpose is protecting and advancing its own consumer interests will take a stand on an unrelated issue, but when this occurs most members of the group are not very concerned with the matter. The probability that an interest group will successfully influence the implementation of a judicial policy may also depend on the nature of the changes required. Handler argues that an organization that supports a judicial policy requiring changes will be more successful in positively influencing those changes under circumstances where a policy requires action by only a few top-level administrators; where the required action is a one-time event; where the action is technically simple; and where the discretion of the agency is limited.[39]

If the implementing organization is relatively closed to outside pressures, then the impact of interest groups may also be limited. Jon R. Bond and Charles A. Johnson, relying on the health services literature—which reports that most hospitals ignore public pressures—and on their own survey data, conclude that pro- and antiabortion groups have little impact on the provision of abortion services. This is particularly true for privately operated hospitals.[40]

Finally, the financial resources of interest groups are important. Money can affect the longevity of groups and their ability to initiate follow-up litigation or projects to educate consumers of the decision. Similarly, lobbying activity requires financial resources that some groups may not have. The National Right to Life Committee, for example, is substantially better financed than are those groups favoring abortions, and it has given substantial assistance to like-minded members of Congress seeking reelection.

In recent years various "public interest" law firms, funded either by wealthy foundations or self-financed through legal fees generated by victorious litigation, have sprung up around the country. These firms usually have an ideological bent or emphasize certain causes such as consumer protection. Because of their stable income—and their legal expertise—such firms can be quite efficient at following through on the implementation of judicial policies.

MEDIA COVERAGE OF JUDICIAL DECISIONS

Although the media sometimes are consumers of judicial decisions, they most frequently are members of the secondary population. Newspapers, general and specialized magazines, and radio and television all cover governmental affairs, including court decisions. But here the similarity ends. One leading communications scholar, Doris Graber, remarks that "reporting of Supreme Court activities seems to be more superficial and flawed than its presidential and congressional counterparts."[41] The same assessment holds for other courts, be they state or federal, trial or appellate. As a general proposition, courts are difficult to report on because of the high number of decisions, the use of technical language, lengthy opinions that are difficult to "boil down into catchy phrases and clichés," and the mundane nature of judicial issues.[42]

Whether the media can report on the judiciary adequately is open to some debate; nevertheless, reports of major appellate court decisions as well as of major trials in lower courts do appear on local and national broadcasts and in daily newspapers. The media serve two primary functions as part of the secondary population: first, they convey information to relevant and interested populations that might otherwise be uninformed of judicial policies or actions, and second, they convey information to the court and to others about the reactions of different groups to previously announced judicial decisions. In performing each of these functions, the media have a potential impact on the implementation of judicial decisions. However, as we will see below, determining the nature and degree of that impact is very difficult.

The Media as Conveyers of Judicial Policies

The popular media are the principal means by which both the general public and most elites learn of court decisions.[43] Popular media, of course, consist of a variety of outlets; but for the U.S. Supreme Court, the actual reports about decisions are done primarily by a small band of reporters working for the major wire services, for a few national newspapers such as the *New York Times* and *Washington Post,* and for the major television networks. A study by Chester Newland indicates that in the 1960s less than a dozen regular reporters covered the Supreme Court and provided the news used by most newspapers and broadcast media. Other reporters may appear at the Court from time to time; however, they are usually interested in a specific decision and may not be well prepared to handle the technical nature of both the Court's announcement process and the Court's opinion.[44] No other court has media reporters assigned exclusively to it. Other judicial decisions are covered by political reporters or by unspecialized reporters.

While journalists covering the Supreme Court must report its decisions accurately, they are always under the pressures of a fast-approaching deadline. Newland's study reveals that wire service reporters frequently prepare alternative news stories of soon-to-be-announced decisions *before* the Court actually renders the decisions. At other times, preliminary stories are prepared with some gaps for quotations and potential implications. Reporters for national newspapers may have a bit more time before a story must be filed. Nevertheless, their reports must also be rushed. Newland gives the following account of *New York Times* reporter Anthony Lewis's work in 1962 to meet an early evening deadline for the next day's edition of the paper:

> The "box" summary went out at 4:15 pm [for the standard *Times* feature, "Supreme Court's Actions"].... This was followed at 4:45 pm by a report largely written in advance on a ceremony honoring Mr. Justice Black's twenty-five years on the Court. The story on the Prayer case [*Engel v. Vitale*] went out at 5:12 pm; the Brown Shoe case [*Brown Shoe Co. v. United States*] report at 6:16 pm; the Obscenity case [*Manual Enterprises v. Day*] report, at 7:26; and the Narcotics Addict case [*Robinson v. California*] report, at 8:03.[45]

Thus, in the space of less than four hours a summary of several court decisions was prepared, along with major stories on four leading decisions.

At the time of Newland's analysis, in 1964, the Court did not make a great effort to accommodate reporters. Since that time some changes have been made, such as the preparation of summaries of opinions by a Court official. Moreover, the Court now spreads decisions across the entire week, rather than announcing them only on Monday, as was the case prior to 1965. Nevertheless, the pressures of deadlines and caseloads still result in rushed filing by a few reporters for most media outlets in the country, especially in May and June, when the Court announces most of its important decisions.

In spite of the deadline pressures, the reporting of judicial decisions appears to be reasonably accurate, though reports may be sketchy and the media arbitrary in choosing which decisions to report. Richard Johnson found that the newspapers in the communities he studied were accurate in their summaries of the *Engel v. Vitale* (1962) and *Schempp* decisions on schoolhouse religion. However, headlines were responsible for some measure of distortion. Thus, "the conscientious observer had ample opportunity to be appraised of the Court's policies and the reasoning behind them. But the more casual observer might have received a partial and somewhat distorted view of what the Court had said." [46]

Judicial decisions have at times been misunderstood and therefore distorted by the media. A famous example of such a misunderstanding involves a story reporting that the Supreme Court had declared segregation on buses illegal, which led several bus companies to drop their segregation rules. The Court had, in fact, dismissed an appeal because the lower court had not reached its final judgment.[47] However, distortion is more likely to occur as a result of inaccurate or misleading headlines, as noted above, or through reports of the reactions of individuals who misinterpret the judicial policy. Newland found that the first report of the Court's actions tended to be fairly accurate and straightforward, and a second report focused on reactions to the decisions. The second story was usually given more prominence than the initial story.[48]

Follow-up coverage focusing on reactions is frequently supplemented by articles on the editorial pages. The follow-up coverage may also include reports on the implementation of judicial policies. Most often such tracking is done by local media; unfortunately, few scholars have the resources to compile and analyze such accounts. However, Richard Pride and David Woodward conducted a study of media coverage of local desegregation efforts involving busing in Louisville and Nashville; they found that the local media tended to be unsensational and evenhanded in their reporting of these events. In fact, reports by the local media were in marked contrast to the treatment afforded the busing story by the national television networks, which tended to emphasize opposition to desegregation moves through stories about local opponents and an emphasis on the potential for violence.[49]

The Impact of the Media on Reactions to Judicial Policies

Most communications scholars agree that the media's impact on our political system involves setting the agenda for political discussion.[50] By this they mean that whatever topic the media choose to focus on becomes the topic being discussed by the general public and the decision makers. To some extent, the media serve the same function for judicial policies. Reporters must decide what decisions to cover. While the media may not set the agenda for the implementation of court decisions, they may often play a role in focusing public attention on where implementation is or is not done faithfully. This discretion can affect the reactions to judicial policies by implementors, consumers, and members of the secondary population.

Larry Berkson's survey of several occupational groups in Florida found that virtually all groups relied on newspapers for information on judicial decisions. Table 5.2 presents a summary of his findings on the channels by which these groups obtain information about Supreme Court decisions. Berkson notes that two different groups emerge in his analysis: first, individuals who feel the need to be continuously informed of the Court's actions (attorneys, judges, law enforcement officers, and lawmakers), and second, individuals who have "only an intermittent interest in Supreme Court decisions."[51] However, the first group supplements its information by relying on original sources or specialized publications for information; the second group largely ignores other sources. Berkson also found that

Table 5.2 Channels by Which Various Publics Usually Obtain Reliable Information about Supreme Court Decisions

Occupational group	Newspapers	TV or radio	Specialized Memoranda	General periodicals	Special journals	Opinion itself
Doctors (N=70)	90%	80%	30%	86%	41%	6%
Attorneys (N=84)	60	51	81	50	87	81
Judges (N=115)	48	39	74	44	76	87
Clergy members (N=62)	89	89	42	77	48	16
Schoolteachers (N=104)	91	95	43	83	43	25
Law officers (N=30)	75	71	80	48	53	44
Bookstore operators (N=30)	90	93	33	83	40	17
Moviehouse operators (N=16)	81	88	19	62	31	6
School board members (N=27)	89	85	63	70	41	4
Lawmakers (N=106)	80	67	61	59	53	35
Total (N=1111)	76	71	66	58	55	42

Source: Larry C. Berkson, *The Supreme Court and Its Publics* (Lexington, Mass.: Lexington Books, 1968), 64. Reprinted by permission of the author.

these occupational groups differed in the degree to which they could correctly describe the law in policy areas that might affect their professional lives. As one might expect, the individuals in the continuously informed group were much more likely to know the law than those in the intermittent group. Unfortunately for his readers, Berkson does not say whether differences in knowledge are a result of more sources or of different sources of information.

Milner's study of police responses to the *Miranda* decision revealed that a variety of sources of information were used by these implementors. He reports that there was "no difference in the average number of sources of information received by each group of police officers approving and disapproving the *Miranda* decision. Both approvers and disapprovers received information from an average of 5.6 sources. Both groups ranked the best sources of information in a similar manner." [52] Like Berkson, he does not consider how levels of knowledge might relate to the number or nature of sources of information. The only difference in acceptance noted by Milner did not involve the media per se. Officers who attended informational conferences that used FBI materials emphasizing the limits of the *Miranda* decision were more likely to approve of the decision than were those who relied on other sources of information.

Whether the media's accounts of judicial decisions and of reactions to them affect either the originating court or the other responding populations is an unanswered question. At varying times members of the Supreme Court have indicated some displeasure about the way the press has reported a decision. Justice Tom Clark, for example, complained of the press's treatment of the *Engel* decision, blaming distorted news accounts for widespread misunderstanding and discontent with the Court's decision.[53] Such complaints, however, are rare, though Bob Woodward and Scott Armstrong suggest that some members of the early Burger Court were quite concerned over press coverage of the Court as well as over leaks to the press.[54] Nonetheless, there is little evidence that judicial decisions are affected by reactions of the press or by press reports of reactions of others.

In the areas of criminal justice and civil rights, media accounts of lower court activities and of the implementation of judicial decisions are occasionally investigated. Robert Crain notes that disturbances in New Orleans associated with desegregation efforts were widely reported in the national press and that some observers went so far as to accuse the press of provoking the protests. Whether the press exacerbated the disturbances or was merely covering them as they occurred is still unclear, but it is doubtful that press coverage actually affected the course of desegregation of that city's schools.[55]

A more direct evaluation of the impact of press coverage on desegregation efforts in Louisville and Nashville found no differences attributable to how the local and national media reported the events. Specifically, white flight in these two cities was more directly tied to structural differences in the cities' desegregation and busing plans than to treatments of the issue by the media.[56]

ATTENTIVE AND MASS PUBLICS

At various times individuals may respond to a judicial decision even though they are not involved either in its implementation or in its consumption. Under these circumstances, the public at large is part of the secondary population, which means that it is not directly affected by the judicial decision, though it may react to the policy or to the implementation of the policy by others in the political system. We also exclude from the public at large individuals associated with interest groups described earlier in this chapter.

We divide the public at large into two groups: the attentive public and the mass public. Public opinion research and surveys regarding judicial topics reveal that a small segment of the population is much more interested in and informed about political topics.[57] This segment is called the *attentive public*. Dolbeare and Hammond's research on public opinions toward the Court leads them to conclude that "the Court is in effect exclusively an object of elite attention— that elites are more responsive to, more knowledgeable of, and more confident in the Court, and therefore more likely to be channels by which Court-initiated policies become transformed into local practice or at least are acted upon some way." [58] Thus, we make a distinction between an informed attentive public and a largely uninformed mass public as we discuss the public at large as part of the secondary population. As we will discuss below, it is likely that the attentive public has a greater influence on the impact of judicial policies.

To consider the importance of the public at large as well as how it influences the impact of judicial policies, we need to evaluate the following questions. First, what do members of this subgroup know about the judiciary and judicial policies? And second, what effect do attentive and mass publics have on the implementation and impact of judicial policies?

Who Knows What about Judicial Policies?

Researchers can find out who knows what about the judiciary and judicial policies fairly easily by conducting a scientific public opinion poll that asks questions to ascertain the respondents' knowledge in this area. Several such polls have been conducted, and most of these have produced similar findings. Most citizens are willing to express some level of understanding about the judiciary and about what it does or should do. A survey of "elites" by Berkson found that 76 percent of the respondents knew that there were nine members of the Supreme Court, and nearly an equal percentage identified

Warren Burger as the chief justice. A slightly smaller percentage (64 percent) could also name at least one associate justice on the Court.[59] Walter Murphy and Joseph Tanenhaus found that 70.6 percent of citizens polled in the mid-1960s actually held some kind of opinion relating to the U.S. Supreme Court.[60]

While most people are willing to talk about the Supreme Court, how informed their opinions are about what the Court does or ought to do is open to some question. Murphy and Tanenhaus found that a majority of the 70.6 percent of the respondents with an opinion about the Court could *not* specify any single thing they liked or disliked about what the Court had done recently or offer an opinion about the main job of the Court.[61] Thus, the basis for their opinions was obscure.

Inadequate knowledge about judicial policies was also revealed in Wisconsin during the mid-1960s by Dolbeare and Hammond. They asked whether the Supreme Court had decided cases in eight issue areas (four in which it had and four in which it had not). Only 2 percent of those surveyed were entirely correct, while 12 percent were entirely incorrect. Only 15 percent of the sample were accurate four or more times. Moreover, when asked to be specific about their likes and dislikes in regard to the Court, only 19 percent responded in terms of policies such as civil rights decisions or school prayer cases.[62]

Similar findings are reported by Berkson for his survey of elites listed in Table 5.2. In this study, when Berkson asked whether the Court had made policies in 24 issue areas, 69 percent of the responses were correct, 9 percent were incorrect, and 22 percent were classified as unsure or no answer. While these figures are substantially better than those reported by Dolbeare and Hammond, as one might expect for elite respondents, the surprising finding by Berkson was that these elites were not especially aware of the *direction* or the *content* of the judicial policies. For example, 50 percent or more of the members of only three groups were able to describe the direction of occupationally relevant decisions—police officers (80 percent), lawyers (58 percent), and judges (64 percent). Less than half of the members of the remaining groups correctly described the contents of relevant decisions—lawmakers (34 percent), clergy (26 percent), schoolteachers (26 percent), and school board members (25 percent). On a more general question regarding a recent Court decision that denied states the authority to set lengthy residential requirements for voting, only 20 percent of the total sample gave a correct interpretation.[63]

Considering that most respondents in these polls had an opinion about the Court, Dolbeare and Hammond's comment is particularly appropriate: "Far more people express attitudes toward the Court than could be said to have any substantive degree of knowledge about it." [64] In this regard, Murphy and Tanenhaus venture the explanation that individuals are concerned only about judicial policies that are salient to them, such as those that "can be viewed in an intensely personal fashion: race, religion, and security of life and property." [65] The Court rarely renders a decision that can qualify for such attention. Moreover, when such decisions do occur, those involved are more likely to be in the consumer population than in the secondary population.

However, there are some occasions where certain members of the public at large may react intensely to a judicial policy. Local desegregation orders, for example, may qualify as "intensely personal" for persons who live in affected neighborhoods but have no children in school. Likewise, individuals who have recently been victims of a crime may react strongly to a court decision broadening the rights of suspects.

Public Opinion and the Implementation of Judicial Policies

Because public opinion about judicial policies is so vague and ill-informed, and because researchers and pollsters rarely ask questions about specific Court decisions, it is difficult to discuss what impact the public may have on the implementation of judicial decisions. To a limited degree, the scholars we have mentioned have suggested that public concerns about judicial policies occasionally influence the judiciary itself. The "switch in time" in 1937 is a prominent example, but here political pressures from Congress and the president were also present, and many attribute the public's belief in the mythology of the Court as the decisive factor saving the Court from President Roosevelt's court-packing plan. Other research, such as that by James Kuklinski and John Stanga and by James Gibson also indicates some correlation between public opinion about an issue and judicial policies in that area.[66] However, on the whole, research on the impact of public opinion on the implementation of judicial policies is not well developed.

To the degree that there is any research on such matters, the findings seem to suggest that public opinion has only a potential impact on the implementation of judicial decisions. Dolbeare and Hammond's research in five communities showed little evidence that the local community was concerned about school prayers. School boards considered local sentiments in making their decisions about school prayer policies only to the extent that school officials evaded the issue enough to avoid arousing community concern over school-house religion.[67] Bond and Johnson's research on hospital abortion policies reveals that local public sentiment about abortion had little impact on whether a hospital offered any level of abortion services.[68] Of course, where the mass public is already aroused about an issue, as the South was about desegregation, implementators can ignore it only at their political peril. From a different perspective, the absence of opinion about most decisions may reduce the impetus to take any particular type of action about judicial policies. That is, the range of action available to responding agencies may be greater when the public has no precise opinion on an issue.

While the influence of the general public is usually minimal, the influence of attentive publics is hard to determine. Dolbeare and Hammond, for example, suggest that local elite concerns are impor-tant in accounting for the inaction of school boards on the religious is-sue. They write, "If local elites are acquiescent, effectuation of the Court policy is more likely. If they are opposed, effectuation may be a long time in coming, perhaps not until some other elite at some other level is induced to act in support of the Court's policy." [69] As is true in regard to civil rights policies, the attitudes of local elites in the civic and business communities have been identified as critical to success-ful desegregation efforts. In contrast, Bond and Johnson's research indicates that abortion policies by hospitals were not so influenced by the attitudes of local elites.[70]

Whether attentive public opinion influences members of either the interpreting or the implementing population probably depends on several factors. First, if the mass public is unmoved by a judicial policy, then the attentive public may affect implementation processes to the degree they normally influence either judges, affected agencies, or possibly others such as Congress. Second, if the mass public is uninterested in a judicial policy, then the attentive public may have considerable difficulty in generating popular opposition to the policy because the mass public is "simply unaware of, but generally favorable toward, the Supreme Court." [71] Thus, in instances where public approval or disapproval of a policy could influence its imple-mentation, attentive publics are likely to have a limited impact either on the mass public or on the implementation of the judicial policy. Fi-nally, if the mass public is moved in one direction or another by a ju-dicial policy, then individuals in the attentive public may have little say over the implementation of a judicial policy unless they are in basic agreement with the policy and the mass public—assuming that those who officially respond to the judicial policy are influenced by public opinion, which may not be true.

SUMMARY

The secondary population is a residual category that we have divided into four groups: public officials, interest groups, the media, and the public at large. Of course, members of these groups sometimes fall in the implementing and consumer populations, but our focus here is on circumstances when they are not directly affected by or involved in carrying out judicial policies.

Because they serve in a representative capacity, public officials often find it politically necessary to react to judicial decisions—especially unpopular ones. Congress and state legislatures can change those policies involving statutory interpretation, but it is not so easy for them to do so in matters of constitutional interpretation. Legislators have two basic options in the latter situation. First, they can directly change the policy, for example, by proposing a constitutional amendment; or by trying to restrict its scope, as Congress did in refusing to fund abortion payments for poor women. Second, they can strike at the offending court more generally, for example, by not raising judges' salaries or by trying to alter the court's personnel. There have been many attempts to use both options throughout our history, particularly against the Supreme Court during this century, but they have seldom met with success. Some scholars hypothesize that at bottom public officials hold the courts, and most of all the Supreme Court, sacrosanct and thus are unwilling to impair their authority seriously. For its part, the Court will sometimes back off from policies that generate enduring hostility among public officials, but on occasion it will stand firm.

The president can pursue several avenues when he disagrees with a Supreme Court policy. He can use his leadership position to persuade the public and Congress to change laws or even pass a constitutional amendment; he can appoint new justices with different policy positions; and he can have the Justice Department argue for discontinuation or modification of the offensive policy.

Judicial policies often lead to the creation of new interest groups or give a new dimension to existing ones. These groups become vehicles for mobilizing attentive but unaffected publics to help or hinder the implementation of judicial policies. For instance, many young whites ventured south in the 1960s to help establish desegregation, and a large number of males have pressured politicians on behalf of one side or the other of the abortion question. Often interest groups will increase the number of consumers of judicial policies through publicity about potential benefits. Groups opposed to a judicial policy may offer counseling about or help establish alternatives to the offending policy.

The media perform two basic functions: informing the public about judicial policies and informing the courts and the public about reactions to these policies. Media reporting of judicial decisions seems to be generally accurate but often sketchy. At times, the media may perform an agenda-setting function because of their selective coverage of court cases and public reactions. Little research exists as to what effect the media coverage has either upon public knowledge about and reactions to judicial policies or upon how courts follow up initial decisions.

Poll evidence indicates that based upon their knowledge of judicial policies, the public as a whole varies from a small number of attentive individuals to a larger number of uninformed persons. However, individuals display a propensity to express opinions about the courts and their policies regardless of knowledge. It is unclear whether public opinion alone (without much support from public officials or interest groups) has any influence on the implementation of judicial policies.

NOTES

1. Beth M. Henschen, "Statutory Interpretations of the Supreme Court: Congressional Response," *American Politics Quarterly* 11 (October 1983): 441-458.
2. John R. Schmidhauser, Larry L. Berg, and Albert Melone, "The Impact of Judicial Decisions: New Dimensions in Supreme Court-Congressional Relations, 1945-68," *Washington University Law Quarterly* 1971 (1971): 209-251. The data noted in the text were extrapolated from Appendix I.
3. Note, "Congressional Reversals of Supreme Court Decisions: 1945-57," *Harvard Law Review* 71 (1958): 1336.
4. For an in-depth discussion of congressional reactions to Supreme Court decisions regarding internal security see C. Herman Pritchett, *Congress versus the Supreme Court, 1957-1960* (Minneapolis: University of Minnesota Press, 1961); and Walter Murphy, *Congress and the Court* (Chicago: University of Chicago Press, 1962).
5. The Eleventh Amendment negated *Chisolm v. Georgia* (1793), the Fourteenth Amendment negated *Scott v. Sandford* (1857), the Sixteenth Amendment negated *Pollock v. Farmers' Loan & Trust Co.* (1895), and the Twenty-sixth Amendment negated *Oregon v. Mitchell* (1970). A proposed Child Labor Amendment was passed by Congress following *Hammer v. Dagenhart* (1918), but it fell a few states short of the three-fourths required for ratification.

6. Harry P. Stumpf, "Congressional Response to Supreme Court Rulings: The Interaction of Law and Politics," *Journal of Public Law* 14 (Fall 1965): 379.
7. Ibid.
8. Stephen L. Wasby, *The Impact of the United States Supreme Court: Some Perspectives* (Homewood, Ill.: Dorsey Press, 1970), 207.
9. Cited in Dean L. Yarwood and Bradley C. Canon, "On the Supreme Court's Annual Trek to the Capitol," *Judicature* 63 (February 1980): 324.
10. William W. Crosskey, *Politics and the Constitution in the History of the United States* (Chicago: University of Chicago Press, 1953), vol. 2, 1243-1246.
11. Cited in John A. Schmidhauser and Larry L. Berg, *The Supreme Court and Congress: Conflict and Interaction, 1945-1968* (New York: Free Press, 1972), 10. *Sims* was mispelled in the *Congressional Record*.
12. Jon R. Bond, "The Politics of Court Structure: The Addition of New Federal Judges, 1949-1978," *Law and Policy Quarterly* 2 (April 1980): 181-188.
13. For a description of the Chase and Douglas impeachment efforts see *Guide to the U.S. Supreme Court* (Washington: Congressional Quarterly Inc., 1979), 658-663.
14. Schmidhauser and Berg, *The Supreme Court and Congress,* 150-176.
15. Pritchett, *Congress versus the Supreme Court;* and Murphy, *Congress and the Court.*
16. Pritchett, *Congress versus the Supreme Court,* 119.
17. Max Lerner, "Constitution and Court as Symbols," *Yale Law Review* 46 (1937): 1293.
18. Harry P. Stumpf, "The Political Efficacy of Judicial Symbolism," *Western Political Quarterly* 19 (June 1966): 295.
19. Stumpf, "The Political Efficacy of Judicial Symbolism"; and Stumpf, "Congressional Response to Supreme Court Rulings."
20. Schmidhauser and Berg, *The Supreme Court and Congress.*
21. Richard Lehne, *The Quest for Justice: The Politics of School Finance Reform* (New York: Longman, 1978) focuses on the consequences of the New Jersey Supreme Court's decision. More generally, see Mary Cornelia Porter, "State Supreme Courts and the Legacy of the Warren Court: Some Old Inquiries for a New Situation," in *State Supreme Courts: Policymakers in the Federal System,* ed. Mary Cornelia Porter and G. Alan Tarr (Westport, Conn.: Greenwood Press, 1982), 3-22.
22. Quoted in C. Herman Pritchett, *The American Constitution,* 3d ed. (New York: McGraw-Hill, 1977), 123.
23. The letter is reprinted in Walter F. Murphy and C. Herman Pritchett, eds., *Courts, Judges, and Politics,* 3d ed. (New York: Random House, 1979), 135-137.
24. Robert Scigliano, *The Supreme Court and the Presidency* (New York: Free Press, 1971), 177.
25. Ibid., 180.
26. David B. Truman, *The Governmental Process* (New York: Knopf, 1951).
27. Stuart Scheingold, *The Politics of Rights: Lawyers, Public Policy and Political Change* (New Haven, Conn.: Yale University Press, 1974), 85.
28. Ibid., 131, 132.

29. Karen O'Connor, *Women's Organizations' Use of the Courts* (Lexington, Mass.: Lexington Books, 1980), 125-126.
30. Stephen Halpern, "Assessing the Litigative Role of ACLU Chapters," in *Civil Liberties,* ed. Stephen Wasby (Lexington, Mass.: Lexington Books, 1976), 165.
31. O'Connor, *Women's Organizations' Use of the Courts,* 18-19.
32. Kenneth Dolbeare and Phillip Hammond, *The School Prayer Decisions: From Court Policy to Local Practice* (Chicago: University of Chicago Press, 1971), 58.
33. Joel Handler, *Social Movements and the Legal System: A Theory of Law Reform and Social Change* (New York: Academic Press, 1978), 128-129.
34. See Harrell R. Rodgers and Charles Bullock III, *Coercion to Compliance* (Lexington, Mass.: Lexington Books, 1976).
35. See Lehne, *The Quest for Justice.*
36. Neal Milner, *The Court and Local Law Enforcement* (Beverly Hills: Sage, 1971); Stephen Wasby, *Small Town Police and the Supreme Court: Hearing the Word* (Lexington, Mass.: Lexington Books, 1976).
37. Milner, *The Court and Local Law Enforcement,* 65-66.
38. See Dolbeare and Hammond, *The School Prayer Decisions,* 59.
39. Handler, *Social Movements and the Legal System,* 22.
40. Jon R. Bond and Charles A. Johnson, "Implementing a Permissive Policy: Hospital Abortion Services after *Roe v. Wade,*" *American Journal of Political Science* 26 (February 1982): 1-24.
41. Doris Graber, *Mass Media and American Politics* (Washington: CQ Press, 1980), 217.
42. Ibid., 217-218.
43. Larry C. Berkson, *The Supreme Court and Its Publics* (Lexington, Mass.: Lexington Books, 1978); and Richard Johnson, *The Dynamics of Compliance* (Evanston, Ill.: Northwestern University Press, 1967).
44. Chester A. Newland, "Press Coverage of the United States Supreme Court," *Western Political Quarterly* 17 (March 1964): 15-36.
45. Ibid., 21.
46. Johnson, *The Dynamics of Compliance,* 95.
47. David L. Grey, *The Supreme Court and the News Media* (Evanston, Ill.: Northwestern University Press, 1968), 105-106.
48. Newland, "Press Coverage of the Supreme Court," 29.
49. Richard A. Pride and J. David Woodward, "Busing Plans, Media Agenda, and White Flight: Nashville and Louisville" (Paper delivered at the Annual Meeting of the Southwestern Political Science Association, Houston, Texas, 1978), 17-18.
50. See Maxwell E. McCombs, "The Agenda Setting Approach," in *Handbook of Political Communication,* eds. Dan Nimmo and Keith Sanders (Beverly Hills, Calif.: Sage, 1981), 121-140.
51. Berkson, *The Supreme Court and Its Publics,* 65.
52. Milner, *The Court and Local Law Enforcement,* 201.
53. Newland, "Press Coverage of the Supreme Court," 15.
54. Bob Woodward and Scott Armstrong, *The Brethren* (New York: Simon and Schuster, 1979), 237-238, 356.
55. Robert Crain, *The Politics of School Desegregation* (Chicago: Aldine Press, 1968), 284-287.

56. Pride and Woodward, "Busing Plans, Media Agenda, and White Flight," 17.
57. Our conception of attentive publics is drawn from Donald Devine, *The Attentive Public* (Chicago: Rand McNally, 1970).
58. Dolbeare and Hammond, *The School Prayer Decisions,* 23.
59. Berkson, *The Supreme Court and Its Publics,* 16.
60. Walter Murphy and Joseph Tanenhaus, "Public Opinion and the United States Supreme Court: Mapping of Some Prerequisites for Court Legitimation of Regime Changes," in *Frontiers of Judicial Research,* ed. Joel Grossman and Joseph Tanenhaus (New York: Wiley, 1969), 290-291.
61. Ibid.
62. Kenneth Dolbeare and Philip Hammond, "The Political Party Basis of Attitudes toward the Supreme Court," *Public Opinion Quarterly* 31 (Spring 1967): 20.
63. Berkson, *The Supreme Court and Its Publics,* 18, 79, 86.
64. Dolbeare and Hammond, "Attitudes toward the Supreme Court," 21.
65. Murphy and Tanenhaus, "Public Opinion and the Supreme Court," 278-279.
66. James Kuklinski and John Stanga, "Political Participation and Government Responsiveness: The Behavior of California Superior Courts," *American Political Science Review* 73 (December 1979): 1090-1099; and James Gibson, "Environmental Constraints on the Behavior of Judges: A Representational Model of Judicial Decision Making," *Law and Society Review* 14 (Winter 1980): 343-370.
67. Dolbeare and Hammond, *The School Prayer Decisions,* ch. 6.
68. Bond and Johnson, "Hospital Abortion Services after *Roe v. Wade.*"
69. Dolbeare and Hammond, *The School Prayer Decisions,* 23.
70. Bond and Johnson, "Hospital Abortion Services after *Roe v. Wade.*"
71. Kenneth Dolbeare, "The Public Views the Supreme Court," in *Law, Politics, and the Federal Courts,* ed. Herbert Jacob (Boston: Little, Brown, 1967), 210.

CHAPTER SIX

Judicial Impact Theory

We have discussed in Chapters 2 through 5 the responses of different populations to judicial policies, and we have offered explanations for these responses culled from the research on judicial policies and their impact. The explanations themselves do not fit into any simple framework: some are drawn from investigations of particular settings or circumstances; others are speculation about results that were unanticipated by the researchers; still others appear to confirm specific theories that guided research. In this chapter we hope to bring order to these diverse explanations by evaluating the role of theory in judicial impact research, reviewing several theories of judicial impact, and discussing applications of the theories.

WHY BOTHER WITH JUDICIAL IMPACT THEORY?

Among most social scientists, the search for theory is an accepted and ever-present goal. But while theory is a leading concern, explaining what theory is or why it is so important is difficult without becoming philosophical or overbearing. This book is not about theory or theory development, but we feel it is important to discuss briefly what we believe theory is, what role it may play in understanding judicial impact, and why we are devoting an entire chapter to theories about the impact of court decisions.

Empirical Theory

When we review different judicial impact theories we will be reviewing *empirical* theories, not *normative* theories about the impact of judicial decisions. In social science, an empirical theory is one that offers an explanation for the causes of observed behavior. A normative theory is one that prescribes how people ought to behave in certain situations. A normative theory of judicial impact might be that lower courts and implementing agencies ought to obey Supreme Court decisions because they come from a legitimate policy maker in our political system. That is, the theory argues that since the decision maker is legitimate, people should respond positively because our system is based on the idea that governmental institutions like the Supreme Court have the authority to decide how our society should be ordered and what behavior is appropriate for individuals in the society. Such a theory is normative because it deals with questions about "ought to" or "should," instead of with questions about whether responses actually are compliant or under what conditions compliant responses might be found.

Empirical theories of judicial impact are concerned with the questions of whether and when compliant responses occur. An empirical theory based on the concept of legitimacy might hold that lower courts and implementing groups respond positively to a judicial policy if it is viewed as coming from a legitimate decision maker. That is, because individuals generally respond positively to statements coming from a source they respect and most people respect institutions such as the Supreme Court, we can expect most people to accept and comply with Supreme Court policies. Both normative and empirical theories may use the concept of legitimacy (or a related concept), but only the empirical theory is *testable*. For example, we can test the hypothesis that if police officers view the Supreme Court as a legitimate source of criminal justice policy, then they will comply with the Court's decisions, and if they do not view the Court as legitimate, then they will not comply with its decisions. If data collected in a systematic way show that the police officers who recognize the legitimacy of the Supreme Court as a source of particular policies—for instance, *Mapp v. Ohio* (1961) and *Miranda v. Arizona* (1966)—are compliant and that those who do not recognize the Court's legitimacy are not compliant, then the hypothesis would be confirmed. Such confirmation in turn increases our confidence that the theory is correct. If the data show no difference in compliance rates between officers who recognize the Court's legitimacy and those who do not, then the hypothesis is not supported and the accuracy of the theory is drawn into question.

Either of these findings would contribute to our empirical knowledge of how the police respond to Supreme Court decisions. If the hypothesis were not supported, then legitimacy theory would probably be discarded, at least as an explanation for police response, and the search for another theory would be initiated. But even in this instance, future researchers would be informed that whether the Court was viewed as legitimate made little difference in accounting for police reaction to Supreme Court decisions. If the hypothesis were supported, then we would have more confidence in legitimacy theory to explain responses to Supreme Court decisions.

Developing this theoretical understanding, whether it involves legitimacy theory or other theories, has several benefits that warrant giving our studies a theoretical focus. Most important is that theories provide an *explanation* for variations in responses to judicial policies, which may prove useful in a variety of research circumstances. If we observe police officers enforcing Supreme Court policies in spite of opposition within their ranks, then a theory such as legitimacy theory may provide an explanation for the compliant behavior under circumstances where noncompliance might be expected. Further, if some police were observed complying with the Court policy and others not complying, we could gather data on the officers' views of the Court's legitimacy to test whether legitimacy theory is an appropriate explanation for the difference in compliance.

In addition to providing *post hoc* (after the fact) explanations for responses to judicial decisions among a single responding group, impact theories can also explain responses among other populations or groups. For example, if legitimacy theory explains police reactions, it may also explain variations in acceptance behavior by consumer groups or adjustment behavior by lower court judges. Thus, an important feature of a well-developed theory is that the explanations are applicable to similar events or behavior in a variety of settings. Of course, the more widely applicable or generalizable the theory, the "better" the theory from the perspective of most social scientists.

Another important advantage of empirical theories is that they tend to identify the variables that are relevant for explaining impact phenomena. If we were constructing a questionnaire to be sent to public officials about their responses to a particular Supreme Court policy and if legitimacy theory were the leading theory in this area, then questions should be included about the respondent's views of the Supreme Court's role as a policy maker and the perceived legitimacy of particular Court policies. We would not ask questions about the respondents' shoe size, salaries, or attitudes about higher education because we have no theoretical reasons for why such characteristics might affect responses to judicial decisions. Thus, theories help us in identifying important information and filtering out irrelevant information.

Finally, theoretically focused research is important because new research questions are usually suggested by old theories. For example, if legitimacy theory were supported by a number of impact studies for various populations and judicial policies, one might be prompted to ask why some respondents view the Court as legitimate and others do not. Similarly, one could ask whether some institutions are viewed as more legitimate than others, and if so, how the perceived legitimacy of courts compares with that of legislative or administrative institutions—or with that of religious, commercial, or social institutions. Answers to such questions indicate how people will respond when judicial policies conflict with policies of other institutions. Another research question could concern whether perceived legitimacy varies across policies. Are judicial policies concerning clearly articulated parts of the Constitution (for example, freedom of religion) viewed as more legitimate than policies concerning rights unarticulated in the Constitution (for example, the right to personal privacy)? Each of these research questions is based on the original theory that legitimacy plays a major role in accounting for responses to judicial decisions. Answers to these questions would expand the original theory to cover a broader range of events and behavior and enable us to explain in more detail what happens in particular situations.

Depending on theory to identify relevant variables has both positive and negative consequences. On the positive side, having a theory substantially simplifies doing research and explaining judicial impact events and behavior. As we have mentioned, theory points to the relevant variables and questions that might be asked in an impact study. On the negative side, however, the researcher may occasionally be blinded to variables and linkages that were not anticipated by the theory but that might also explain an event or behavior. For example, if legitimacy theory were the leading theory and one focused only on questions pertaining to it, then one could easily miss instances where environmental pressures, such as local public opinion preferences, affect the responses to judicial decisions. Of course, no single theory is yet dominant in explaining the impact of judicial decisions, so we frequently try different theories; even so, theory-directed studies run the risk of missing connections not anticipated by those theories. However, as bad as ignoring some relevant data may be, the consequences of having no theories or of having only idiosyncratic explanations are far worse. Without theories, our knowledge might be encyclopedic, but it would not be organized, nor would it prompt cumulative research in the future.

The Role of Empirical Theory
in Judicial Impact Research

Despite the commitment of social scientists to organized and cumulative research, theory has played only a modest role in judicial impact research. Such research began in the 1950s and 1960s with a descriptive focus. The findings of widespread noncompliance with Supreme Court decisions by early investigators, such as Gordon Patric, Frank Sorauf, Walter Murphy, and others, were rather startling and seemed to demand explanation.[1] By around 1970 some scholars were developing or applying theories to explain noncompliance or other judicial impact phenomena and to establish directions for future research. Some theories were relatively comprehensive and offered explanations for patterns of behavior in a wide variety of situations. Others were quite narrow, offering simple explanations of how one variable affected another in particular circumstances. Some of the latter, in fact, can probably be deemed theories only by a generous use of the term. (Of course, not all subsequent judicial impact research has been guided by these theories. Much research is still descriptive, and explanation for the findings is either ignored, presumed, or at best, loosely speculative.)

We discuss below a number of theories that have been advanced to explain judicial impact phenomena. Some are derived from psychology, some from economics, some from the study of communications, some from the study of organizational behavior, and some from political science and sociology. For the sake of an orderly discussion, we have divided them by these focuses. Remember that these theories are not mutually exclusive. They are interactive—they may reinforce each other in some situations and be at odds in others—and all are probably operative to some degree. However, there is virtually no research on the interactions of two or more theories. For this reason, our review concentrates on simple statements of the theories, rather than on their interaction.

PSYCHOLOGICAL THEORIES OF JUDICIAL IMPACT

Researchers contend that our responses to a new policy are shaped by our preexisting attitudes toward the policy or toward things symbolized by or associated with the policy or the agency making the policy. Such attitudes may be acquired from a variety of sources, such as parents, peers, churches, community norms, magazines, and television shows. These attitudes may be based upon actual facts or upon misinformation; they may stem from accurate or from erroneous versions of history. Attitudes may or may not be logically connected with the policy at issue. Regardless, they become embedded in our outlook on life and politics and are difficult—though by no means impossible—to change. They color our reactions to judicial decisions as well as to other political events. Nonetheless, we all have a zone of indifference (see pp. 38-39) in relation to some policies. That is, for some policies either we have no preexisting attitudes or we hold them so weakly that they do not significantly affect our acceptance and response decisions. Obviously, whether a policy falls inside or outside the zone depends upon some nonattitudinal factors such as external pressures on us and how the policy affects our daily lives. But it is also affected by some general attitudinal patterns that researchers have noted. These patterns are explained by what we call psychological theories of judicial impact.

Psychology and political science offer similar theories about attitude development and change which have some potential for explaining reactions to judicial decisions. For instance, there are psychoanalytic theories about attitude change and about compliance with authority; and there is a growing body of research about the socialization of children and adolescents which offers explanations of why we tend to obey the law and view our political institutions positively. These theories may prove at some point to be important in explaining reactions to judicial decisions, but currently the literature developing these perspectives and using them to explain reactions to court decisions is too hypothetical or too remote to be connected with reactions to judicial policies.[2] Consequently, we will not review these broader theories here. Rather, we first consider two theories as they are specifically applied to judicial impact: legitimacy theory and cognitive dissonance theory. Then we consider the potential usefulness of explanations that relate attitudes toward a policy and reactions to the policy.

Legitimacy Theory

We have introduced the concept of legitimacy previously in this book. In Chapter 2 we identified legitimacy as one of the variables that affect a lower court judge's willingness to accept a higher court decision. In Chapter 5 we noted the arguments about what role Congress's perception of the Supreme Court's legitimacy had in defeating or modifying most of the Court-curbing bills considered in the 1950s. Legitimacy theory has several facets. These facets can relate to either of two things: the institution making the policy (the court) and the substance of the policy. In this section, we will discuss three related but distinguishable facets. Our focus is primarily on how they relate to the courts themselves, but sometimes institutional legitimacy is intertwined with the legitimacy of specific policies.

Generally speaking, we are more likely to respond positively to commands from those who we believe have the right to issue such commands to us. The legitimacy we accord to the source of the command affects the nature of our response. The success of political institutions and even of governments themselves depends in large part on whether or not citizens believe that the institutions are behaving legitimately. Legitimacy is not synonymous with approval or even with correctness. Rather, a decision is legitimate in the respondent's eyes if he or she concedes that the court's proper function in society is to make such a decision and that the decision itself is not grossly biased or totally absurd.

Legitimacy theory—explaining individuals' acceptance of and response to institutional policies as a function of their attitudes toward the institution's authority and role in the governance of society—is a familiar one in political science through the works of such scholars as Seymour Martin Lipset and David Easton.[3] In very general terms, judicial scholars such as Alexander Bickel, Charles Black, and Michael Petrick have used legitimacy theory to explain why a court, particularly the Supreme Court, is able to secure the psychological acceptance of and appropriate behavioral responses to its decisions.[4] Legitimacy theory is quite comprehensive in the sense that it can be applied to explain the behavior of persons in the interpreting, implementing, consumer, and secondary populations. It should be noted, however, that legitimacy theory does not purport to explain acceptance or, more particularly, behavioral responses completely. Legitimacy is a background factor that interacts with more immediate factors in any given situation. For example, most of us accept the legitimacy of a highway speed limit, but many of us also exceed 55 miles an hour on the interstate when we are in a hurry to get somewhere. Conversely, even those who deny the right of the federal government to set a maximum speed limit may proceed at 55 miles an hour when a state trooper is cruising along behind them.

Legitimacy as Social Distance. Courts engage in various activities that by design or coincidence enhance the perceived legitimacy of their decision-making role by maintaining a social distance from the other participants in the political system. Considerable drama and ritual enhance this distance. Judges wear robes, everyone rises when they enter the courtroom, and they are addressed as "Your Honor." The distance is augmented by the absence of lobbyists in the courts, by the rule that judges cannot talk with anyone about a pending case, and by the norm that they cannot even appear to be involved in partisan politics.

The Supreme Court's legitimacy is reinforced not only by the various rituals and the social distance, but as Richard Johnson observes, by the fact that it is *the* Supreme Court. As the highest court in the land, there is no judicial appeal of its decisions. In particular, "it is perceived as having a legal and constitutional right to do what it does." Johnson argues that the maintenance of a visible social distance from other political actors is particularly important for the Court because it is "in a position to enunciate broad social principles and in turn take the brunt of the criticism when those nearer the scene of battle implement the principles." [5] Thus Johnson believes that the superintendent in the school system he studied was successful in calling for an end to prayers in school by citing the Court as the source of the policy. Here the Supreme Court's legitimacy reinforced the acceptance decision and behavioral changes on the part of an implementing population.

Not everyone accepts the Supreme Court's legitimacy uncritically. Some people believe that the Court's power of judicial review, which allows it to overrule legislation, violates the principle of majority rule upon which democracy is based. Indeed, this view was widely shared in the nineteenth century and was an integral part of both President Thomas Jefferson's and President Andrew Jackson's concept of the Supreme Court's proper role. While judicial review has few prominent opponents today, the idea is still not necessarily well understood or accepted among the general public. Other people may accept the Court's authority in general but feel that Court decisions in particular areas are not legitimate because they violate some cherished principle, such as federalism, separation of powers, or the protection of national security.

Legitimacy as Finding the Law. Another facet of legitimacy involves people's perceptions of how courts function. Many people believe that courts do not make policy, that they simply serve as vehicles by which the law is determined and applied. This belief is sometimes referred to as the myth of the courts. Jerome Frank, a prominent legal scholar and federal judge in the 1930s and 1940s, was the leading analyst of this myth.[6] Frank argued that even adults who are engaged in politics and legal disputes have a psychological need for a father figure. In other places or times, religious authorities, kings, or the leaders of totalitarian parties fulfill this need. In modern, secular America, where the ideal is a government of laws and not of men, we turn to our judges to fulfill this need—we impute to them wisdom, concern, and capabilities beyond those possessed by other political actors. As one judicial scholar puts it, this myth "transforms courts from instruments of naked power to legitimate authorities capable of proclaiming and implementing policies without the use of force." [7]

As it relates to constitutional law, the myth is that Supreme Court justices are particularly qualified to determine the "true" meaning of the Constitution and apply it in specific cases. Thus judicial decisions are not acts of policy making or even of discretion, but are preordained and mechanical impositions of enduring constitutional principles. At one time the myth of mechanical jurisprudence was so pervasive that even many justices accepted it. In 1936 Justice Owen Roberts wrote what has become a classic statement of mechanical jurisprudence:

> When an act of Congress is appropriately challenged in the Courts as not conforming to the constitutional mandate the judicial branch of the Government has only one duty—to lay the article of the Constitution which is invoked beside the statute which is challenged and to decide whether the latter squares with the former. All the Court does, or can do, is to announce its considered judgment upon the question. This Court neither approves nor condemns any legislative policy. [8]

There exists a somewhat analogous myth about the immutability of the common law, which held that judges did not make decisions or policies, they merely "found" the correct principle through proper deductive reasoning.

To the extent that such myths permeate our thinking, they shelter the courts from public scrutiny and induce members of the various populations to accept and respond positively to judicial policies. Of course, the uncritical acceptance of such myths is not so widespread today, especially among the political elite. Nonetheless, the myths still retain considerable influence on our thinking. After all, most judges try to be impartial and most of us want to believe that we live under a government of laws and not of men.

As the power of the myth declines, so may the legitimacy of the courts, which in turn could jeopardize the acceptance of judicial policies. A crucial link in this argument is that while myth sustains legitimacy, familiarity with the reality of judicial decision making may diminish the myth. [9] If citizens come to understand that the courts make policy decisions, acceptance and compliance may become more dependent upon individual attitudes toward the particular policies involved.

Legitimacy as Fairness and Realism. Stephen Wasby offers a slightly different perspective on the legitimacy of the courts, especially that of the Supreme Court. He notes that if the Court is perceived as "not ruling fairly on a subject or on the basis of adequate knowledge," then the reception given the decision may be negative.[10] In the same vein, if people perceive that a court's past policies have been unfair, were made without proper procedure, or seem unrelated to the real world, they will not accept the court's legitimacy. In other words, legitimacy is a product not only of how people view the court's function in society, but also of how well they think a court is fulfilling its function. A court can undermine its legitimacy by making seemingly unfair or unrealistic decisions. Conversely, a court that is perceived as having a strong record of impartiality and knowledgeability may win acceptance of an unpopular decision.

While different, these three facets of legitimacy—legitimacy as social distance, as the myth of finding the law, and as being fair and realistic—are closely connected. A court that loses one facet of legitimacy may well lose the other two. For instance, in the wake of numerous antilabor decisions in the years from 1890 to 1935, organized labor and its sympathizers came to believe that the Supreme Court was not keeping any distance from the political system, that the Court's policies were not merely mechanical applications of the Constitution, and that the justices were deliberately hostile to the workers' interests. All three perspectives on legitimacy are based on the underlying hypothesis that the greater the perceived legitimacy of the court, the greater the probability that its policies will be accepted and faithfully implemented.

Comparative Legitimacy. Legitimacy theory may also be used in comparing the efficacy of courts to that of other institutions. That is, people may perceive the courts as more legitimate or less legitimate than other institutions, such as Congress and the presidency. When the policies of two institutions clash, individuals will presumably accept the one from the agency they consider more legitimate and reject the other. As we saw in Chapter 5, for instance, the Supreme Court had sufficient legitimacy in the public mind to withstand President Franklin Roosevelt's 1937 attempt to pack it— although it gave ground in the political dispute during the process. On the other hand, on issues involving foreign policy and military security, the public is probably less likely to view decisions of the

Court as legitimate in relation to those of the president. Indeed, some people might argue that the need for a father figure posited by Jerome Frank has been redirected in the last half of the twentieth century from the courts to the presidency as foreign policy and military concerns have become predominant in our political life. Similarly, people may attribute reduced legitimacy to court decisions when they conflict with important policies maintained by nonpolitical institutions, such as the church, the family, or community tradition. The widespread unwillingness to accept the Supreme Court's desegregation and abortion decisions results from such a situation.

Research on Legitimacy Theory. Although legitimacy theory is hardly new, little empirical research has been done in the area. One study by Walter Murphy and Joseph Tanenhaus directly assessed public opinion about the Supreme Court's legitimacy. They found that fewer than half of the respondents knew about the Court and its functions and that perhaps only a third of the public viewed the Court as an "impartial and competent" adjudicator of constitutional issues.[11] Gregory Casey concludes from his study that large segments of the public continue to hold what he describes as mythical views about the Supreme Court's function.[12] Of course, as we noted in Chapter 5, there have been other public opinion surveys conducted about the Court, but most measure knowledge of or attitudes toward the Court's specific policies instead of how the respondents regard the Court per se. Most of these found low levels of knowledge about the Court's decisions.[13] Indeed, it appears that those who know the most about the Court's specific decisions are those who dislike those decisions. One survey suggests that the public's regard for the Supreme Court doesn't differ much from that for the presidency or for Congress, implying that perhaps judicial legitimacy has little existence independent of general governmental legitimacy.[14] While these results do not refute the general proposition that perceptions of legitimacy have a role in shaping responses to judicial decisions, they do cast doubt on the idea that the Supreme Court has a special capability to legitimize its own policies in the eyes of the public. This argument is made most pointedly by David Adamany, based on his close examination of both current opinion studies and the historical events surrounding Supreme Court decisions in earlier eras.[15]

Though the general public may not accord the Supreme Court special legitimacy, one might wonder about political elites in particular. It can be argued that political elites are crucial to the operation of judicial policies because they make up the entire interpreting population, much of the implementing population, and the key elements of the secondary population insofar as feedback is concerned. While there is evidence that such elites tend to support civil liberties to a greater extent than the public at large,[16] there are no empirical data showing that elites believe the Supreme Court is particularly legitimate or that they are more supportive of its decisions than those of other agencies. Indeed, elites, at least nowadays, are not fooled by the myth of mechanistic jurisprudence, and on occasion readily make negative acceptance decisions and behavioral responses. Most of the examples in this book of defiance, evasion, and avoidance of judicial policies involve political elites.

Cognitive Dissonance Theory

Cognitive dissonance theory is based on the widely accepted psychological tenet that an individual's opinions on a particular subject need to be internally consistent with his or her behavior. When inconsistencies occur tensions arise within the individual, who then takes conscious or unconscious steps to reduce the tension. Two of the most informative early studies of judicial impact employed cognitive dissonance theory to understand better how and why school personnel reacted as they did to the Supreme Court's decision banning prayers in public schools (*Abington School District v. Schempp,* 1963). Both Richard Johnson and William Muir have suggested that a decision such as this would be likely to fall outside many persons' zone of indifference and thus motivate them to respond in some manner.[17] Johnson argues that a directive from a court that a person respects ordering that person to cease practices to which he or she is committed is likely to create a cognitive imbalance and generate tensions to return to some form of cognitive consistency. A variety of means may be employed to return to cognitive consistency, including the changing of behavior consistent with the court order, but such a change or any other reaction is likely to lead to a new imbalance between personal attitudes and personal behavior. It is at this point, Johnson maintains, that cognitive dissonance theory "gains specific relevance." [18]

Several means may be employed to reduce the dissonance that may result from the response to a judicial decision, as we will outline below. Cognitive dissonance theory is concerned with these means, by which an individual either increases the desirability of the chosen alternative or decreases the desirability of the rejected alternative. The theory does *not* predict which alternative an individual will choose or why, just that some change in attitude or behavior will occur.

Muir and Johnson identify several postreaction patterns in individuals who experience cognitive dissonance. Both authors draw heavily from the original work of Leon Festinger, who outlined a theory of cognitive dissonance.[19] Muir's list of possible ways individuals may handle dissonance includes

1. Denying the existence of the judicial decision
2. Depreciating the decision by interpreting it to be inapplicable
3. Dissociating himself or herself from the field covered by the decision
4. Becoming indecisive
5. Keeping the original attitude and exaggerating the coercive effects of the law
6. Accentuating the original attitude and derogating the law
7. Converting to the legal attitude
8. Diminishing the importance or eliminating an originally equivocal attitude

The first five of these responses Muir labels the *nullist* reaction, and the remaining three patterns he terms *backlash, conversion,* and *liberating,* respectively.[20]

Johnson offers a somewhat more compact list of responses. His terms are: *bolstering,* where additional positive elements are seen in the chosen alternative; *denial,* where the positive elements of the rejected alternative are denigrated; *transcendence,* where the dissonant elements are reorganized in a different scheme, which reduces or eliminates dissonance—for example, a higher principle is invoked; and finally, *differentiation,* where the cause of the dissonance is distinguished from one or more of the existing elements—for example, previous practices are redefined and become acceptable to the individual under the new rule.[21]

Both scholars found that school personnel used some of these patterns of behavior to work out any dissonance they experienced after deciding how to react to the Court's school prayer decision. Although these scholars list particular response categories, they explain individual responses by idiosyncratic variables, so their research does little to satisfy our search for a systematic explanation of the circumstances that cause individuals to reduce cognitive dissonance in a particular manner.

Attitudes toward Judicial Policies

Throughout this book we have noted the importance of a person's attitude toward a particular judicial policy. Regardless of how an individual feels about the Supreme Court as a policy maker, the nature of the policy itself is likely to have a substantial effect on his or her reaction to the judicial decision. For example, a person may not like the fact that the Supreme Court in *Roe v. Wade* (1973) announced a liberalized policy regarding abortion because he or she believes that such a decision should be made by legislative bodies Nevertheless, the same individual may agree with the policy itself and therefore may react positively to it. Substantive policy likes and dislikes are what the zone of indifference concept is all about.

The most straightforward hypothesis employing personal atti-tudes suggests that individual policy preferences influence reactions; that is, individuals with positive attitudes toward a judicial policy will be more likely to respond positively to the policy than individuals with negative attitudes toward the policy. While this hypothesis would seem trite because it should be obvious, there have been few tests of it, and those that have been made do not always support it. One public opinion poll found few respondents who were willing or likely to act on their opposition to a court policy.[22] Neal Milner reports a 78.9 percent opposition to the Supreme Court's *Miranda* decision among police officers in four Wisconsin cities; yet the officers' behavioral reactions were for the most part positive, that is, compliant. Thus, even though the officers held negative attitudes toward the policy, their reactions were contrary to the attitudes hypothesis, which predicts that compliance would be minimal.[23] Of course, in some instances personal policy preferences do make a difference. Racial attitudes have no doubt influenced people's reactions to desegregation rulings. And in the school systems studied by Johnson and by Muir, the key decision makers' basic agreement with the Supreme Court's prayer-banning decisions resulted in compliance.

The challenge is to account for the differences between occasions when attitudes are influential and occasions when they are not. It may be that there is a psychological theory waiting to be developed or applied to judicial impact. At times attitude is modified by pressures external to the individual, which can overwhelm pressures to react consistently with one's attitudes. Police officers may dislike the *Miranda* decision, but if they do not comply with it, their cases will probably be dismissed. School officials may wish to comply with the Court's decisions regarding prayers, but they may fear strong adverse community reactions. Where response is solely a product of an individual's attitudes, his or her policy preferences will be likely to be influential. Where the reaction is affected by external factors, individual attitudes become only one factor influencing reactions to judicial policies.

UTILITY THEORY:
A PSYCHOLOGICAL—ECONOMIC APPROACH

Cost-Benefit Analysis

Utility theory, in which a cost-benefit analysis of alternatives explains responses to judicial policies, has been advanced largely by Robert Stover and Don Brown and by Harrell Rodgers and Charles Bullock.[24] Basically, utility theory is borrowed from the work of nineteenth-century British philosopher Jeremy Bentham[25] and from the classical or rational calculation theories of economists. Bentham's central assumption is that individuals seek to maximize pleasure and minimize pain; the economists' main assumption is that people seek to maximize financial gain and minimize financial losses. Each approach postulates that individuals will make rational decisions that they believe will best achieve these goals.

Historically, these two approaches are treated as separate theories because Bentham included and emphasized psychic well-being while economists concentrate on monetary profits and losses. However, judicial scholars, especially Stover and Brown, have tended to combine the two approaches into a single theory. We will treat utility theory as a single entity which combines both psychological and economic aspects—as well as others that might be viewed in terms of maximizing the achievement of goals or minimizing obstacles to their accomplishment. In fact, such a combination is quite appropriate here because public policies, whether made by courts or by other agencies, often have both economic and psychological aspects. In regard to judicial policies, Stover and Brown argue that "given the capacity to comply or not comply, individuals' responses to legal directives will vary with the expected value of various compliant and noncompliant actions." [26]

Scholars generally conceptualize the process of maximizing values in terms of the idea of utility. The concept of utility underlies Bentham's approach, and it is frequently used in modern economics to describe a person's or firm's interests in selecting a particular strategy or outcome. If a business were making a 25 percent profit, then there would be a positive utility for the businessperson to continue the same behavior (all other things being equal). If the business were operating at a loss, then the utility would be negative and the person would presumably be looking for ways to improve the business or change markets. As Stover and Brown put it regarding judicial policies:

Utility refers to the net benefit or loss which the individual *expects* to result from reactions to a particular law. The utility in this situation is a product of a person's values and his/her expectations of eventual outcomes. Their values refer to their attitudes toward relevant objects such as the court, the policy, or significant others affected by the policy. The expectations refers to perceived probabilities that taking a particular course of action will actually result in a benefit or a cost to oneself.[27]

While the calculations for the expected utilities may not be rational in the sense that complete information is available to or even sought by the decision makers, rationality is assumed insofar as individuals are expected to make choices maximizing pleasure or profit instead of pain or loss based on the information they do have. Thus, Stover and Brown offer the basic postulate of this theory: "A person with the capacity to either comply or not comply with a given law will not comply when the utility of noncompliance is greater than the utility of compliance." [28]

Rodgers and Bullock note that the range of factors considered in the utilities calculation can be expressed in the inequality

$$Bn + Cn <?> Bc + Cc$$

where

Bn = benefits of noncompliance
Cn = costs of noncompliance
Bc = benefits of compliance
Cc = costs of compliance

Noncompliance is expected if the net value of $Bn + Cn$ is greater than the net value of $Bc + Cc$. Compliance is expected if the reverse is true. Explaining these elements in more substantive terms, Rodgers and Bullock suggest that the benefits of noncompliance (Bn) could include "financial gain, expected power and prestige, or simply convenience." The costs of noncompliance (Cn) could include the certainty and severity of "formal or informal sanctions." The benefits of compliance (Bc) may involve "maintaining personal esteem, financial gains, or . . . the esteem of others." And finally, the costs of compliance (Cc) may include "inconvenience, ostracism, or increased responsibilities." [29]

Utility Theory and Law-Abidingness

Utility theory particularly complements legitimacy theory. Legitimacy theory largely explains a person's decision whether or not to accept a judicial policy. This acceptance decision in turn influences the behavioral response. Utility theory, by contrast, looks at a person's behavioral response rather than the acceptance decision. A person may feel that a policy is legitimate but that his or her own interests are best served by noncompliance. For instance, some persons cheat on their income tax even though they would not argue that the tax is unconstitutional or even unfair. They cheat because it maximizes their financial gain and they feel that the probabilities of getting caught are sufficiently low to take the risk of underpaying their taxes. (The converse is also true. Some persons may consider the income tax illegitimate but carefully pay every penny due in order to avoid the negative utility of going to prison or paying a large fine if they are audited.)

Rodgers and Bullock nicely highlight the opposite perspectives of the two theories. Studies exploring the concept of legitimacy, they note, indicate that most citizens tend to be law-abiding, that respect for the law and obedience to it are characteristic of most individuals from early childhood on. But they also note that in some areas noncompliance or disobedience is widespread and widely accepted. Thus, they conclude, "Individual attitudes about law and law-abidingness do not provide a very accurate guide to behavior where specific laws are concerned." [30] Instead of following their inclinations to be law-abiding, most individuals engage in some type of cost-benefit calculus before reacting to a decision—at least when their own preferences are important. For example, a teacher's attitudes toward school prayers would probably affect his or her acceptance decision to an order to cease praying in class. If the teacher felt that classroom prayers gave great psychological pleasure and it seemed that sanctions could be avoided or minimized, he or she might well continue the prayers. If the teacher derived little satisfaction from the prayers or if sanctions were expected to be severe, he or she would most likely stop the prayers. An individual might make either response, in spite of a general inclination to be law-abiding. Rodgers and Bullock suggest that this incongruence between general law-abidingness and specific noncompliance is not unusual among Americans.[31]

Rodgers and Bullock highlight an individual's commitment to law-abidingness as a factor that is frequently included in the calculations of the cost-benefit inequality we set out earlier. Individual commitments to law-abidingness may vary, of course, but when an individual is considering disobeying a judicial decision, these authors maintain that "the psychic costs of violating the commitment [to law-abidingness] could be a highly constraining factor." [32] A positive attitude about law-abidingness could be so strong that the costs of noncompliance with a judicial policy would exceed the benefits of noncompliance, thus pushing the individual toward compliance. But, as many have pointed out, these pressures may be overcome under some circumstances. If the individual can rationalize the noncompliance, then psychic costs of noncompliance may be reduced and the pressures for law-abidingness neutralized. In such an instance, through a process much like the balancing notion used in cognitive dissonance theory, noncompliance is rationalized, commitments to law-abidingness neutralized, and equilibrum restored for the individual.[33]

Rodgers and Bullock hypothesize that the norm of law-abidingness is least constraining when the individual "(1) disagrees with a law; (2) believes that he would benefit from breaking the law; (3) doubts that he would be punished for breaking the law; and (4) perceives that he would suffer little public sanction for breaking the law and might even be esteemed by important peers for doing so."[34] This combination of factors, the authors contend, was what came about in the South during efforts to desegregate public schools. School officials frequently opposed the Supreme Court's *Brown v. Board of Education* (1954) decision, were reasonably certain that little would happen to them if they did so, and actually were applauded for opposing the law by local citizens. Under these circumstances, individuals normally committed to law-abidingness were able to ignore a judicial policy and still maintain a sense of mental balance.

Applicability of Utility Theory

One shortcoming of utility theory is that it is not easy to test empirically in many situations. The theory argues that the net utility of an action will be related to responses to a judicial decision and tells us that this utility is the product of an individual's values and expectations. However, the theory does not specify what values or expectations are important, nor what their net worth may be. Moreover, comparisons between individuals are difficult to make because each individual may give different net worths to different values and expectations, and the particular values and expectations they think are important may also differ dramatically. For example, one school superintendent may value community support highly, while another may instead value the support of school personnel. Both superintendents may decide to continue prayers in schools, and both may have maximized their utilities, but the factors affecting their decisions are different. From this perspective, any decision to allow or ban school prayers could be explained by identifying the values important to the decision makers, determining whether they were maximized, and concluding that utility theory explains reactions to court decisions. The difficulty, of course, is that unless one specifically states what factors are hypothesized to be the focus of the superintendent's thinking, there is no way to falsify the theory. Such overarching generalizations have no meaning to our analyses.

Utility theory is most easily tested when the values and expectations involved are economic ones. Economists advance and test cost-benefit theories frequently. Some legal scholars have advanced propositions that purport to explain judicial decisions and their impact—particularly those in tort and contract law—as being basically cost-benefit calculations, but the propositions have not been subject to serious testing.[35] Most political scientists, however, are more interested in decisions involving public policies that do not primarily involve economic allocations and that often are not measurable on any dimension.

Rodgers and Bullock applied utility theory in explaining the desegregation of southern schools. They found, in brief, that as the financial costs—especially the loss of federal funds—of maintaining segregated schools increased, resistance declined.[36] Similarly, as we noted in Chapter 4, Micheal Giles and Douglas Gatlin found that financial considerations were the most determinative of whether white consumers of court-ordered busing actually avoided sending their children to integrated schools.[37] These studies indicate the value of using utility theory to explain judicial impact. Moreover, they suggest the importance of economic factors over psychological factors in utility calculations, when the two clash. Of course, the comparison of psychological and economic factors cannot be rigorous because one cannot quantify most psychological values in terms of dollars and cents.

It seems, however, that utility theory is most valuable as an explanatory device when it is applied to decisions whose impact is primarily economic. Courts make many such decisions in fields such as labor relations, antitrust, and public utility regulation, and there is no reason political scientists cannot apply this theory in assessing the reactions of various populations to such decisions. In the short term at least, the most fruitful application of utility theory is likely to be in the realm of economic or other quantifiable variables. Combining the psychological and economic roots of utility theory is conceptually acceptable, but it has the drawback of making empirical tests difficult.

In some instances it is very difficult to test whether individuals engage in a series of cost-benefit calculations after a judicial decision; but Stover and Brown propose another hypothesis which is both important and testable. They observe that focusing on the cost-benefit inequality (p. 200) forces us to consider the range of factors that may influence compliance and that may be manipulated to achieve behavioral change. According to these researchers, as an institution's ability to manipulate terms in the inequality increases, its influence over reactions will also increase. The authors suggest that, unlike legislatures, courts have little control over the costs of noncompliance with their own general policies. Nor do courts have the same ability to dispense benefits to or limit the costs of those who do comply. In a general sense, then, courts are less likely than legislatures to achieve changes in behavior, especially if they limit themselves only to issuing orders and perform little or no follow-up.[38]

The main focus of explicit utility theory and research has been on explaining compliance/noncompliance decisions. Thus to date the theory has been applied almost exclusively to the implementing population, largely because social scientists with a theoretical and empirical orientation have been more interested in explaining compliance than in any other aspects of impact. Conceptually, however, there is no reason to limit utility theory to the implementing population. In fact, we have touched on the notion of utility (without using the term) in our chapters describing the other populations. Lower court judges, we noted in Chapter 2, are governed in part by a concern for their professional reputation and their social and political status in their local area. In Chapter 4 we discussed the Florida Atlantic University study, which showed that white parents' reactions to busing orders were influenced to a considerable degree by the cost of alternatives. And some members of the secondary population, such as members of Congress, may base their response behavior on a political calculation of votes to be gained or lost. Indeed, to the extent that the psychological aspects of utility theory are considered, utility theory could be applicable to all populations because of its universal explanatory nature. But even if utility theory is limited to its economic aspects or to aspects that are measurable in some manner, utility theory obviously has a good deal of applicability to the consumer population and some applicability to the interpreting and secondary populations. Social scientists need to expand on the heretofore narrow focus of the theory.

COMMUNICATIONS THEORY

The communication of judicial decisions is a haphazard, multi-stage process which, according to many observers, inadequately informs others in the political system about the decisions or the expectations of the courts. Stephen Wasby, for example, found that police officers learn of judicial decisions from a variety of sources, including personal friends, the general media (considered ineffective sources), and training sessions and bulletins from law enforcement agencies (considered very effective communications channels).[39] Wasby's analysis of communications channels from the Supreme Court to local police officers found that information came from many sources and passed through several levels of the interpreting and implementing populations. Were we to include the secondary and consumer populations as sources of information, the process would be even more complex.

The term *theory* as applied to the communications that link judicial decisions with their consequences is something of a misnomer. There is no overarching or well-recognized theory. Rather, we have a number of separate propositions about the relationship between the nature of the communication of a judicial policy and the responses to that policy. Nonetheless, researchers have given considerable attention to various aspects of the communication of judicial decisions, and it is reasonable to assume that the communicative process has particular effects on the chain of events following a judicial decision.

Existing research establishes that sources and levels of information vary from population to population, and from group to group within the respective populations. We have noted some of these variations in the previous chapters. However, it is less clear whether levels or sources of information are related to variations in responses to judicial policies.

There are two features of the communications process that affect responses to judicial decisions.[40] First, the context of the decision itself can be important, since some responses may be affected not only by what the decision is, but also by how it is "packaged." Second, the channels through which the decision is communicated will affect how people perceive the message. Each of these features of the process lends itself to hypotheses, which we discuss below.

Context of the Decision

How a court chooses to announce a policy can be very important to the reception of the policy by affected groups. Speaking primarily of compliance with Supreme Court decisions, G. Alan Tarr suggests that responses may be "a function of the perceived finality of the standards enunciated by the Supreme Court, the clarity of those standards, and the persuasiveness of the Court's justification of its decisions."[41] This perspective, shared by many legal scholars, holds that responses to a Supreme Court decision are affected by the persuasiveness of the opinion announcing the decision, and is analogous to the belief that a president must be persuasive to be effective.[42] What constitutes a final, clear, and persuasive policy is not, however, easily identified.

Tarr suggests that the perception of finality of a policy is governed by three factors. First, the level of support for the policy on the court may be important. If the policy is announced with only minimal support, a five-to-four vote on the Supreme Court, for example, then changes or modifications in policy could occur with changes in personnel or even changes in the policy preferences of one justice. If support for a policy is marginal, its finality is open to question and its implementation may be ineffective. In the early 1970s the future of *Miranda* looked doubtful after President Richard Nixon appointed four conservative justices to the Supreme Court. Many judges, prosecutors, and police officers expected *Miranda* to be overruled shortly and did not worry too much about its implementation. However, the Court eventually chose to retain the basic *Miranda* policy. Second, finality may be evident from the degree to which the policy has been enforced and applied by a court in the past. Longstanding policies and those to which a court has expressed a firm commitment will be seen as more permanent than will novel policies or older ones that have been questioned or surrounded with exceptions. For instance, in the 1970s the Supreme Court began questioning or making exceptions to the exclusionary rule in search and seizure cases (*Bivens v. Six Unknown Named Federal Narcotics Agents*, 1971; *United States v. Calandra*, 1974; *Stone v. Powell*, 1976), and the rule's viability is more uncertain now than it was 15 or 20 years ago. Third, the perception of finality may be affected by whether a decision is subsequently used by a court to support other decisions. Continued use of a particular decision or standard by the court would demonstrate a commitment to the particular policy involved, thus indicating a sense of closure regarding the policy. Conversely, failure to mention the decision again leaves its finality uncertain.[43]

The clarity of a decision refers most basically to whether there are doubts about what is to be done. Clear decisions minimize the leeway available to the interpreting and implementing populations, so that it is more difficult for someone, especially a judge, to argue that the decision means something the court did not intend. Clarity also provides a basis for "sanctions such as strongly critical [judicial] opinions" against noncompliant judges.[44] While clear opinions are not more likely to lead to acceptance and positive responses, such opinions do set forth the expectations for affected groups. Unless those expectations are clearly articulated, implementors will not know what behavior is called for and interpreters will not know how to evaluate responses that are made. For example, the police and other criminal justice officials were uncertain about what behavior was required after *Escobedo v. Illinois* (1964), but their uncertainty was erased in the *Miranda* decision, which set forth precisely what the police were to do upon arresting a criminal suspect. Many people may have disliked *Miranda,* but few have misunderstood it.

Clear decisions not only minimize leeway, they also minimize distortion in the communication of the decision to relevant groups. Richard Johnson points out, for example, that "behavior congruent with the message depends in large measure upon whether the ruling is received in a relatively undistorted state by those who are affected." [45] Thus, for those in the zone of indifference a clear statement of expectations is more likely to be met with acceptance and positive responses than one that is ambiguous. And for those who are not inclined to obey a court policy, a clear policy statement provides a standard against which nonacceptance or noncompliance can be evaluated and perhaps sanctioned.

The persuasiveness of a judicial opinion refers both to the quality of the arguments and to other devices that may be included to induce acceptance. Presumably a persuasive argument would be logically sound and, as applicable, abide by the canons of judicial construction, be supported by demonstrable historical or social facts, be buttressed by precedent, show proper deference to constitutional principles— such as separation of powers or federalism—and be felicitously written. In short, it should make "construction of contrary legal arguments more difficult and render those arguments less likely to gain other adherents." [46] Even within these parameters, a persuasive decision is not always easily identified. However, some decisions are widely viewed as unpersuasive. Justice Harry Blackmun's opinion in *Roe v. Wade* (1973) was criticized for its unconvincing qualities by many who had no quarrel with the Court's abortion policy. In the obscenity area, the Supreme Court has occasionally abandoned even minimal efforts at persuasion (see *Redrup v. New York,* 1967).

In addition to constructing quality arguments, a majority opinion can include incentives and disincentives that affect acceptance and compliance. These could include references to individual or societal rewards to be gained by compliance or speculation about the unpleasant consequences that may result from noncompliance.[47] At times, incentives can affect subsequent behavior to a far greater extent than logic. *Mapp* and *Miranda* are classic examples. Although the police may not be persuaded of the rightness of these decisions, they stand in danger of losing convictions when they violate their commands. The disincentives announced in these opinions is what makes them controversial; earlier Supreme Court admonitions to the police to restrain their behavior were largely ignored.

While it is reasonable to believe that final, clear, and persuasive decisions receive greater compliance than those lacking such qualities, scattered research indicates otherwise. Studying state court reactions to a series of religion decisions by the Supreme Court, Tarr found no such relationship. By way of explanation, Tarr notes that knowledge about court decisions is fairly low among the general population, and he believes there is little reason to think that judges are any better informed about the policies, especially in regard to the quality of the opinions. Tarr believes that few judges actually read an entire Court opinion, much less pay attention to the details that could indicate some measure of finality, clarity, or persuasiveness.[48]

Additional support for this negative conclusion is provided by the research of Charles Johnson on treatments of over 300 Supreme Court decisions by lower federal courts. His analysis related positive and negative treatments by these lower courts to such attributes as size of the majority, number of dissenting opinions, and whether the chief justice authored the majority opinion. Less than 5 percent of the variance in lower court reactions was accounted for by any of these indicators of finality or persuasiveness.[49] While Tarr's suggestion that judges do not read higher court opinions very carefully has not been fully substantiated, it may be that the substance of the decision is more important as a determinant of reactions than is the way it is phrased, especially beyond the interpreting population.

Channel of the Communication

In reviewing legitimacy theory, we have already seen how people's reactions can depend upon the perceived legitimacy of the court making the policy. However, except for the interpreting population, most people do not obtain their information directly from the originating court. The policy, rather, is mediated through some channel—perhaps a lower court, perhaps a newspaper article or television news report, or perhaps by word of mouth from a lawyer, friend, or employer.

In considering the effects of the communications process, our basic concerns are: Who transmitted the message? What was its content? Was it received by the affected groups in a relatively unaltered state? Clearly, some of the features we discussed earlier affect these concerns. For example, it is obviously easier to transmit a clear, unambiguous policy statement than one characterized by poor writing or multiple opinions. However, even the same decision may receive different treatments from different sources. Although few have proposed theories on this matter, some scholars believe that different responses are likely to follow when different channels are used to send the same message because distortions are introduced, producing different messages at the end of the process.

Knowledge received on a second- or thirdhand basis is subject to distortion—often unconscious and unintended—by those in the channel from origin to destination. Such distortion is often a function of *selective perceptions;* that is, people within the channel pay attention to the aspects of a decision that affect them and ignore those that appear to be inapplicable to them or too difficult to comprehend. A recipient of this distorted version of the decision may, in turn, apply a different selective perception to it so that a third recipient has a doubly distorted message.

News reports, an essential source of information in our society, can be misleading. By their nature the media tend to simplify things, and their reporting of court decisions is no exception. Reports often concentrate on who won or lost the decision and ignore the court's rationale, which is essential to the impact of the decision; at best, a lengthy opinion will be condensed into a few sentences. Similarly, there is often a tendency on the part of the media to exaggerate the potential consequences of decisions. Or, contrariwise, some important Supreme Court decisions may be virtually ignored if they occur— along with so many others—at the end of the Court's term in June, or if they happen to be announced when an international or domestic crisis is dominating the news.[50]

Oral communication is subject to even greater distortion. Lawyers are perhaps the main channel of dissemination of word-of-mouth communications. Being busy, lawyers often read decisions hastily and only with a view of a particular client's interest in mind. Thus, the client (or others to whom the attorney talks) may receive a narrow perspective on the decision—a perspective that may emphasize his or her hopes or fears and that may distort the decision as it is passed on. Interest groups, such as environmental or civil rights organizations, can also exaggerate the potential consequences of decisions in their internal communications to members.

Distortion is most likely to occur when the channel has a particular bias. Recalling the multitude of sources of information for law enforcement officials we mentioned earlier, it seems reasonable to suggest that the police may not have obtained unbiased information about criminal justice decisions, which, of course, would affect their responses to those decisions. An additional factor in the relationship between sources and responses is attentiveness to the media. For example, Richard Johnson reports that while the headlines reporting the *Schempp* decision were largely negative, "the conscientious observer had ample opportunity to be appraised of the Court's policies and the reasoning behind them." But "the more casual observer might have received a partial and somewhat distorted view of what the Court had said [and if he] had a commitment on the issue, . . . he could selectively expose himself to materials which would tend to reinforce his commitment." [51]

Individual policy preferences may lead people to select different sources of information. Existing research has not yet clearly identified the relationship between these sources and the individuals' eventual reactions. Milner reports that the sources and levels of information varied between four Wisconsin communities; the most professional police department depended on other law enforcement agencies, such as the FBI, as sources of information. However, while departments relied on different sources of information and some of that information gave different accounts of the Court's expectations regarding *Miranda,* the behavioral responses of police in each of the communities did not differ dramatically. [52]

Distortion of the nature of a judicial decision can be minor and relatively harmless, but it can sometimes produce serious misperceptions about the nature of a court decision—especially when the distortion is reinforced by cognitive dissonance or by vague or ambivalent phrases in the court's opinion. We have already noted in Chapter 3 that many of Kenneth Dolbeare and Phillip Hammond's rural respondents believed the school prayer decision allowed voluntary, organized prayer in the classroom. [53] Similarly, most juvenile judges in rural Kentucky had only the haziest notions of the provisions of *In re Gault* (1967)—the Supreme Court's most important juvenile justice decision. [54] It is not clear where these respondents received their information from, but it is clear that they did not obtain it from reading the relevant Supreme Court decisions.

ORGANIZATIONAL THEORIES

Most judicial policies are implemented through organizations. Individuals may make acceptance and compliance decisions, but they do so in the context of organizational goals and policies. Moreover, judicial policies are most often implemented by public organizations (such as police departments, school systems, and welfare departments) or by quasi-public organizations (such as hospitals and labor unions). All these organizations are subject to several different policies from within government—for example, from Congress, state legislatures, and high-level agencies. As Martin Shapiro argued some years ago, a court is just another government agency trying to implement a preferred policy, and it must compete with other agencies, which often prefer different policies.[55] In practice this means that organizations are not likely to accord judicial policies any special consideration unless the courts can bring special pressures to bear. Thus courts must act with appropriate knowledge and fore-thought if they are to be successful—especially if they are trying to induce a significant change in organizational behavior. As a student note in the *Yale Law Review* put it, courts must be aware that "the implementation of new policies and procedures often involves the behavior of public bureaucracies: a plan will be successful largely to the extent to which the court appreciates the particular characteristics of the organization it is scrutinizing." [56]

The study of organizational behavior and of how public policies are implemented by organizations is a common feature of such disciplines as political science, sociology, and public administration. While few studies have focused on the implementation of judicial policies, there is reason to believe that organizational theories are applicable to court-made policies. This point is made explicitly by Lawrence Baum, who argues that judicial impact scholars should treat the implementation of court decisions not as a unique phenomenon, but as a variant of how all public policies are carried out. Baum goes on to note that many public policies are only partially implemented, and that they have various degrees of success in accomplishing their goals. We should not expect judicial policies to fare any better, he argues; a 100 percent compliance or success rate is an unrealistic expectation.[57]

Of course, the relationship between the courts and the implementing organizations is not exactly the same as that between legislative bodies or executives and such agencies. Courts have little in the way of monetary sanctions or incentives and a very limited ability to monitor the day-to-day activities of an implementing organization. On the other hand, they have some special weapons, such as the injunction and the ability to assess liability. At any rate, in this section we shall look at how two basic categories of organizational theories, policy tensions and organizational inertia, apply to judicial impact and then take a brief look at how some judicial policies requiring positive actions by an agency are implemented in light of organizational constraints.

Policy Tensions

If an organization realizes that it is not serving its constituents or customers satisfactorily and that this is costing it support or profits, then the organization faces a "performance gap" and it will look for ways to improve services.[58] However, Charles Johnson has pointed out that when an external actor, such as a court, decides that the agency is performing inadequately (for example, contrary to the law or the Constitution), change in the organization does not follow these classic lines. Since the organization is likely to be committed to its defined goals and preferences, which differ from the judicial policy, *and* since it is legally bound to follow a court decision, the agency is caught between two opposing forces. The tension between these two forces substantially affects the agency's responses. These forces are: "a commitment to agency programs and [the] threat of sanctions or loss of resources if changes are not made in those programs." Under such circumstances, "the agency is expected to preserve existing programs to the extent that this is possible." [59] An intervening factor that may affect agency responses is whether the agency has the resources to resist orders to change, pay for the required changes, or influence the court to the extent that the court moderates or relinquishes its demand for change.

Johnson provides an illustration of this explanation for responses to judicial decisions in a figure (our Figure 6.1), which "represents a continuum of alternative programs constituting a single dimension of policy." [60] In this figure, point A represents the present program of the agency that has been overruled by a judicial decision; point B represents the programs the court may wish the agency to adopt; and points C^1, C^2, and C^3 represent alternatives the agency might consider and adopt. Under certain circumstances, the agency may choose to remain with the original program (point A), for example, if the agency is highly committed to a program, if it believes the risks of enforcement or sanctions are reasonably low, or if the agency believes it has sufficient resources to resist court efforts to require change. Another reason for remaining at point A may be that the agency simply cannot financially afford to change its policies or practices. On the other hand, if the agency is not highly committed to the program; if the court's policy is not perceived as endangering the program significantly; if risks or sanctions are too great for the agency; or if resources are insufficient to resist change but sufficient to support it, then movement to alternatives near point B would be likely.

The most likely outcome of the circumstances anticipated by this theory is that the agency will not try to retain the status quo,

Policy gap between agency and the court

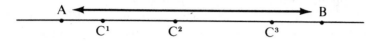

Where   A = Policy preference of agency
         B = Policy preference of court
         C^i = Policy alternatives after a court decision

Figure 6.1   Organizational policy choices that lead to policy tensions.

nor will it change completely to the court's policy preference. The compromise is likely to be at a point C^i, the particular location of which is a function of the three factors mentioned above: commitment, perception of threat from the court, and resources for resistance. If commitment is high, external pressures and threat are low, and resources for resistance are low, then the agency may respond by moving only slightly beyond point A. If the reverse is true, then movement goes far toward point B.

Martin Shapiro's study of a long-running policy clash between the Patent Office and the Supreme Court illustrates this process well.[61] Put briefly, the Court believed the Patent Office's standards for what constituted an invention were too lenient—that many patents were granted for items that lacked an innovative idea or were based on ideas already in the common domain. Over the years the Court invalidated many patents that it believed were too loosely granted, but it lacked the ability and resources to get the Patent Office to change its general policy. After all, the Court did not itself make initial judgments about patent applications, nor did the situation permit it to give precise, detailed commands about the standards by which the applications should be judged. Shapiro tells us:

> ... the Patent Office had clearly won the war since it continued its operational policies unchanged in the face of Supreme Court opposition. . . . [It makes little] difference that the highest court would invalidate when it hardly ever sees a patent so long as it cannot get the Patent Office to invalidate at the point where the mass of patent policy decisions are made, the point of application.[62]

In short, the situation gave the agency the resources for resistance and denied the Court the ability to put much pressure on the recalcitrant organization.

On the other hand, Shapiro's study of the Federal Power Commission (FPC) in the 1950s illustrates a situation where considerable judicial control of agency policy was possible. Because of loopholes and ambiguous statutory language, the FPC's ability to make policies regulating the price and uses of natural gas was tenuous. Shapiro shows how the Supreme Court was able to interpret statutes to widen somewhat the FPC's power to make natural gas policy. The Court still held the leash and interpreted laws to steer the FPC's expanded power in directions it preferred. Here the Court's power to interpret statutes was a resource the agency desperately needed.[63]

Inertia in Organizations

The idea that organizations develop inertial forces behind their policies and practices is not a new one. Since inertia plays an important role in most organizational theories, it deserves a closer look. The sources of inertia in organizations are several, and judicial impact scholars have focused on two broad categories: sources that are system based and sources that relate to individuals who occupy various positions within the organization.

System-Based Inertia. Most organizations are structured to carry out a particular mission or to attain a particular set of goals. Police departments, for example, are devoted to the maintenance of order and law; school systems try to transfer cognitive skills and cultural values from one generation to another. Normally, organization officials will come to accept and defend the mission or goal of the organization and behave accordingly. The impact of these goals and the commitment of officials to them may be substantial when officials are considering responses to judicial decisions. One commentator notes, "In an organization that has successfully instilled a sense of mission, those who believe in the bureaucracy's mission are likely to resist judicial efforts to alter it." [64] Such beliefs are inertial—that is, they are difficult to overcome, even when support from clientele groups or other government agencies is weak and an adverse judicial policy has been handed down.

The adverse impact that organizational goals and missions may have on the implementation of judicial decisions is perhaps best shown in the area of criminal justice. Several reports of police resistance to court decisions expanding suspects' rights may be found in the literature (see Chapter 3); there is considerable conflict between the roles a police officer assumes as protector of law and order and as protector of the rights of defendants. In many instances

214

these two roles are not compatible, and police officers are understandably troubled when they must implement such decisions as *Mapp* and *Miranda.*

There is more to inertia than commitment to organizational policies. Organizations also develop subsidiary goals, such as saving money, protecting their clientele, maintaining their prestige, avoiding excessive work, and more generally continuing their existence without a fundamental change in function or activities. Judicial decisions that threaten the status quo run up against a reluctance to change—in other words, inertia. For example, in the 1970s the Supreme Court held that public schools could not suspend students and that welfare agencies could not terminate benefits without a hearing (*Goss v. Lopez,* 1975; *Goldberg v. Kelly,* 1970). Hearings can be quite time consuming. Accordingly, school systems and welfare agencies have developed mechanisms for holding "quickie" or pro forma hearings and for discouraging clients from requesting full-blown hearings. Similarly, several state alcoholic beverage control agencies have resisted a Supreme Court decision that eliminated their authority to establish minimum fair trade prices for the sale of liquor (*California Liquor Dealers v. Midcal Aluminum,* 1980). Obviously, this decision eliminates one of the agencies' main functions and in the process both lowers their prestige and hurts their clientele. For that matter, the continuation of prayers and other religious practices, at least as reported by Dolbeare and Hammond, is to a large extent attributable to organizational inertia.[65]

Inertia from Individual Commitments. Another source of inertia arises from the individual commitments and preferences of organizational personnel. Baum highlights some of these preferences. Although he specifically addresses the responses of judges, his comments are equally applicable to agency officials. Baum hypothesizes that "the more subordinates' interests are favored by faithful implementation of appellate decisions, the more faithful their implementation will be." Baum offers two reasons for such a relationship. First, there are "psychic and material costs of policy change," and resistance is likely to be a function of the degree to which the affected policies or behavior are "institutionalized." Second, when no particular policy exists in an area, subordinates will "tend to adopt policies which maximize their interests." However, when a court comes along and requires that they abandon "the interest-maximizing policies, then the court is likely to be resisted."[66] Thus, if an employee receives some material or psychic gain from his or her behavior, then continuing with that behavior is likely to be in his or her interest even if a court has said that the behavior must change.

It is difficult to separate the effects of individual attitudes from organizationally induced commitments to the organization's mission and goals. However, a few studies apparently have done so, revealing that even if the organization's goals and mission have been altered to be consistent with the court decision, individual commitments may still control behavorial responses to a judicial policy. Teachers in some school systems, for example, conducted certain religious exercises despite rules to the contrary, and some police officers continued to act as though the Supreme Court had not issued rulings in cases such as *Mapp* and *Miranda.* Nevertheless, it is likely that where agency policy is altered to be consistent with the court policy, then the appropriate behavioral responses are likely to be made, overriding individual preferences among organizational personnel.

The explanatory power of the concept of inertia extends beyond organizational behavior. For example, despite the Supreme Court's decisions limiting the ability of professional associations to prohibit public advertisements, few professionals have availed themselves of this new freedom. Lawyers and physicians, for example, still rarely run ads in local newspapers, and those who do are often looked upon with skepticism by the public and disdain by fellow professionals. In short, even when the courts legitimize some activity, change does not necessarily follow.

While inertia in organizations may be a powerful force, it is not insurmountable. It can be overcome by various judicial sanctions. The role of sanctions is usually addressed in two contexts: the perceived authority of the policy maker and the actual use of sanctions to encourage compliant behavior. The first context is an application of legitimacy theory to the organization or individuals responding to the judicial decision, and the second involves the variety of sanctions and the likelihood of their use by external actors to move the organization toward a policy or practice consistent with the court decision.

As we have noted, the perceived legitimacy of a policy maker can affect how individuals respond to court decisions. On this subject Baum writes, "Subordinates' interests and preferences often incline them against obedience to higher officials, but the authority which they attach to those officials' decisions tends to counteract these centrifugal tendencies and to provide an important motivation for faithful implementation." [67] We have already discussed legitimacy theory, and there is no point in reviewing it here. Suffice it to say that judicial claims to legitimacy constitute a major source of power, though the applicability of legitimacy to any given organizational situation can vary considerably.

In addition to being perceived as legitimate, most courts have an array of tools they may employ to enforce their actions. However, as Baum points out, some sanctions, such as selective hiring or firing of recalcitrant subordinates, are not generally available to judicial bodies. Thus, while courts possess such powers as the injunction (including contempt authority) or the ability to assess damages, these powers are "far from overwhelming." [68] Moreover, courts are often reluctant to use extreme sanctions, such as contempt citations or heavy fines, and final judgments can often be delayed for years through appeals. In sum, such sanctions are generally sufficient to overcome inertial forces when they are limited or localized and a plaintiff is willing to pursue the matter vigorously, but they are less successful when inertia is widespread and the plaintiff is not willing or able to press for fundamental changes. The clear findings of both Rodgers and Bullock's and of Giles's studies are that judicial sanctions themselves were not sufficient to overcome inertial resistance to desegregation by southern school systems; segregation collapsed only when federal executive agencies actively pursued change and developed their own extrajudicial sanctions. [69]

Positive Policies, Judicial Capabilities, and Organizational Theories

Until recently most court decisions affecting organizational behavior were restrictive—that is, the court put limits on a business or agency by telling it that it could not do something it wanted to do. Other decisions prescribed procedural steps that organizations had to follow in carrying out their policies, for example, due process requirements such as holding hearings or considering certain types of evidence. Courts seldom dictated in any positive manner the substantive policies that agencies had to carry out.

In the last two decades or so, this has changed. While courts still often make decisions in the traditional mold, they are coming more and more to require organizations to carry out positive, substantive policies. Often the court will spell out in considerable detail what the agency must do. *Miranda* was perhaps the first major such instance of positive substantive policy making, although its burden on police time and resources was mild and, as we saw in Chapter 4, its impact on police functioning was minimal. But following *Swann v. Charlotte-Mecklenburg County Board of Education* (1971), federal district courts began issuing detailed orders regarding crosstown busing, racial ratios among teachers and pupils, curriculum offerings, and other features of the school system thought necessary to achieve desegregation. Federal district courts also began issuing detailed orders to end discrimination in employment and housing. In the 1970s the federal courts began requiring states and localities to improve conditions in penitentiaries, mental hospitals, halfway houses, and other institutions. In addressing prison conditions, for instance, courts would often prescribe such things as the minimum number of square feet of cell space to which an inmate was entitled, the minimum dietary and exercise requirements, and the details of a vocational rehabilitation program. Many states, in fact, had to reduce their prison population in order to meet the judicially imposed requirements. Others dramatically increased appropriations to build new prisons or renovate old ones. State courts also joined in the trend to making positive, substantive policy by reforming tax assessment policies or the financing of public schools.

Much of the discussion over this new type of judicial policy making focuses on the proper role of the courts—the merits of judicial activism versus judicial restraint—and is beyond the scope of this book. Some of the discussion, however, takes the position that courts cannot successfully engage in positive, substantive policy making. The leading proponents of this position are perhaps Donald Horowitz and Nathan Glazer.[70] They argue that courts by their very nature lack the capacity to supervise agencies closely enough to ensure compliance in spirit as well as in letter, and that, moreover, the substitution of policies made by courts for those made by legislators or agency professionals will have serious unintended consequences for society generally and an agency's clientele in particular. For example, Horowitz points out that the District of Columbia school board complied with a court order to equalize teacher-per-pupil expenditures at each school by transferring the teachers who were most easily moved, regardless of the schools' subject area needs. And when Alabama had to increase its expenditures on mental hospitals, much of the money came from funds that would have been spent on prisons and welfare.

Little real theory has been yet advanced about the limits or consequences of the courts' making positive, substantive policy. The position that courts are exceeding their capabilities by doing so is largely drawn from particular experiences or based upon speculation. But Glazer has advanced five "hypotheses" that are certainly open to empirical testing.[71] The new trend in judicial policy making, he believes,

1. Will reduce agency administrators' and case workers' discretion and responsibility
2. Will reduce agencies' authority
3. Will give greater weight to theoretical considerations than to practical ones
4. Will give greater weight to abstract speculations and social science research in the formulation of policy
5. Will increase the power of the legal profession in the formulation of policy

The verdict on the limits of judicial capability is not yet in. Certainly there have been some judicial successes. Richard Lehne in his book *The Quest for Justice* details how the New Jersey Supreme Court virtually compelled the state legislature to pass an income tax to enhance the financing of an underfunded public school system.[72] Other policies are subject to debate. We have already discussed in Chapter 4 the scholarly dispute over the side effects, such as white flight, of court-ordered busing. Similar debates rage on *Miranda* and *Mapp*. And certainly there have been a few failures. For instance, by reducing taxes legislative bodies have often thwarted the intended impact (enhanced revenues for education) of court-ordered tax assessment reforms.

What is clear is that as courts continue to make positive, substantive policies, scholars will need to develop and test theories that explain when courts are capable of successfully imposing these policies on bureaucratic organizations and when they are not.

ENVIRONMENTAL THEORIES

In our review of the explanations for reactions to judicial decisions among the various populations we have frequently pointed to the apparent importance of forces or influences surrounding the responding population. These include the opinion of the local community, the opinion of local elites, and the prevailing traditions of the community. All of these factors are external to the respondents; that is, they are in the environment of the actors, groups, or populations affected by the judicial policy. In Chapter 2 we noted the strong influence of local segregationist sentiment on federal district judges in the South; likewise, we have several times discussed Dolbeare and Hammond's research showing how elites and local traditions in the towns they studied combined to forestall compliance with the school prayer decisions by teachers and administrators.

The underlying assumption of such research is that environmental pressures shape or influence reactions to judicial policies. Unfortunately, we have no well-developed theories to predict either when environmental factors (as compared to personal or communications factors) will be important or what particular environmental factors will be the most important in accounting for the reactions.

To the extent one can identify a theory concerning these environmental factors, the discussion of "triggering" factors by Dolbeare and Hammond offers a potentially useful theoretical perspective. After finding that none of the school systems they studied had actually stopped schoolhouse religious activities, Dolbeare and Hammond argue that compliance "requires some decisive trigger." In this case, the trigger could have been "clear cues from state enforcement authorities, strong determination on the part of key local actors, . . . or thick-skinned commitment on the part of local citizens." [73] Positive responses by any of these actors, they believe, could have had an effect on the local systems; but since no actions were taken, nothing was done by any of the local school systems.

Dolbeare and Hammond are referring to compliance, but the same argument can be made in regard to negative responses to a judicial decision. Much of the resistance to civil rights decisions and laws was undoubtedly triggered by negative statements by governors, U.S. senators, and others who did not like the *Brown* or later desegregation decisions. Likewise, police departments seemed readier to resist *Mapp v. Ohio* if they were supported by a "law and order" mayor or city council.[74] Viewed from this perspective, the basic thesis is that groups responding to a judicial decision are directly affected by the direction and nature of environmental pressures prompted by the decision. While the most attention has been focused on the interpreting and implementing populations, presumably these triggers also affect decisions in the consumer and secondary populations. Indeed, in Chapter 5, we saw that Congress's responses to Supreme Court decisions were often triggered by constituent reactions.

At least two major assumptions underpin an environmental trigger theory of judicial impact. The first assumption is that if environmental pressures are influential, then they must first be received or perceived by the responding population. That is, a judge, school administrator, student, or other actor must first be aware of environmental pressures before responding to those pressures in reacting to a Court decision. Evidence regarding the degree to which individuals are aware of environmental pressures concerning judicial policies is limited and mixed. In controversial policy areas, environmental pressures stemming from public opinion or even elite opinion seem to be quite apparent to the judges and public officials who must implement the policy. Robert Crain tells us that local judges and school board members in New Orleans knew of southern attitudes toward desegregation following *Brown,* and it is hardly surprising that environmental factors had such a strong impact on their behavior.[75] Attitudes toward issues such as prayers in the schools or the exclusionary rule may be more varied, especially in heterogeneous communities, and triggering may depend upon which group makes the most noise or who the individual generally looks to for guidance. For policies with low visibility, there may be no triggering at all.

The second assumption is that responding groups and populations are relatively open to and potentially influenced by these forces. Of course, responding populations are not always open to environmental pressures. Judges, for example, are supposed to decide matters before them only on the basis of the relevant facts and law. We noted in Chapter 2 that for some judges environmental pressures are influential, but often judges are unwilling to be influenced by outside pressures. Some organizations have also been successful in insulating themselves from environmental pressures. Jon R. Bond and Charles A. Johnson found that few hospitals included community representatives in discussions about their abortion policy following *Roe v. Wade.*[76] By design or by accident, some responding groups that could be affected by environmental pressures are not so affected because those pressures either are unnoticed or are effectively blocked.

SUMMARY

The development and testing of theories are essential parts of social science research, for only with theories can scholars explain what they have observed and decide where to proceed with further research. In this chapter we have reviewed nine major theoretical perspectives that we believe can be tested empirically in regard to judicial impact. These theories have for the most part been borrowed from other social sciences or from other branches of political science. Table 6.1 summarizes aspects of each of the nine theories: to what extent the theory has been applied to a population in the literature and whether the theory has been supported by research.

The entries in Table 6.1 are, of course, rough and somewhat subjective approximations, but the table provides a basic summary of the status of the theories relative to the various populations. It is clear that the theories are most often discussed in relation to the interpreting or implementing populations, especially the latter, where the

Table 6.1   Status of Theories of Judicial Impact

Theories	*Population*			
	Interpreting	Implementing	Consumer	Secondary
Psychological				
Legitimacy	*	*		*
Cognitive dissonance		+[a]		
Attitudinal	+[b]	+[c]/−[d]	+[e]	+[f]
Utility				
Psychological/ economic		+[g]	+[e]	
Communications				
Context	−[h]	*		
Channels	+[i]	+[j]/−[d]	*	
Organizational				
Tension	*	+[k]		
Inertia	+[l]	*	*	
Environmental				
Environmental trigger	+[m]	+[j]/−[n]	*	*

* = Theory discussed in the literature as relevant to the particular population, but no hypotheses specifically tested
+ = Theory supported by tests of hypotheses for specific populations
− = Theory not supported in tests of hypotheses for specific populations
+/− = Theory received mixed support in tests of hypotheses for specific populations
No entry = Theory not discussed in the literature as relevant to specific populations

[a] Muir, see note 17.   [b] Kathleen L. Barber, "Partisan Values in the Lower Courts: Reapportionment in Ohio and Michigan," *Case Western Reserve Law Review* 20 (1969): 401-416.   [c] R. Johnson, see note 5.   [d] Milner, see note 23.   [e] Giles and Gatlin, see note 37. [f] This relationship appears to be axiomatic and thus has not been the focus of empirical testing. As members of the secondary population have by definition no interpreting, implementing, or consuming roles, the presumption is that any reactions they have to judicial policies are motivated by their attitudes. [g] Rodgers and Bullock, see note 32.   [h] Tarr, see note 41.   [i] Canon and Kolson, see note 54.   [j] Dolbeare and Hammond, see note 55.   [k] Charles A. Johnson, "Judicial Decisions and Organizational Change: Some Theoretical and Empirical Notes on State Court Decisions and State Administrative Agencies," *Law and Society Review* 14 (1979): 27-56.   [l] Neil Romans, "The Role of State Supreme Courts in Judicial Impact Analysis," *Western Political Quarterly* 27 (1974): 38-59. [m] Micheal Giles and Thomas Walker, "Judicial Policy-Making and Southern School Segregation," *Journal of Politics* 37 (1975): 917-936.   [n] Bond and Johnson, see note 76.

literature has covered all nine theories. It is equally clear that most empirical research on the theories has been conducted largely on the interpreting and implementing populations. By contrast, the theories have been discussed considerably less often in relation to the consumer and secondary populations, and empirical tests here are quite infrequent. This contrast, though dramatic, is not necessarily surprising. A focus on the interpreting and implementing populations seems a natural beginning point for those interested in explaining the impact of judicial policies; and to some degree the smaller, more discernible populations make it easier to develop and test theories.

Table 6.1 also demonstrates that some theories have a broader applicability than others. As might be expected, attitudinal and environmental theories, which are the least well developed and rigorous, have been freely suggested as explanations for the responses of all populations. Indeed, not surprisingly, attitudes have been found to relate to responses in all four population categories, though contrary results have also occurred in research on the implementing population. On the other hand, cognitive dissonance may be limited to the implementing population. Similarly, organizational tension theory is largely limited to the interpreting and implementing populations (though it might apply to occasional instances in which organizations engage in disadvantageous consumption choices). Communications theories have been similarly limited to the interpreting and implementing populations, but there is no apparent reason why they could not be used to explain the behavior of consumer or secondary populations.

Some of the theories are more easily tested than others, a factor which may account for the lack of empirical tests for some theories. Attitudinal theory, which requires little more than correlational analysis, falls in the former category. So does utility theory, where the countervailing gains and losses are often easy to posit. On the other hand, it is difficult to make legitimacy theory operationally testable, especially for the interpreting and implementing populations. Organizational inertia is another concept that is difficult to measure, so tests of that theory are also difficult.

An important point not revealed in the summary table is the comparative strengths and weaknesses of the nine theories. For instance, both cognitive dissonance and utility theory have been found to explain the reactions of the implementing population, but we cannot determine which theory is stronger. Which theory prevails when they point in opposite directions? While various theories may have some role in explaining the reactions of people to judicial decisions, the explanatory power of some theories is likely to be greater than that of others. The task of future scholars is not only to provide research to fill in the cells of this table, but to develop a new table which assesses the comparative power of the theories within each population.

Unfortunately, research comparing theories is not likely to be done in the immediate future. Theory development in the judicial impact field is still in its infancy. Much remains to be done in giving the existing theories greater substance and in developing more sophisticated methods of testing them. But ultimately we need to have not only well-developed theories explaining reactions to judicial policies, but a well-developed understanding of how they interact.

NOTES

1. Gordon Patric, "The Impact of Court Decisions: Aftermath of the *McCullom Case*," *Journal of Public Law* 6 (Fall 1957): 455-464; Frank Sorauf, "*Zorach v. Clauson:* The Impact of a Supreme Court Decision," *American Political Science Review* 53 (September 1959): 777-791; and Walter Murphy, "Lower Court Checks on Supreme Court Power," *American Political Science Review* 53 (December 1959): 1017-1031.
2. Sheilah R. Koeppen, "Children and Compliance: A Comparative Analysis of Socialization Studies," in *Compliance and the Law,* ed. Samuel Krislov et al. (Beverly Hills: Sage, 1973), 161-180.
3. Seymour M. Lipset, *Political Man* (New York: Doubleday, 1960); and David Easton, *A Systems Analysis of Political Life* (New York: Wiley, 1965).
4. Alexander Bickel, *The Least Dangerous Branch* (Indianapolis: Bobbs-Merrill, 1962); Charles L. Black, *The People and the Court* (New York: Macmillan, 1960); Michael Petrick, "The Supreme Court and Authority Acceptance," *Western Political Quarterly* 31 (March 1968): 5-19.
5. Richard Johnson, *The Dynamics of Compliance* (Evanston, Ill.: Northwestern University Press, 1967), 27, 41.
6. Jerome Frank, *Law and the Modern Mind* (New York: Brentano, 1930). See also Max Lerner, "Constitution and Court as Symbols," *Yale Law Review* 46 (May 1937): 1290-1319.
7. Gregory Casey, "The Supreme Court and Myth: An Empirical Investigation," *Law and Society Review* 8 (Spring 1974), 386.
8. *United States v. Butler,* 297 U.S. 1 (1936) at 63.
9. Casey, "The Supreme Court and Myth," 388.
10. Stephen Wasby, *The Supreme Court in the Federal Judicial System* (New York: Holt, Rinehart and Winston, 1978), 234.
11. Walter Murphy and Joseph Tanenhaus, "Public Opinion and the United States Supreme Court," *Law and Society Review* 2 (May 1968): 359.

12. Casey, "The Supreme Court and Myth."
13. Kenneth Dolbeare, "The Public Views the Supreme Court," in *Law, Politics, and the Federal Courts,* ed. Herbert Jacob (Boston: Little, Brown, 1967), 194-212; and John Kessel, "Public Perceptions of the Supreme Court," *Midwest Journal of Political Science* 10 (May 1966): 167.
14. Dolbeare, "The Public Views the Supreme Court," 197-198.
15. David Adamany, "Legitimacy, Realigning Elections and the Supreme Court," *Wisconsin Law Review* 1973 (1973): 790-846.
16. David G. Lawrence, "Procedural Norms and Tolerance: A Reassessment," *American Political Science Review* 70 (March 1976): 80-100; see also Michael Corbett, *Political Tolerance in America* (New York: Longman, 1982), ch. 7.
17. Johnson, *The Dynamics of Compliance;* and William Muir, *Prayer in Public Schools* (Chicago: University of Chicago Press, 1967).
18. Johnson, *The Dynamics of Compliance,* 18.
19. Leon Festinger, *A Theory of Cognitive Dissonance* (Evanston, Ill.: Row, Peterson, 1957).
20. Muir, *Prayer in Public Schools,* 10.
21. Johnson, *The Dynamics of Compliance,* 19-20.
22. Dolbeare, "The Public Views the Supreme Court."
23. Neal Milner, *The Court and Local Law Enforcement* (Beverly Hills: Sage, 1971).
24. Robert Stover and Don Brown, "Understanding Compliance and Noncompliance with the Law: The Contributions of Utility Theory," *Social Science Quarterly* 56 (1975): 363-375; and Harrell R. Rodgers and Charles S. Bullock III, *Law and Social Change: Civil Rights Laws and Their Consequences* (New York: McGraw-Hill, 1972).
25. Jeremy Bentham, *An Introduction to the Principles of Morals and Legislation* (New York: Hafner, 1948).
26. Stover and Brown, "Understanding Compliance," 368.
27. Ibid., 369.
28. Ibid., 369-370.
29. Rodgers and Bullock, *Law and Social Change,* 4.
30. Ibid., 183-184.
31. Ibid., 184.
32. Harrell R. Rodgers and Charles Bullock III, *Coercion to Compliance* (Lexington, Mass.: Lexington Books, 1976), 69.
33. Ibid., 69-70.
34. Ibid., 70.
35. Richard Posner, *Economic Analysis of Law,* 2d ed. (Boston: Little, Brown, 1977).
36. Harrell R. Rodgers and Charles S. Bullock, "School Desegregation: A Multivariate Test of the Role of Law in Effectuating Social Change," *American Politics Quarterly* 4 (April 1976): 153-175.
37. Micheal Giles and Douglas Gatlin, "Mass Level Compliance with Public Policy: The Case of School Desegregation," *Journal of Politics* 42 (November 1980): 722-746.
38. Stover and Brown, "Understanding Compliance," 371-372.

39. Stephen Wasby, "The Communication of the Supreme Court's Criminal Procedures Decisions: A Preliminary Mapping," *Villanova Law Review* 18 (June 1973): 1086.
40. Johnson, *The Dynamics of Compliance*, 26.
41. G. Alan Tarr, *Judicial Impact and State Supreme Courts* (Lexington, Mass.: Lexington Books, 1977), 89.
42. See Richard Neustadt, *Presidential Power* (New York: Wiley, 1960).
43. Tarr, *Judicial Impact and State Supreme Courts*, 89-90.
44. Ibid., 91.
45. Johnson, *The Dynamics of Compliance*, 60.
46. Tarr, *Judicial Impact and State Supreme Courts*, 92.
47. Johnson, *The Dynamics of Compliance*, 42.
48. Tarr, *Judicial Impact and State Supreme Courts*, 102.
49. Charles A. Johnson, "Lower Court Reactions to Supreme Court Decisions: A Quantitative Examination," *American Journal of Political Science* 23 (November 1979): 792-804.
50. Chester Newland, "Press Coverage of the United States Supreme Court," *Western Political Quarterly* 17 (March 1964): 15-36; and David Grey, *The Supreme Court and the News Media* (Evanston, Ill.: Northwestern University Press, 1968).
51. Johnson, *The Dynamics of Compliance*, 95.
52. Milner, *The Court and Local Law Enforcement*, 219-220.
53. Kenneth M. Dolbeare and Phillip Hammond, *The School Prayer Decisions: From Court Policy to Local Practice* (Chicago: University of Chicago Press, 1971).
54. Bradley C. Canon and Kenneth Kolson, "Compliance With Gault in Rural America: The Case of Kentucky," *Journal of Family Law* 10 (Winter 1971): 300-326.
55. Martin Shapiro, *Law and Politics in the Supreme Court* (New York: Free Press, 1964).
56. Note, "Judicial Intervention and Organization Theory: Changing Bureaucratic Benavior and Policy," *Yale Law Journal* 89 (January 1980): 513-537.
57. Lawrence Baum, "Implementation of Judicial Decisions: An Organizational Analysis," *American Politics Quarterly* 4 (January 1976): 86-114.
58. James March and Herbert Simon, *Organizations* (New York: Wiley, 1958); and Anthony Downs, *Inside Bureaucracy* (Boston: Little, Brown, 1968).
59. Charles A. Johnson, "Judicial Decisions and Organizational Change," *Administration and Society* 11 (May 1979): 31-32.
60. Ibid.
61. Martin Shapiro, *The Supreme Court and Administrative Agencies* (New York: Macmillan, 1968), 143-226.
62. Ibid., 200.
63. Ibid., 227-261.
64. Note, "Judicial Intervention and Organization Theory," 523.
65. Dolbeare and Hammond, *The School Prayer Decisions*.
66. Baum, "Implementation of Judicial Decisions," 97, 98.
67. Ibid., 101.

68. Ibid., 105.
69. Rodgers and Bullock, "School Desegregation"; and Micheal Giles, "HEW versus the Federal Courts: A Comparison of School Desegregation Enforcement," *American Politics Quarterly* 3 (January 1975): 81-90.
70. Donald Horowitz, *The Courts and Social Policy* (Washington: Brookings Institution, 1977); and Nathan Glazer, "Should Judges Administer Social Services?" *The Public Interest* 50 (Winter 1978): 64-80.
71. Glazer, "Should Judges Administer Social Services?" 80.
72. Richard Lehne, *The Quest for Justice: The Politics of School Finance Reform* (New York: Longman, 1978).
73. Dolbeare and Hammond, *The School Prayer Decisions*, 139.
74. Bradley C. Canon, "Testing the Effectiveness of Civil Liberties Policies at the State and Federal Levels: The Case of the Exclusionary Rule," *American Politics Quarterly*, 5 (January 1977): 57-82.
75. Robert Crain et al., *The Politics of School Desegregation* (Chicago: Aldine, 1968).
76. Jon R. Bond and Charles A. Johnson, "Implementing a Permissive Policy: Hospital Abortion Services after *Roe v. Wade*," *American Journal of Political Science* (February 1982): 1-24.

CHAPTER SEVEN

The Impact of Judicial Decisions as Public Policy

Most people assume that judicial decisions have an important impact on the political, economic, and to some extent the social structure of the nation. Since the nineteenth century, scholars have written numerous books and articles focusing on the implications of various decisions and policies of the U.S. Supreme Court. In fact, as much scholarly work (if not more) has been written about the Supreme Court as about the president of the United States—which surely indicates that scholars believe that the high Court's decisions have a large effect on our public life. Politically active citizens, too, see the Supreme Court as having a powerful impact. Their belief is manifest in the campaigns against such Court actions as the desegregation decisions, the school prayer decisions, and the abortion decision. These grass-roots campaigns have been at least as broad and enduring as those relating to any congressional or presidential decision, and they certainly imply a perception of the Court as having a large impact on society.

Measurement of this presumed impact is not easy. As we saw in Chapter 4, much of the Court's influence is effected through permission and suggestion rather than through command. More important, the Court's decisions and policies interact with those of other government agencies. If Congress or state legislatures pass laws reinforcing a Supreme Court policy, is the impact attributable to the legislative or to the judicial body, or can credit be divided between them? Similarly, who gets the credit or the blame when Supreme

Court decisions complement those of Congress, state legislatures, or the president?

In the last several decades some scholars have tried to measure the Supreme Court's impact on American public policy. Some of their findings indicate that the Court's impact is not nearly so pervasive as many people presume. Needless to say, these findings and the methods from which they were derived have generated considerable discussion.

In the first section of this chapter we focus on these findings and the controversy surrounding them. We also discuss briefly the degree of impact that state supreme courts, state trial courts, and lower federal courts have on public policy. At times the lack of research and clear evidence forces us to infer the impact of a policy from its substance; in the rest of this book we have tried to probe and explain the exact nature of the impact of a decision, and we have pointed out that the impact cannot always be predicted from the substance of the court's opinion. But even though we may at times speculate, we believe it is essential to attempt a discussion of the courts' general impact on society.

To draw together some of the strands of discussion about policy impact from the entire book, in the second section of this chapter we make a brief overall assessment of the impact of the courts on four major policy areas: freedom of expression, criminal justice, equality in America, and regulation of the economy. We ask what kinds of decisions courts have made in these areas, how these decisions have tied in with those of other public agencies, and to what extent these decisions have had any real impact on public policy and behavior. Again, systematic investigation of these questions is scarce, and much of what we say will be speculative.

THE OVERALL IMPACT OF THE COURTS

The Supreme Court

As we have noted, measuring the overall impact of the Supreme Court is not an easy task; in some ways it is impossible. In order to have research and evidence available, we focus here on the impact of Court policies that have drawn substantial opposition from the nation's political institutions, particularly Congress. Obviously, such a focus does not tell the whole story of the Supreme Court's impact. We will not look at opposition from nonpolitical institutions, such as businesses, labor organizations, churches, and the like. Nor will we look at situations where the Court's policies are not seriously opposed.

Considerations of space, existing research, and measurability have more or less dictated our choice of focus. Moreover, we feel that the degree to which the Court prevails when in opposition to other political institutions is a strong test of how much impact it has in American society.

Finding Acts of Congress Unconstitutional. Throughout its history the Supreme Court has been viewed as a champion of political minorities. For its first century and a half the Court was seen as a bulwark for the propertied interests against populist majorities. More recently, the Court has been portrayed as the shield of the oppressed groups in society, championing their rights and liberties against invasion by overweening majorities. But regardless of whether the privileged or the underprivileged are the minority under consideration, the Court's function has commonly been seen as the protection of minority interests.

Not everyone believes that the Supreme Court is primarily a protector of minorities. Some argue that it changes positions with major shifts in the political winds. As Peter Finley Dunne's turn-of-the-century barroom philosopher, Mr. Dooley, remarked, "The Supreme Court follows the election returns." [1] However, the first empirical challenge to the presumption that the Supreme Court is a check on the other branches of government was advanced by Robert Dahl in 1957. [2] He argues that the perception of the Court as the protector of minorities of any type against an overriding majority is not very accurate. Instead, the Court is an integral part of the political majority and often assists in imposing the majority's will upon minorities.

Political majorities are those who elect the national lawmakers, Congress and the president. The main interests in the electorate are stable over long periods of time, and control of Congress and the presidency is based upon coalitions or alliances of these interests. Dahl calls a dominant coalition "the law-making majority." An example of law-making majority is the New Deal coalition forged by President Franklin D. Roosevelt. It consisted of such interests as the labor movement, big city political machines, ethnic and racial minorities, and the South. Similar successful coalitions were developed by presidents Jefferson, Jackson, and Lincoln and by the Republicans at the turn of the century; each coalition commanded national politics for a generation or more. Such an alliance eventually breaks up in the face of a crisis, like the Civil War or the Great Depression, and a new law-making majority develops after a short transitional period. [3]

The Supreme Court is normally in harmony with the law-making majority because its members are appointed by the president, who naturally appoints justices with similar political views to his own. On the average, a Supreme Court vacancy occurs every 22 months. Though a law-making majority just coming to power may face a potentially hostile Court, it should have a sympathetic one before a decade is out (and perhaps earlier, as there is likely to be a sympathetic justice or two already on the Court). Thus it follows that "the policy views dominant on the Court are never for long out of line with the policy views among the law-making majorities in the United States." [4] One way of testing this proposition is to look at cases where the Court has declared an important act of Congress unconstitutional and then determine whose policy has ultimately prevailed, the Court's or the law-making majority's. When Dahl made such a test, he excluded laws that had been voided more than four years after enactment because the particular law-making majority that had passed the measure might no longer exist or might no longer be particularly interested in the policy involved. Most major policies, he believes, would most likely be challenged within four years of adoption. Of course, only laws with policy implications for the law-making majority's program should be considered in the test. For the Supreme Court to strike down routine legislation concerning such matters as river navigation or Indian reservations is hardly a challenge to the powers that be. Admittedly, the distinction between important and unimportant laws is somewhat arbitrary, but doubtful cases can be resolved in favor of the important category.

Dahl found 23 instances in which the Supreme Court struck down an act of Congress important to the law-making majority within the four-year period. He also found that Congress ultimately prevailed in 17 of these instances—or 74 percent of the time. In another four cases, it was unclear who had prevailed. In only two cases during 168 years (1790-1957) had the Court successfully blocked the enactment of policies desired by the law-making majority[5]—two cases that involved Reconstruction laws penalizing Confederate officers.

How was it possible for Congress's policy making to prevail over the seemingly final power of judicial review? The answer usually involves time. At some later date after the Court's decision Congress would pass essentially the same legislation and the Court would uphold it. In some instances minor differences between the laws would allow the Court to save face, but usually the real explanation for the Court's approval of the second law was changes in personnel on the bench. Indeed, at times the Court would not even bother with the face-saving charade, but would overrule directly or by implication its earlier decision. Only once was a constitutional amendment necessary: the Sixteenth Amendment authorized a national income tax after the Court had found an earlier such tax unconstitutional (*Pollock v. Farmers' Loan & Trust Co.,* 1895).

Between 1957 and 1983 only a handful of Supreme Court decisions declared an act of Congress void within four years of enactment. Perhaps two can be considered major. *Oregon v. Mitchell* (1970), which struck down a federal law lowering the voting age to 18 in state elections, was reversed by adoption of the Twenty-sixth Amendment to the Constitution. *National League of Cities v. Usery* (1976), which nullified a law extending the federal minimum wage to state employees, has so far not been reversed or evaded by Congress. These cases raise to 25 the number of the Supreme Court's declarations of unconstitutionality within four years of enactment, with 18 such decisions being reversed, 3 prevailing, and 4 unclear. Activity in this quarter century clearly has not seriously altered the data underlying Dahl's conclusion about the Court's relationship to the law-making majority.

Many of the 18 cases in which Congress prevailed related to major pieces of controversial legislation of their time, such as workmen's compensation laws, child labor laws, and New Deal agricultural and economic programs. Both sides felt strongly about both the substance and the philosophy of these policies. Thus Congress's 72 percent success rate is an impressive indicator of the Court's inability to stand against the firm desires of a law-making majority. The crisis between the Court and the Roosevelt administration over the constitutionality of the New Deal is illustrative. Unluckily for Roosevelt, no Supreme Court seats became vacant during his first term (1933-1937) and a Court dominated by appointees of the old coalition struck down eight important New Deal laws. In Roosevelt's second term, however, the law of averages caught up with him and he was able to appoint five justices. By 1941 the eight anti-New Deal decisions, as well as the constitutional philosophy underlying them, were unceremoniously swept under the rug.[6]

"By itself, the Court is almost powerless to affect the course of national policy," Dahl concludes.[7] Of course, no one denies the ability of the Court to make many policies—only that it can make fundamental policy. The Court is not a mere rubber stamp for the dominant coalition, but is, in Dahl's words, "an essential part of the political leadership." Thus it can often "determine important questions of timing, effectiveness and subordinate policy,"[8] especially when the elements of the coalition are not united in their enthusiasm for a particular policy.

The Court as Legitimizer. What, then, is the impact of the Supreme Court in the American political system? Several scholars have argued that its primary function is to confer legitimacy upon the controversial policies adopted by the political majority. When the Court applies its stamp of constitutional approval, these policies are withdrawn from debate and become acceptable to the citizens, including those who originally opposed the policies. Again the New Deal serves as an example. Programs such as Social Security and the Agricultural Adjustment Act that were bitterly resisted by the old Republican coalition during the 1930s became markedly less controversial within a few years after the Supreme Court found them constitutional. Law professor Charles Black's historical study, *The People and the Court,* is the leading work to stress legitimization as the Court's primary function.[9] Another law professor, Arthur S. Miller, studied the Supreme Court's impact on the economy and concluded that its direct impact was "about like that of a snowflake lofting down on the bosom of the mighty Potomac."[10] He, too, believed that the Court's primary role has been one of approving other agencies' economic policies and quieting controversies about them.

Political scientist David Adamany, however, denies not only the Court's ability to block important policies favored by the law-making majority, but also that the Court has much ability even to legitimize acts of Congress.[11] He supports his contention by citing public opinion polls (see Chapter 6, p. 195) that reveal low public respect for the Supreme Court and many of its decisions. To the extent that the Court has an impact on the political system, Adamany argues, it is to destabilize the policies of a newly installed law-making majority in the transition period between its taking control of the legislative and executive branches and its obtaining enough justices on the court to control judicial decisions.

Other Supreme Court Policy-Making Activities. The view that the Supreme Court was relatively impotent as a policy maker predominated until the mid-1970s.[12] But in 1975 it was challenged by Jonathan Casper. Casper does not address the legitimization issue, being instead interested in the Court's direct role in policy making. He believes that focusing only on instances where the Court considers the constitutionality of acts of Congress "excludes from consideration a large body of evidence that seems highly relevant to determining the Court's role in national policy-making."[13]

One contention is that it is misleading to ignore the nearly 50 cases in which the Court declared federal legislation unconstitutional more than four years after enactment. These constituted over 60 percent of the declarations of unconstitutionality between 1803 and 1957. Moreover, since 1957, 27 out of 30 cases have been in this category. Many of these are controversial decisions with important policy implications, and it cannot be concluded without investigation that the law-making majority was no longer interested in maintaining the policies found in such laws. Certainly Congress was concerned in 1983 when the Court declared one of its major policy tools, the legislative veto, unconstitutional, despite the fact than it had been in use since 1932 (*Immigration and Naturalization Service v. Chadha*). Moreover, as the Court's workload increases, it may not always be possible to dispose of constitutional challenges within a four-year period. For example, in 1976 the Court declared parts of the Federal Election Campaign Act of 1971 unconstitutional (*Buckley v. Valeo*). By eliminating the more-than-four-year cases, we fail to consider well over half the evidence bearing on the effectiveness of judicial review at the federal level.

A more important point, however, is that we should not equate Supreme Court policy making with negative action only. Policy making is more than merely thwarting someone else's efforts; it also involves imposing your own preferences. There is evidence, Casper argues, that the Court has acted positively when the national law-making majority was divided on an issue or when its preferences were not well formulated.

One situation where the Court may well make considerable policy involves statutory construction of acts of Congress. Sometimes this occurs in a constitutional context. In *United States v. E. C. Knight Co.* (1895), for example, the Court ruled that the Sherman Antitrust Act could not be applied to manufacturers because production of goods was not within the scope of the Constitution's commerce clause. Here the Court effectively limited the law's coverage but did not find it unconstitutional. Congress could not, however, legally get around the Court's decision. When statutory construction is not done within a constitutional context, Congress can reverse the Court's interpretation through passage of a more explicit statute. However, it often fails to do so even in areas of major importance. During the 1950s and 1960s, for instance, the Court was successful in gutting a number of federal laws aimed at prosecuting or otherwise constraining alleged subversives (*Yates v. United States,* 1957; *Jay v. Boyd,* 1956; and *Communist Party v. Subversive Activities Control Board,* 1961). More recently, without adverse congressional reaction, the court construed the Civil Rights Act of 1964 to permit special promotion programs for minorities despite the seemingly contrary wording of the law (*Kaiser Aluminum & Chemical Corp. v. Weber,* 1979). During the Vietnam War the court interpreted the Selective Service Act to permit nonreligious conscientious objectors to be exempt from the draft (*United States v. Seeger,* 1965), and when Congress reenacted the law to make it clear that this was not what it intended, the Court again interpreted the statute to exempt nonreligious objectors (*Welsh v. United States,* 1970).

Another major area of the Court's work is judicial review of state and local laws or practices. Of course, the law-making majority usually has no clear preferences in cases arising from particular localities. Many such cases deal with unusual laws or obscure practices. Nonetheless, some instances of judicial review at the state or local level involve situations common throughout the nation; then the Court's decision has a widespread impact and often becomes far more controversial than do exercises of judicial review at the federal level. This has been especially true in the last several decades. Certainly the Court's decisions on desegregation, school prayer, legislative reapportionment, defendant's rights, and abortion have generated more political heat than any recent decision finding an act of Congress unconstitutional. Proposed constitutional amendments to reverse or modify decisions in four of these areas have received serious consideration in the last quarter century; such decisions have also been featured issues in presidential campaigns. It may not be easy to pinpoint precisely the law-making majority's preferences on these issues, but it cannot be denied that the Court—and not other agencies of government—has established the fundamental national policy in these areas. Making major national policies by striking down state or local laws is not a new phenomenon: later in this chapter we focus briefly on how the court shaped the nation's economic policies in the nineteenth and early twentieth centuries through such decisions as *Gibbons v. Ogden* (1824) and *Lochner v. New York* (1905).

Finally, it should be noted that while Congress has reversed the Supreme Court on numerous occasions when laws have been struck down, sometimes the Court has made its policy prevail for many years. For instance, the Court successfully prevented the adoption of a national law prohibiting child labor for 25 years. The *E. C. Knight* doctrine limiting federal regulation of manufacturing prevailed for over 40 years. Most spectacular of all, the Court frustrated a national civil rights law for over 80 years. Policies are never expected to last forever. Surely, the Court must be given some credit for having an impact on society in those cases where its preferences prevailed for a generation or longer.

State Supreme Courts

Judging from the attention local media give to state supreme courts and their decisions, it seems fair to conclude that the statewide policy impact of these courts is considerably less than is the national policy impact of the U.S. Supreme Court. State supreme court decisions are seldom prominent. Most people could probably not name or describe a single decision their state supreme court has made in the last 25 years. Lawyers aside, very few people organize to support or overturn state supreme court decisions.

These observations are just impressions. The fact is that virtually no one has studied the policy impact of state supreme courts. Researchers have looked at other features of these institutions, such as how justices are recruited, how they vote once on the bench, and how they react to U.S. Supreme Court decisions, but no one has examined what their policies are and how much impact these policies have.[14] No one has followed in Dahl's footsteps and analyzed how often state supreme courts have nullified acts of their state legislatures and, in cases of such conflict, whose policy preferences have ultimately prevailed.

One difference between state supreme courts and the U.S. Supreme Court is that the former make considerable policy through their common law decisions. There is little federal common law, and at any rate the U.S. Supreme Court has not given it much attention in the last half century. But in many states common law policies have been significantly altered during this same period. In tort law, particularly, the courts have fashioned new remedies or expanded existing ones for accident victims and consumers of defective products.[15] The establishment and alteration of common law doctrines constitutes one area where the courts have a relatively free hand at policy making. State legislatures can override common law by enacting statutes, but they do not often do so. Most legislators see the common law as the province of jurists.

Although our example is not necessarily typical, we can focus briefly on one state supreme court's policy-making activity. A graduate seminar conducted by Bradley C. Canon studied the Kentucky Supreme Court between 1965 and 1980. The study found that the court during this period decided just over 300 cases that made reasonably important policy.[16] Table 7.1 shows the proportion of policy-making cases in various areas. Like the U.S. Supreme Court, the Kentucky Supreme Court is heavily involved in making criminal justice policy and constitutional law. Unlike the nation's highest court, however, the Kentucky Court is also heavily involved in

Table 7.1 Public Policy Cases Decided by Kentucky Supreme Court, 1965-1980

Issue	Number of cases[a]	Percentage of total[b]
Criminal law	46	15
Tort law	42	13
Cities and counties (including zoning)	42	13
U.S. or state constitutional law	36	11
Administrative law	30	9
Workmen's compensation	27	9
Taxation and fiscal policy	24	8
Domestic relations	18	6
Health, safety, and environment	18	6
Schools and educational policy	16	5
Insurance law	14	4
Elections	12	4
Property law (including mineral rights)	10	3
Miscellaneous[c]	43	14

[a] There was a total of 316 cases, and the percentages are based on this figure.
[b] Total exceeds 100 percent because some cases involved two or more issues.
[c] Includes alcoholic beverages, attorneys, banking and finance, contracts, corporations, highways, labor law, landlord-tenant relations, and trusts and estates.

such areas as tort law, workmen's compensation, and domestic relations.[17]

In the area of public law, the Kentucky Supreme Court seems to best fit the role of legitimizer. This is especially important in Kentucky, which, like many states, is governed by a nineteenth-century constitution containing many explicit restrictions on the legislature. Kentucky's highest court has upheld such things as implied consent laws, no-fault insurance laws, malpractice insurance pool laws, laws permitting city-county merger, and laws establishing local development commissions in the face of constitutional provisions that could well be construed to prohibit them. Indeed, the Kentucky constitution provides that no state employee can be paid more than $12,500 per year, and it took the state supreme court's "rubber dollar" decision (declaring that this provision is to be interpreted with inflation in mind) to keep the state in a position to employ professionals and administrators (*Matthews v. Allen,* 1962). Major acts of the legislature are seldom struck down, although the court did negate the lawmakers' effort to give surface owners control over strip mining of coal under their land that had been deeded to another party (*Department of Natural Resources v. No. 8 Limited of Virginia,* 1975). This law would have voided the state's highest court's earlier "broad form deed" doctrine (Chapter 2, pp. 36-37), which holds that owners of subsurface minerals can use any means necessary for extraction, even if the method was not known at the time the mineral rights were acquired. The Kentucky Court also struck down a law establishing a work-release program for prisoners as violative of the ancient constitution (*Hancock v. Holmes,* 1974). Neither of these decisions has been reversed by the legislature. The state's highest court was more often willing to negate special legislation designed for particular cities or counties, often related to such things as the creation of special taxing districts or the sale of alcoholic beverages.

The Kentucky Supreme Court was largely ineffective in its biggest venture into policy making. In 1965 the court ruled that property, which until then had been assessed at 10 to 40 percent of its market value, must be assessed at full value (*Russman v. Lockett*). It should be noted that a good number of other state supreme courts have made 100 percent assessment decisions in the last 25 years. This decision was particulary important in Kentucky because the state ·constitution sets specific dollar maximums on local tax rates, and virtually all school districts, financially strapped, were at the upper limit. The court's decision would enable the schools to increase their revenue substantially. Meeting in special session, however, the legislature passed a "rollback" law which prohibited taxing districts from increasing actual revenues by more than 10 percent. Although the constitutionality of the rollback law was on the face of it dubious, the state supreme court saw the political handwriting on the wall and upheld it (*Rea v. Gallatin Co. Fiscal Court,* 1967; *Miller v. Nunnelly,* 1971). Even at that, two justices were defeated for reelection in the aftermath of the 100 percent assessment controversy.

While the Kentucky Supreme Court has not been an initiator in reforming common law, it has generally been quick to adopt controversial innovations.[18] In the 1960s and 1970s it accepted most of the consumer-oriented changes in tort law which impose greater liability on physicians, hospitals, municipalities, manufacturers, and construction firms. In the most controversial area of tort law, however, the court steadfastly resisted pressures to overturn the venerable doctrine of sovereign immunity.

It is likely that there is considerable variation in the policy-making impact of the 50 state high courts. The California Supreme Court, for instance, has a reputation for being a policy maker and is one of the few whose recent decisions have received significant attention beyond legal circles. It has made many controversial decisions, such as one requiring equalization of per capita spending for all school districts in the state regardless of their taxable wealth (*Serrano v. Priest,* 1971). It has also taken the lead in changing common law policies by establishing the doctrines of comparative negligence (*Li v. Yellow Cab Co.,* 1975) and of strict liability for defective products (*Greenman v. Yuma Products Co.,* 1963), and by abolishing the doctrine of sovereign immunity (*Muskopf v. Corning Hospital District,* 1961). It is also the only state supreme court to have declared the death penalty unconstitutional (*People v. Anderson,* 1972), an action that was later reversed by an amendment to the state constitution.[19]

High courts in a few other states, such as New Jersey and Michigan, also have a reputation for engaging in considerable policy making. In most states, however, the state supreme court appears to have only a modest policy impact, and a few state supreme courts seem virtually dedicated to the status quo.[20]

State Trial Courts

As is the case with state supreme courts, scholars have paid little attention to the kinds of policy that state trial courts generate. Nor can they tell us much about the impact these courts have on the communities they serve. One reason for this is that trial courts are presumed to have little impact. Table 7.2 shows the proportion of cases in various areas of the law filed in urban Alameda County (Oakland) and rural San Benito County, California, in 1970. These distributions are probably reasonably typical. Family (mostly divorce) cases predominate and tort cases (mostly automobile accidents) run second. Government or public policy issues are infrequent. Five out of six cases do not even go to trial. In those that do, most involve issues of fact and the outcome is of little concern beyond the parties involved. In those few where legal policy is central, the assumption is that the loser will appeal; therefore the policy will be resolved by an appellate rather than a local court.

Kenneth Dolbeare conducted an extensive study of the effect of trial courts in Nassau County, New York.[21] Of course, a county that consists of suburbs of New York City is not necessarily typical, but there is no reason to believe that the impact of its courts is

Table 7.2 Types of Cases Filed in Trial Courts in Alameda and San Benito Counties, California, in 1970

Type of case	Alameda County	San Benito County
	(N = 236)[a]	(N = 188)
Family law	51.7%	61.7%
Torts	27.1	19.2
Contracts	15.7	9.1
Property	2.3	3.2
Government	1.3	1.1
Corporations/labor	1.3	3.2
Miscellaneous	0.4	1.1
Total[b]	99.8	98.6

[a] N is a 2 percent sample of total population.

[b] Totals do not equal 100 percent due to rounding or to the inclusion of unknown types of cases in the total.

Source: Adapted from Lawrence A. Friedman and Robert V. Percival, "A Tale of Two Courts: Litigation in Alameda and San Benito Counties," *Law and Society Review* 10 (Winter 1976): 281-282, by permission of the publisher, the Law and Society Association.

significantly different from that of courts in other suburban locales. Through interviews and newspaper articles, Dolbeare determined the most important policy disputes in the county from 1949 to 1964. He then looked at the local court records and found that there were 388 decisions relating to these disputes or to more general policy areas such as schools and taxes. Criminal cases were excluded from his study.

Dolbeare found that "in the overwhelming proportion of the cases, the local trial court was the final determining authority." Only one quarter of the decisions were appealed; on appeal, the decisions of the trial courts were upheld by a better than two-to-one ratio. Thus Dolbeare believes that "for most practical purposes, the local trial court *is* both the [U.S.] Supreme Court and state court of last resort." [22]

Table 7.3 shows the main substantive areas in which the Nassau County trial courts made policy and gives a thumbnail sketch of the general nature of the policy. Note that more than half of the cases involve zoning for land use disputes. Here, especially because the

Table 7.3 Summary of Court Impact in Major Substantive Areas, Indicating Major Elements Relevant to Outcome

Subject area	Total cases	Percent support for govt.	Nature of claims involved and basis of resolutions	Overall character of court involvement in area
Nonzoning Area				
Nominations and elections	16	75	Intraparty contests by insurgents, resolution controlled by election law.	Courts endorse technical determinations, appellate review immediately available.
Education	25	80	Challenges to school budgets, employee reinstatements, parental claims, decided by education law.	Courts irrelevant except as safety valves, but enforce parental rights.
Taxation	9	33	Claims for reductions in assessments or attacks on local nonproperty taxes. Decided on facts of valuations and authorizations.	Courts establish valuations at sharp variance with county and void local taxes. Major policy-making role.
Licensing, other regulations	30	43	Businesses oppose local regulations, challenge administrators of state regulatory authorities.	Courts support business freedom, scrutinize procedures of state agencies. Effect is to stress economic rights.
Government powers and procedures	34	62	"Constitutional" powers of county government, Democratic party use; control by general laws of state.	Courts allocate power and define government structure, control incorporation and annexation. Primary area of court impact.

Zoning and Land Use Area				
Business permits	63	Applicants allege prezoning rights, special privileges, arbitrariness of denial of business use. Decided on basis of factual support for findings.	44	Courts protect rights to use property when they have vested character. Constant tension between courts and government standards.
Residential permits	38	Applicants seek to build on substandard lot. Facts as to date of ownership control rights vs. zoning.	47	Courts enforce vested rights against government efforts to maintain standards.
To annul grant of permit	25	Applicants attack extension of business use into residential area and grants to build on substandard lots. Factual support in record controlling.	68	Courts uphold governments more readily, grantee seen as having the vested rights.
Injunctions	18	Efforts by governments to enforce zoning standards in affirmative fashion.	50	Courts grant governments no special advantage and appear unreceptive to such efforts.
Declaratory judgments	46	Plaintiffs attack constitutionality of ordinance control over use of property. Due process of law standards control.	54	Courts void ordinance where it precludes all reasonable uses, restrain upzoning, insist on comprehensive rather than spot zoning.

Source: Kenneth Dolbeare, *Trial Courts in Urban Politics: State Court Policy Impact and Functions in a Local Political System* (New York: Wiley, 1967), 108-109. Reprinted by permission of the publisher.

outcome is related to the courts' finding of facts, trial courts are likely to have an important impact on their communities.

While Table 7.3 indicates that the trial courts were involved in a reasonably broad scope of areas, Dolbeare notes that of the five most important specific issues of public concern in Nassau County over the 15-year period, the courts were involved in only one. Issues such as transportation and labor disputes never reached the courts. Dolbeare found that "the impact of the courts on the substance of policy is narrow, specialized and distinctively individualistic. When the economic opportunities of an individual or business [are] involved, the courts are invocable and effective." [23] In effect, the trial courts were oriented to the economic status quo. They would prevent or at the very least delay the constriction of business operations and opportunities, and they would block threats to the value of property.

The trial courts did protect the rights of political minorities, often the local Democratic party, through enforcing the election laws fairly and by preventing governmental bodies from adopting popular but illegal policies—or even legal policies by means of procedural shortcuts. Dolbeare also noted that the trial court served as a safety valve in some community disputes, especially those involving school policies, by allowing the losing side to have its day in court, though the courts rarely overturned or altered the policies involved. In these two observations, we can see both the minority shield and the legitimizing role present at the trial court level.

One can say, then, that the trial court's policy impact tends to be negative—the court can veto or delay the actions of government, often forcing either the adoption of alternative methods of accomplishing a goal or the abandonment of a project altogether. In such actions, the courts especially favor businesses and property owners in zoning and regulatory disputes, but otherwise, in Dolbeare's words, "no clear pattern of direction . . . emerges." [24] The trial courts are reactive. They do not initiate much policy. In contrast, the U.S. Supreme Court has recently initiated much policy in such areas as desegregation, abortion, and criminal justice, and many state supreme courts have recently been active initiators of new common law policies. Perhaps the differences may reflect the constraints upon trial courts as opposed to the freedom of courts of last resort, but they probably also reflect the conservatism of state trial judges.

Lower Federal Courts

No study comparable to Dolbeare's has been written on modern federal district courts or even on the U.S. courts of appeals.[25]

Nonetheless, we can make a few comments here upon the general impact of these courts. As with state trial courts, the impact of federal district courts is limited because of appeals. However, the vast majority of the appeals end at the U.S. court of appeals; taken together, the district courts and courts of appeals have considerable discretion in formulating judicial policy.

For the most part, the impact of these courts has paralleled that of the Supreme Court, since these courts impose Supreme Court decisions to a greater or lesser degree on activities within their jurisdiction. Before World War II the impact was often in the economic realm as the federal courts struck down state or local regulatory laws or broke strikes through injunctions. In the last three or four decades the major impact has shifted to the civil rights and liberties area—the courts have struck down local laws and policies that discriminate by race or sex, that constrain freedom of expression, and that appear to short-circuit due process. State courts, by contrast, make considerable economic policy but enter the civil rights and liberties area less often. In some instances the law gives sole jurisdiction to the federal courts in civil rights cases; but it is also true that most plaintiffs in such cases believe they have a better chance of prevailing or of obtaining greater relief in the federal courts.

Sometimes federal courts make policy independent of the Supreme Court. At the court of appeals level such policies are known as *the law of the circuit.* Usually these involve issues the Supreme Court has not yet addressed and which in many instances it declines to settle. For example, in the 1960s and 1970s some parents sued in federal courts to overturn school board regulations limiting the length of pupils' hair. The law of the circuit in five courts of appeals was that such regulations were basically unconstitutional, while in five others the "law" was that they were basically constitutional.[26]

At the district court level, independent policy making depends considerably on the circumstances. The impact can be substantial in complex local situations where the Supreme Court has given district judges a good deal of discretion in fashioning remedies for racial discrimination in schools, housing, and employment. The impact is much less where the law or Supreme Court policies are independent of local situations. Beyond delegated discretion, however, some federal judges have taken to developing innovative and often detailed policies affecting public institutions in their districts. The classic example of this is Judge Frank M. Johnson, Jr., of the Northern District of Alabama, who, in the absence of any guidance in Supreme Court precedents, during the 1970s singlehandedly imposed sweeping reforms on the state's prison system and its mental hospitals.[27] Subsequently, many other district judges, again with little appellate guidance, followed in Judge Johnson's footsteps.

The district judges' personalities and ideologies are also important to the impact of the courts, especially in districts with only one or two judges. But even in districts with a number of judges, the mix can vary considerably. Robert Carp and C. K. Rowland's study of district court decisions shows courts in Minneapolis, Milwaukee, and Boston to be much more liberal than those in St. Louis, Oklahoma City, or Pittsburgh.[28] Differences in ideology depend largely upon the vagaries of the appointment process in a given district. Were most of the judges appointed by Presidents Kennedy, Johnson, and Carter or by Nixon, Ford, and Reagan? Were the senators from that state liberals, moderates, or conservatives? Of course, as we have discussed in Chapters 2 and 6, the local environment also helps shape the court's impact. As Carp and Rowland note:

> [A district] is often synonymous with a particular set of policy relevant values, attitudes and orientations. So in a general sense one would automatically expect that on some issues Mississippi federal judges would act differently from Oregon jurists, not so much because they are from different states, but because they are from a different political, economic, legal and cultural milieu.[29]

Federal courts make much negative policy, but in contrast to state trial courts, they also initiate important policies, especially in the civil rights and liberties area. In many instances, federal district courts fulfill the shield role for the benefit of racial minorities, unpopular causes, and various dispossessed elements of society. The actual impact of federal courts varies considerably depending upon circumstances, but in some instances the courts have a freedom of action that parallels that of the highest courts. Moreover, federal district courts have sometimes come to make detailed policies in a manner that exceeds the reviewing capabilities of appellate courts in such areas as prisons, hospitals, schools, urban renewal, and public housing. Indeed, their engagement in such policy making has had sufficient impact to generate much discussion and not a little criticism in recent years.[30] It is quite telling that there is no parallel controversy over the role of state trial courts.

JUDICIAL IMPACT IN FOUR PUBLIC POLICY AREAS

Throughout most of this book we have concentrated on certain populations concerned with the impact of judicial policies. In this section we turn to four specific policy areas and summarize the impact the courts have had in these areas. The first three areas involve what are often called civil liberties policies: freedom of expression, criminal justice, and equality. In civil liberties, if anywhere, we would expect judicial decisions and policies to have an impact on American society. The fourth policy area is economic policy, an area in which the courts have been making policy since the early days of the Republic.

Because we are summarizing, we will concentrate largely on Supreme Court decisions, especially in the civil liberties areas. Our review will not be exhaustive, since we will limit ourselves to major cases and to exemplary areas. Other, more scholarly and extensive, studies of judicial policies in each of these areas are available; but we are interested particularly in the impact of these policies on the political system. As we have stressed throughout this book, there is a difference between a policy and the policy's actual impact. Here we are asking, To what extent have judicial decisions changed people's attitudes and behavior? How have they done this? A corollary question is also appropriate: To what extent are judicial decisions responsible for such changes as have occurred? Would these changes have taken place along much the same lines at the behest of some other government agency or in the normal course of social change?

In none of the four areas can we answer these questions very conclusively. Systematic studies that deal with these questions are rare, scholarly speculation is infrequent, and data are sparse. We will report the findings that are available. However, sometimes we will engage in our own speculation, which we would like to believe is penetrating, though it is certainly not conclusive. And sometimes we simply pose the questions without trying to answer them.

Freedom of Expression

Political Expression. It is difficult to assess the impact of court decisions in this area. Obviously, Americans can and do express themselves through a wide variety of means. The crucial issue for evaluating political freedom is the degree to which unpopular opinions can be expressed. In general, Americans have a tradition of tolerance for unpopular viewpoints, but the tradition is punctuated with numerous exceptions, especially in times of crisis. It is difficult to tell whether our tolerance has actually increased over time and, if so, how much change has been caused by the courts.

Until World War I the courts rarely heard freedom of expression cases, and they made virtually no policy in this area. In fact, it was not until after World War II, with the McCarthyism of the 1950s and the Vietnam War protests of the 1960s, that the Supreme Court began hearing a steady stream of such cases. Nearly all freedom of expression policy has been made by the Supreme Court, and there is no doubt that that body has expanded the constitutional parameters of freedom of speech, of press, and of association considerably. Because of the Court's decisions, it appears that today district attorneys, police, school officials, and others are less likely to prosecute or harass persons expressing unpopular viewpoints than they might have been just a few decades ago.

Consider the fate of those who opposed U.S. foreign policy over the years. Opponents of our entry into World War I were hounded from college professorships and other jobs on the flimsiest of charges.[31] Few dared to speak up in anything but the most ambiguous language, and those who did were often given long jail sentences for such activities as distributing literature that would not merit a second prosecutorial glance by today's standards. (For an example, read the Supreme Court case of *Abrams v. United States,* 1919.) Even during the 1950s many persons associated with communist front groups or far left causes tried to hide the fact. By the time of the Vietnam War, however, opponents carried their protests to the streets loudly and frequently. Prosecution was infrequent. Those who were tried, such as Dr. Benjamin Spock, the Chicago Seven, and the Gainesville Eight, were usually acquitted or had their convictions overturned on appeal. Virtually all faculty and student protestors remained affiliated with their universities.

The changes in government responses to protest suggest that the Supreme Court has developed liberal policies interpreting the First Amendment in recent years and that by and large these policies have gained acceptance. However, we do not know very much about the actual use of the First Amendment guarantees in modern times or about how it compares with uses in earlier eras. Such a comparison is largely unmeasurable, but in the absence of a crisis at least, freedom of expression appears to have been robust in this country throughout its history. Around 1800 it was common for many leading newspapers to print intemperate and sometimes scurrilous attacks on major national leaders, such as George Washington and Thomas Jefferson. In the first half of the twentieth century, anti-Semitic and anti-Catholic attacks (to say nothing of anti-Negro diatribes) were common in many newspapers and magazines. Of course, such material exists today, but it is not prominent or common.

Obviously, the prevalence of scurrilous personal, racial, or religious attacks is hardly the only measure of the breadth of freedom of expression. Investigative journalism is probably more widespread and probing today than at any time in the past. The fear of libel is much less pervasive in the newsroom today than it was in earlier years, although the expenses of a libel suit can often induce self-censorship.[32] And the willingness of people with unpopular views to take to the streets or engage in symbolic protest may well be greater now than in previous years. But on the whole, it is hard to make a case that the dissemination of unpopular or offensive viewpoints is broader or more widespread now, despite recent Supreme Court decisions, than in earlier years. The Court's impact seems to be the narrower, but by no means unimportant, one of reducing the grosser or more official forms of harassment of persons disseminating such views.

Sexually Oriented Material. Sexually oriented material might be an exception to our generalization that court decisions have not dramatically broadened the use of the constitutional guarantees of freedom of expression. Judicial policies relating to obscenity took a dramatic turn around 1960. Until *Roth v. United States* (1957) the Supreme Court was virtually uninvolved with obscenity cases; lower courts almost universally adhered to the *Hicklin* test (established in the English case of *Regina v. Hicklin,* 1868), which defined material as obscene in effect if any part of it had a "tendency to deprave or corrupt" the minds of children. By this standard, reputable literary works (such as James Joyce's *Ulysses*) and even documentary films (such as one showing the birth of a buffalo) were banned. In the 1960s the Court held that the measure of obscenity was whether the work taken as a whole appealed to purient interests; was without redeeming social, literary, artistic, or scientific value; and was offensive to the sensibilities of the average person in the community (see particularly *Memoirs v. Massachusetts,* 1966). No longer could the focus be on isolated parts of a book or on its possible impact on children. Now intent and merit had to be considered. (The Court modified its standards somewhat in the 1973 case of *Miller v. California,* but it did not fundamentally change them.)

One would almost have to be a hermit not to be familiar with the prevalence of sexually oriented material in our society today. Such material is not found only in adult bookstores, X-rated movie theaters, and topless bars, though these certainly thrive in all large and small cities. Many of the novels on sale in shopping malls and supermarkets feature explicit sexual language and torrid love scenes. Many nonfiction books are devoted to surveys of sexual fantasies or to explicit advice on how to become a better lover. *Playboy* and similar publications are available on most magazine racks and circulate by mail to millions of homes. Nudity and lovemaking are common in popular movies. Even television is not immune to this heavy emphasis on sex. Indeed, it is the widespread prevalence of this phenomenon rather than the isolated adult bookstore or X-rated theater that has triggered the recent so-called profamily political campaigns of the Moral Majority and similar groups.

A Rip Van Winkle who had gone to sleep in the mid-1950s would truly be astounded upon awakening today. Best-selling novels then almost never focused on sex directly and did not use dirty language. On the nonfiction side, it was easier to find a guide book to climbing the Himalaya mountains than to find one on the physical aspects of sex. Under rigid self-censorship and prodding from the Legion of Decency (a national Catholic organization), movies were "squeaky clean"; even married couples slept in twin beds, and 1950s heroine Doris Day always remained chaste. Even our clothes were less suggestive in the 1950s.

Can we attribute our hypothetical Rip's astonishment to the Supreme Court? The answer is not clear. Obviously, to some extent, the Court through *Roth* and subsequent decisions has contributed to a legal situation that inhibits the prosecution of activities that would most likely have been prosecuted 30 years ago. But more is involved than Court decisions; a fundamental change in public attitudes has taken place. People are more willing to buy or watch sexually oriented material and to tolerate such activities on the part of others. The crucial questions are, Did the Court's decisions generate this change in attitude or did the change occur more or less independently of the Court (or even serve as indirect cause of the Court's decisions)? Was a new generation of Americans ready to burst the seams of a confining Victorian morality anyway? Did the Court simply loosen a few threads to make the escape easier? To the extent that the answer to the last two questions is yes, we cannot attribute too much impact to the Court. That body would be simply following, if not the election returns, the prevailing social trend. Of course, the Court would accrue some credit for going along with social trends rather than trying to delay them. If the answer is no, then the Court has imposed a major impact on the nation, for as we have seen there is no doubt that there has been a substantial change in this area affecting our everyday life.

We do not know the answer; the relationship is impossible to determine, and no one has addressed the question of cause and effect with persuasive argument. Most likely, the answer lies somewhere in between. It seems reasonably clear that the nation was shedding Victorian morality in the post-World War II years. It also seems reasonable to believe that the Court's decisions made this process more respectable and enhanced its rapidity by lessening fears of prosecution. At bottom, it is fair to conclude the sexually oriented material is one area where the courts—especially the Supreme Court—have had a clearly visible if unmeasurable impact on national behavior.

Criminal Justice Policies

The Due Process Revolution. It might be argued that the courts, and especially the Supreme Court, have had greater success in altering behavior in the criminal justice area than in any other. In one way, this would seem to be an obvious conclusion. After all, the courts are intimately involved in criminal justice. Presumably they ought to have more impact in their own house than anywhere else. In another way, however, such is not a foregone conclusion. For most of the nation's history, courts have refrained from making serious alterations in criminal justice policy. Moreover, other implementing agencies are also involved in the criminal justice field; when the courts began seriously changing policies here, these agencies reacted bitterly.

Traditionally the courts had looked to the forms rather than to the substance of the procedure to determine whether defendants received due process of law. With a few exceptions involving extreme cases (such as *Brown v. Mississippi* [1936], where deputies tortured a suspect until he confessed), the Supreme Court before World War II turned a deaf ear to defendants' claims. Only under Chief Justice Earl Warren did the Supreme Court begin considering the reality of the criminal justice system as well as its forms. In decisions such as *Mapp v. Ohio* (1961) and *Miranda v. Arizona* (1966), the Court recognized that what occurs in the course of police searches, arrests, and interrogations is as much a component of due process as is what occurs at the trial. For that matter, the Warren Court did not forget the courtroom. In its most important decision at this level, *Gideon v. Wainwright* (1963), the Court required that all indigent felony defendants be provided with a lawyer.

Despite President Richard Nixon's appointment of four "law and order" justices, the Court in the 1970s did not retreat from the major thrust of the Warren Court's criminal justice decisions. Indeed, the Burger Court has extended the guarantee of counsel to indigents charged with a misdemeanor who are subject to incarceration (*Argersinger v. Hamlin,* 1972). And during the 1970s the lower federal courts as well have come to make policy in the criminal justice areas. By 1980 prison systems in half the states were under federal court mandates to undertake significant improvements, such as providing more space for prisoners.[33]

A few state appellate courts, particularly those in California, Florida, and Michigan, have acted to broaden the scope of the defendant's rights in recent years. For the most part, however, state appellate courts have not been pioneers in this respect. Indeed, the function of these courts—along with state trial courts—has probably been one of limiting and tempering the impact of the Supreme Court's criminal justice decisions. They have also served as a buffer between the abstract doctrines of the due process revolution and the realities of its application.

No one can deny the manifest improvements (at least from the defendant's viewpoint) in the criminal justice system over the last three decades. Fewer cases are solved at the end of a nightstick or even under the glare of a strobe light. Public defenders and organizations that provide lawyers for poor defendants exist nationwide and in general these attorneys are alert to violations of their clients' rights. Prisons have improved: the chain gangs and torture devices are a thing of the past. Even such a political conservative as Chief Justice Warren Burger is an advocate of extensive prison reform, if for no other reason than to get the burgeoning habeas corpus petitions off the federal courts' already overcrowded dockets. There remain, of course, instances of police brutality and other gross denials of due process. But the outrage these breaches provoke shows them to be exceptional; half a century ago, the reaction would have been, "Ho hum, another dog bites man story."

Certainly a good deal of this change is attributable to the decisions of the Supreme Court and other federal courts. It is hard to believe that the police would have undertaken to formulate and read *Miranda*-like warnings to suspects without the courts' intervention— to say nothing of providing suspects with their own attorney before interrogation. Nor can we believe that in the absence of *Mapp* the police would have curbed illegal searches to the extent they have.[34] Decisions such as *Gideon* and *Argersinger* established the necessity for expanding structures to provide attorneys for defendants, the great majority of whom could not afford to retain one. (It should be noted that most states had established right-to-counsel policies for felony defendants prior to the *Gideon* decision. However, they were often not well implemented. To a considerable extent it was the Court's decisions expanding the right to counsel beyond the trial—for example, *Hamilton v. Alabama* [1961], *United States v. Wade* [1967], and *Miranda*—that served as an impetus to the states' expansion of the free counsel system.) Finally, it is clear that courts moved in the area of prison reform because neither the legislatures nor the prison administrators had been able or willing to make any changes in existing conditions.

Still, the courts cannot take all the credit for the due process revolution. Changes in the attitudes of the implementing population should also be recognized. Police forces, for instance, are much different now than they were 50 years ago. Officers have more general education and receive more professional training. They are more likely to go by the book, and they have a sense of professional pride in doing so.[35] There would probably have been a decline in justice at the end of a nightstick by now, even if the Supreme Court had made no restrictive decisions.

Likewise, there has been a change in the legal profession. Clarence Darrow and Perry Mason notwithstanding, in an earlier era there were few criminal attorneys and they were at the bottom of the professional barrel. In the last two decades, however, a wave of idealism has overtaken law students and many thousands have gone into criminal law. While hardly all the best and brightest have followed this path, the field is now respectable and its practitioners do a credible job of representing their clients. Were it not for this idealist blossoming on the part of many young lawyers, the states might find it difficult to implement *Gideon* and *Argersinger.* Of course, it is possible that it was the Warren Court's reforming decisions that caught the imagination of the students; thus the decisions may have served as a catalyst to their own successful implementation.

What we are saying here is that even when the courts are a major force in bringing about change, as was the case in the due process revolution, the accomplishment of the change is more than a matter of command and compliance. Important alterations in the nature of the implementing population hastened and smoothed the achievement of the Supreme Court's goals. While Court decisions may have been the most important factor in the development of the changes, they were hardly the only one. In short, while the Court's due process decisions were often ahead of the tide, they were running in the same direction.

Rising Crime Rates.   In light of the important causative role of the courts in the due process revolution, can significant blame for rising crime be attributed to their decisions? This charge is often made. Sometimes it is alleged that people violate the law because they are familiar with Supreme Court decisions restraining police and prosecutors.[36] However, no one has offered any evidence that would-be criminals are avid readers of the *U.S. Reports* or that they would even understand the opinions if they read them. Indeed, as we saw in Chapter 4, a large number of suspects could not understand their *Miranda* rights after hearing or reading them. Moreover, while Americans worry considerably about the prevalence of crime today, we also worried about it in the days of Al Capone and John Dillinger, long before the due process revolution. With the exception of murder, data on the incidence of crime are so notoriously unreliable that even a before-and-after compilation would not be very revealing of changes in crime rates.

More probably, the impact of the courts on crime is indirect. Again hard evidence is nonexistent. But it is not unreasonable to argue that the media attention given to appellate court reversals of convictions of the obviously guilty and to the successful habeas corpus petitions of incarcerated prisoners may lead some would-be criminals to believe that even if they were caught, they would have a good chance of escaping punishment. (Of course, factors unrelated to the courts' due process decisions may produce this outlook. One example is the frequency with which probation is granted or parole given after only a small fraction of a sentence has been served.)

Regardless of whether the courts' decisions have encouraged crime, many people have charged that their policies make it more difficult to solve crimes and to obtain convictions. Obviously, the imposition of more stringent due process standards would be expected to have some impact in this direction. The price society pays for due process of law is that some guilty persons will escape justice. Thus the issue is a quantitative one: Are so many escaping that such standards are not worth the price?

In some cities arrests for "search and seizure" crimes declined following *Mapp*. These arrests involve victimless crimes, usually gambling or narcotics possession.[37] Americans are probably more willing to allow some guilty parties to escape justice in such cases than we would be if murder or kidnapping arrests declined and we believed the criminals remained free. (Indeed, tolerance of illegal gambling in some communities is a virtual open secret.) On a overall basis, a General Accounting Office study of *Mapp*'s impact on federal prosecutions shows that successful motions to suppress evidence occur in only 1.3 percent of the cases—and in many of these cases the defendant is nonetheless convicted.[38]

As we saw in Chapter 4, most suspects respond to police questioning in spite of receiving their *Miranda* warnings. Of those who refuse questioning, it is difficult to say how many have been emboldened by *Miranda* and how many would have refused without the warning. We can also wonder how many nonresponders are convicted anyway. While it would not be an easy task to find answers here, these questions can be approached empirically. However, no social scientist has yet taken up the challenge.

Perhaps the most successful and fundamental part of the due process revolution is the provision of counsel for defendants—not only at the trial, but at other stages of the process as well. Competent attorneys are more likely to ensure that police and prosecutors follow the law and to win acquittal or dismissal when they do not. Even where there are no violations of due process, defense attorneys are often able to plea bargain for lighter sentences. Many defense attorneys are overworked, and often they seem to treat defendants on an indifferent, assembly-line basis, but even under less than ideal circumstances, these attorneys constitute an important asset to securing due process.[39] Again there is little evidence as to how much convictions or sentences would increase without the representation of defendants by counsel.

There is another side to the coin. We can ask to what extent the innocent have been protected by the due process revolution. While the due process guarantees are intended in part to extend the rule of law to those in authority and to legitimize the actions of authorities, certainly the protection of the innocent is one of the important benefits society hopes to acquire from the due process system. Unfortunately, data-based analysis of how well the innocent are protected is impossible, if for no other reason than that we have no objective method of determining who is innocent and who is not.

It is clear that *Mapp* and related search and seizure decisions do not protect the innocent from false convictions. The excluded evidence is almost always reliable and is usually sufficient in itself to establish the defendant's guilt. The goal of these decisions is to reinforce the constitutional restraints on authority rather than to prevent false convictions.

In regard to police interrogation, the question is whether in the absence of the *Miranda* warnings innocent suspects are likely to give the police false confessions. The answer depends upon what the police do. Obviously, one can beat or torture a false confession out of a suspect, but this kind of intimidation is not a serious problem nowadays—and even if it were, it would not be likely that *Miranda* would prevent police who were inclined to such brutality from engaging in it. There is not much evidence, even of an incidental nature, that the more common police interrogation techniques induced false confessions prior to *Miranda*.

So we must conclude that there is little evidence that the courts' decisions reforming the criminal justice system have had a large impact on the crime rate, on the ability to obtain convictions, or on protecting the innocent. Many questions of impact in this policy area fairly invite sophisticated social science research. Even so, the nature of the situation most likely precludes obtaining very much revealing data or arriving at more than tenuous conclusions.

Equality in American Life

In contrast to the areas of freedom of expression and criminal justice, in the push for equality the courts have not been the only highly visible and consistent policy maker. We think of *Brown v. Board of Education* (1954) as a great judicial contribution to equality, but we can also think of the 1964 Civil Rights Act and the 1968 Fair Housing Act as landmark legislative contributions. In this section we briefly assess the roles of the courts—especially the Supreme Court—in the effort to achieve equality in American life; but to put the courts' role in perspective we will have to compare their accomplishments with those of other institutions.

The Courts and Racial Equality. Certainly the courts made the first really dramatic move toward racial equality. *Brown* hit the nation like a fire alarm in the middle of the night. To be sure, there had been some political rhetoric and even some action (for example, the integration of the armed forces and of some southern graduate and professional schools) before 1954. But no branch of government had openly and forthrightly adopted a public philosophy of racial integration. The Supreme Court did this in *Brown.*

Because *Brown* was the earliest and most important direct effort by the courts to promote racial equality, it is worth looking at its impact on American society in some depth. We can first ask, What was *Brown*'s direct impact on school integration? The answer is not much. By 1964, ten years after the decision, only slightly more than 1 percent of the black schoolchildren in the 11 states of the Confederacy were attending school with whites;[40] in three states there was no public school integration. Moreover, in the few formerly all-white southern schools that had admitted black students, integration had for the most part been achieved in an atmosphere of high tension or even violence.

Harrell Rodgers and Charles Bullock (along with others) have argued that it was unfortunate that the courts were the first branch of government to make a commitment to racial equality.[41] It was the wrong branch of government, they say, because the public does not believe that unelected judges should make major policy changes and it will often refuse to accept as legitimate policies that are promulgated only by the courts. Even worse, the judiciary itself was ambivalent about the policy. The Supreme Court adopted the ambiguous phrase "all deliberate speed" as guidance for implementing integration (*Brown II,* 1955). Moreover, as we noted in Chapter 2, many federal district and appellate judges in the South dragged their feet as far as integration was concerned. (Indeed, a close analysis of the original *Brown* opinion reveals little judicial commitment to a philosophy of racial equality. The Court ordered integration of the schools only because segregation produced an inferior learning environment for blacks, not on the principle that integration was right in itself.)[42]

The important thing about *Brown* is not what it accomplished directly, but what it accomplished indirectly. The psychological impact of the decision far exceeded its immediate legal consequences. *Brown* stood as a symbol to blacks and whites alike that racial equality now had an institutional champion at the highest level. (This is true despite the Court's cautious and ambiguous language. Not too many people read *Brown* all that closely. Moreover, the justices were or probably became more committed to racial equality than the language indicated. This is suggested by the *per curiam* decisions of the late 1950s declaring segregation unconstitutional in public parks, auditoriums, and so on—where no learning or personality development occurred—on the authority of *Brown.*) In *Brown* the Supreme Court put racial equality on the national agenda; it could no longer be ignored or avoided.

Usually some time must pass before new symbols achieve widespread acceptance and change patterns of thinking. This was the case with *Brown.* During the remainder of the 1950s its symbolic message worked its way into the minds of many blacks—especially younger ones. The new values translated themselves into action when in February 1960 the first sit-in occurred in a Greensboro, North Carolina, dime store. Within a few months sit-ins spread across the South like wildfire, expanding from stores to other segregated establishments. In the next few years, the movement increased in size as thousands of blacks demonstrated in front of state capitols and other public buildings and held parades on the main thoroughfares of cities. Arrests were common, and violence was not infrequent. The Supreme Court treated sit-ins and demonstration cases gingerly. It overturned nearly all convictions it heard arising from them, but it did so on situational grounds. The Court steadfastly avoided the adoption of a policy that would have required businesses to treat all customers alike regardless of race.

In fact, the majority of justices made it plain that they were deferring a general decision in hopes that Congress would pass an antidiscrimination law (see *Bell v. Maryland,* 1964). The justices were undoubtedly aware of how little actual compliance *Brown* had achieved and to what extent resistance was fueled by charges that it was undemocratic for unelected judges to make policy. If the president and Congress could be induced to make major policy commitments in the push toward equality, that charge would no longer be valid.

So, in an indirect manner, the Court's *Brown* decision led to the Civil Rights Act of 1964. As we have noted, *Brown* was an impetus for the civil rights movement. And the sit-ins and demonstrations stirred up so much attention and emotion that the other branches of government could no longer avoid a major policy-making role. The result was the 1964 act, which was proposed by Presidents John F. Kennedy and Lyndon Johnson and passed after a prolonged parliamentary struggle, including a filibuster.

The focus of the civil rights movement was on discrimination in public accommodations; such discrimination was outlawed in Title III of the act. Somewhat surprisingly, there was little resistance from southern businesses after passage. But the act included other sections as well; ironically, one of them, Title VI, carried *Brown*'s indirect impact full circle—back to the schools. Title VI prohibited racial discrimination in all schools receiving federal funds and empowered the Department of Health, Education and Welfare (HEW) to require segregated school systems to draw up plans for accomplishing substantial integration. Title VI became all the more important when, in the following year, Congress passed the Aid to Elementary and Secondary Education Act, which established for the first time a system of substantial federal aid to local school systems.

Title VI worked! As we mentioned in Chapter 3, the increase in school integration throughout the late 1960s and early 1970s was spectacular. Rodgers and Bullock's study of integration in Georgia found that about five-sixths of the state's school districts had achieved substantial levels of integration by 1973-1974 (with some of the others being urban school districts that were rapidly desegregated, and often resegregated, due to white flight).[43] Their study indicates that HEW's threats to cut off federal aid constituted the key variable necessary to achieve this compliance level. It is likely that the findings for Georgia are typical of the deep South, if not the whole region. Indeed, although *Brown* itself applied only to de jure segregation, which existed almost exclusively in the South, its legacy moved north as

Title VI was applied to de facto segregation based upon residential patterns.

There is an old expression, "Money talks." This probably best summarizes the school integration situation. What the Supreme Court could not accomplish very well directly, it accomplished indirectly by bringing Congress into the picture with the carrot and stick of federal funds. There are severe limits on the degree to which the courts can accomplish changes in a public policy when that policy involves such vital and everyday activities as attending schools, using public accomodations, or hiring people. But if the judiciary can draw other government agencies into the policy-making arena on its side, much more can be accomplished.

This is not to say that the courts played only an indirect role in achieving integration in the schools. Later on, the Supreme Court made two important decisions that brought the federal courts effectively back into the integration picture. One, *Green v. County School Board of New Kent County* (1968), required school boards to take "positive steps" toward integration, thus outlawing passive compliance—such as "freedom of choice" plans, which usually resulted in 100 percent of the whites choosing white schools and 80 to 90 percent of the blacks choosing black schools. The other decision, *Swann v. Charlotte-Mecklenburg County Board of Education* (1971), permitted federal district judges to use massive crosstown busing to achieve substantial integration throughout metropolitan school systems.

We are not saying that integration was universal or was always easily accomplished. As we saw in Chapter 4, to avoid heavily integrated schools some families moved out of central cities or sent their children to private schools. We are saying that school integration increased dramatically only after Congress and the executive branch got into the policy-making picture, particularly with their fiscal powers. While the Supreme Court was the major progenitor of the movement toward racial equality over the last 30 years, only a small fraction of what has been accomplished in this area would have occurred by virtue of the Court's direct impact alone.

Perhaps it is fortunate that the Supreme Court made the first dramatic step toward racial equality in *Brown*. While its indirect impact has been more pervasive and substantial than its direct impact, the Court's decision has on an overall basis been reasonably successful in changing public policy and attitudes about racial equality. Moreover, it is hard to see what branch of government could have taken the first step if not the Supreme Court. Congress probably had the legal authority to integrate the schools, but it is difficult to imagine northern members of Congress passing such a law in the face of intransigent opposition from their southern colleagues and indifferent support from their home districts. The president acting alone has no legal authority in this area. It would have been quixotic to expect southern legislatures to act on the issue. Under the circumstances, only the Supreme Court could have taken the first step and set in motion the broader chain of events.

There were no *Brown*-like decisions by which the courts mobilized other ethnic groups into the push for equality. Few in fact suffered the same legal discrimination as was imposed upon blacks. Nonetheless, Hispanics, American Indians, and others were indirect beneficiaries of *Brown*. The success of the blacks led other groups to mobilize themselves into a positive self-consciousness about their role in American society. These groups, too, are now protected by laws designed to ensure equal access to jobs, education, and housing.

It seems clear that America has moved far toward racial equality in the last several decades. Certainly the courts can claim a good deal of credit for this accomplishment. But it is also clear that in many ways America is a long way away from achieving true racial equality. Even the most casual comparison of differences in job opportunities, income, and housing between whites and blacks reveals this. We can ask, then, to what extent these deficiencies in the achievement of racial equality represent the weakness of judicial policies.

The answer is that judicial policies have had mixed results. There are some court decisions that, though they seemed to have great potential, have not altered things very much. A good example is *Jones v. Alfred H. Mayer Co.* (1968), where the Court interpreted the 1866 Civil Rights Law to mean that blacks could recover damages from the developers or owners of private housing who discriminated against them in selling or renting it. There has been no research on the degree to which this decision has actually implemented housing desegregation. Casual observation seems to indicate that even when *Mayer Co.* is considered in conjunction with the Fair Housing Act of 1968, government policies have resulted in little integration in housing comparable to that in schools or even in the job market. One major obstacle is that it takes a good income to buy single-unit suburban housing. Courts and legislative bodies may hold that blacks have a right to such housing, but they do not provide them the money for it. A similar decision requiring private schools to accept blacks (*Runyon v. McCrary*, 1976) seems to have done little to alter the nearly all-white composition of these schools. In a slightly different context, many blacks have difficulty finding jobs, not because the courts have failed to establish policies about their eligibility or even because such policies are resisted by employers, but because fewer blacks have training in fields, such as engineering and computer programming, where jobs are available. This is not to deny, however, that there remains great prejudice against blacks, which often serves as an additional barrier to their taking advantage of employment and housing opportunities.

One can see, then, that there are some limits to what the courts—or any government agency—can do to effect public-policy changes in a short period of time. The American commitment to equality has always been more focused on equality of opportunity than on equality of result. Except in political areas such as voting rights, Americans have never believed that everybody should be equal—that they should have the same income, the same education, or the same kind of housing. Rather, our philosophy has been that everyone should have the same *opportunity* to be educated, make money, and buy material goods. Differences in individual talent, perseverance, and just plain luck will make some people more successful than others.

While courts and other agencies can try to make opportunities equal, they cannot command equal results without running afoul of a basic tenet of American society. They cannot educate the uneducated or make the poor wealthy. This is a particularly frustrating limitation in the first generation or two of desegregation, where educational and skill deficiencies are often the direct result of legal or actual segregation. Indeed, this problem has led to the establishment of affirmative action programs and other attempts to compensate blacks and other minorities for past discrimination. The Court's policy in relation to affirmative action is not entirely clear. In the most salient relevant decision, *Regents of University of California v. Bakke* (1978), the Supreme Court produced an ambiguous result. In two other decisions, a bitterly divided Court has upheld such programs (*Kaiser Aluminum & Chemical Corp. v. Weber,* 1979; *Fullilove v. Klutznick,* 1980).

The Courts and Equality of the Sexes.   The role of the courts in the movement for equality of the sexes has been rather secondary. Gender is a different sort of characteristic from race and ethnic identification, and the women's liberation movement has probably drawn only modest inspiration from the civil rights movement. Rather, it sprang up in the 1960s almost spontaneously, largely because the preceeding two decades had produced large numbers of well-educated women who felt their capacities were underused or unused. Moreover, it was Congress and not the Court that made the first major commitment to equality of the sexes by including prohibitions against sex discrimination in the 1964 Civil Rights Act. (Ironically, these were first suggested by southern opponents of the act who hoped that if they added extra provisions to it, more legislators might be offended and vote against it.) While this particular change was a casual byproduct of the national attention to the issue of racial equality, Congress made more serious commitments to equality of the sexes in 1972 both by passing laws that prohibited sex discrimination in employment and by submitting to the states the Equal Rights Amendment (ERA) to the Constitution. (While the ERA was not adopted, it had great symbolic value to the women's movement. And it was this very symbolism that also served to mobilize the successful opposition to the amendment.)

The courts have never made such a dramatic commitment. The Supreme Court opinion in *Frontiero v. Richardson* (1973) came the closest when it declared that laws making a gender distinction were subject to "strict scrutiny" (a standard by which the Court evaluates racial distinctions). However, only three other justices subscribed to Justice William Brennan's opinion, one short of a majority. Four other justices concurred in the result (equal financial benefits for spouses of members of the armed forces regardless of sex or actual dependency), but specifically refrained from endorsing the "strict scrutiny" standard. Another justice, William Rehnquist, dissented from both the result and the reasoning.

Since 1972 the Court has decided a good number of cases involving gender distinctions. But it has not been entirely consistent in doing so, nor has it articulated a clear philosophy of what distinctions are constitutionally impermissible (see, for example, *Craig v. Boren,* 1976). The impact of the cases has been modest. The most important have either affected the federal treasury by making men eligible for survivor and old age benefits in situations where Congress had previously limited eligibility to women (*Weinberger v. Wiesenfeld,* 1975; *Califano v. Goldfarb,* 1977) or have broadly construed Congress's antidiscrimination laws (*North Haven Board of Education v. Bell,* 1982).

Thus, while the courts have had some impact on the movement for equality of the sexes, they have not been among the primary movers. Nor have they offered much symbolic support. The limited nature of the judicial policies and their subsequent impact may reflect the belief of the courts that discrimination against women in our society is rooted more in sex role expectations than in law. Given such expectations, courts may wait for legislatures to establish fundamental policies and then to refine these policies with judicial interpretations.

Regulation of the Economy

As our fourth major policy area, we look at the impact that the courts have had upon economic activity in America. From one perspective, we would not expect the courts to have much influence, since in comparison with other government agencies, courts are not very adept at making economic policy. They are reactive rather than planning agencies, and they lack both the facilities and the inclination to become involved in developing economic policies. Beyond that, the United States is basically a capitalist society, and the government as a whole has only limited ability to influence economic activity (as most of our recent presidents have learned early on).

On the other hand, many court decisions are economic in nature, transferring money or property from one party to another. (Indeed, there is a school of thought centered at the University of Chicago Law School which considers all court decisions to be little more than the articulation of economic policy.)[44] Moreover, the courts have been intimately connected with the shaping of economic policy throughout the nation's history. Most of the Supreme Court's major decisions in its first 150 years of existence involved economic issues. Potential appointees to the court were supported or opposed because of their economic views. (By contrast, the Court has been making landmark decisions regarding freedom of expression, criminal justice, and equality for only the last 40 to 50 years.) Also, many major common law doctrines are little more than legal statements of economic policies determining which groups in the consumer population shall receive financial advantages and disadvantages. In short, many believe that the courts have made and perhaps still make significant economic policy decisions. It is hard to assess the actual impact of such policies, but we will discuss the matter briefly.

Early Judicial Impact on the Economy. During the first century of American history the courts made many important economic policies through the development of constitutional and common law doctrines. The doctrines established by the great Chief Justice John Marshall in a number of landmark cases, including *Gibbons v. Ogden* (1824), *Dartmouth College v. Woodward* (1819), and *McCulloch v. Maryland* (1819), established the concept of a national economy and of corporate integrity free from state interference.[45] Similarly notable state cases, such as *Farwell v. Boston and Worcester Railroad* (1842), created the common law principles of assumption of risk, the fellow servant rule, and contributory negligence, among others (see Chapter 4, p. 126). These doctrines permitted corporations to avoid liability for injuries to their employees and thus accumulate capital during a period of rapid industrial expansion. Indeed, during this period the courts had a nearly exclusive franchise to make economic policy. State legislatures acted interstitially at best, and Congress did not pass the first major law regulating interstate commerce until 1887.

Few studies ascertain the impact of these decisions with any precision. C. Peter MacGrath wrote an interesting account of the impact of *Fletcher v. Peck* (1810) on those persons actually involved in the Yazoo land scandal (which gave rise to the case), but he was not able to say much about the general effect of *Fletcher*'s principal holding: that the Constitution's obligation of contract clause applies to state as well as to private sales.[46] One presumed consequence of the assumption of risk and similar doctrines is that employers were careless about the danger of industrial accidents; consequently, there were more of them than necessary. Lawrence Friedman and Jack Ladinsky, in their study of industrial accident law, report estimates that by the end of the nineteenth century the annual accident rate was 5 per 100 employees, with over 35,000 persons killed and 2,000,000 injured.[47] It is not clear, however, that the figures would be lower if the common law doctrines had not existed. For the most part, scholars of legal and social history either speculate or offer presumptions about the impact of various decisions and doctrines. Often these explanations are reasonable and believable, but they are not systematically supported.

Late in the nineteenth century Congress and many state legislatures began making economic policy more regularly and the role of the courts changed. On the constitutional level, the courts often made negative economic policy—that is they tried to nullify or minimize the impact of legislation. This can be seen in such now infamous "substantive due process" decisions as *Lochner v. New York* (1905), striking down maximum hours legislation; *Adkins v. Children's Hospital* (1923), striking down minimum wage laws; *Adair v. United States* (1908), striking down laws protecting labor unions; and *United States v. E. C. Knight Co.* (1895), holding that antitrust law could not be applied to manufacturers. Many state courts followed suit. The classic example is *Ives v. South Buffalo Railway* (1911), in which New York's workmen's compensation law (the nation's first) was nullified. On the common law level, the courts continued for the most part to espouse economic policies protective of business, which was largely accomplished by adherence to the rules developed earlier. Indeed, it was this adherence to common law that led legislatures to pass workmen's compensation acts and other statutes overturning or bypassing certain common law doctrines. The courts responded by stressing the doctrine that statutes in derogation of the common law are to be narrowly construed. It is fair to note, however, that not all state courts were happy about broadly applying the doctrine of assumption of risk, the fellow servant rule, or the doctrine of contributory negligence, although few abandoned them altogether.[48] Some state courts began adopting doctrines favoring the consumer over business during this period.[49]

Data-oriented studies of the impact of the court's substantive due process (or related) decisions are virtually nonexistent. Even speculation and presumption are infrequent; legal historians have tended to focus on earlier eras,[50] and political scientists focus on more recent decisions. Still there is little doubt that most people in the period from 1890 to 1940 firmly believed that the courts had a pronounced effect on economic behavior. Never was the economic orientation of potential judges scrutinized and debated more fervently. Witness the bitter opposition of the corporate bar to the appointment of Justice Louis Brandeis, who as a lawyer had defended maximum hours laws, or labor's successful effort to block confirmation of President Herbert Hoover's appointment of Judge John Parker, who had frequently applied the *Adair* precedent in ruling on labor disputes. Witness also President Theodore Roosevelt's feud with his appointee, Justice Oliver Wendell Holmes, after the latter voted "wrongly" in a key antitrust case (*Northern Securities Co. v. United States,* 1904). These beliefs were perhaps best captured by one of the era's leading economists, John R. Commons, when he asserted that the U.S. Supreme Court was the world's "first authoritative faculty of political economy." [51]

Modern Judicial Impact on the Economy. The great struggle between the conservative Supreme Court and the New Deal marked a watershed in the Court's impact on economic activity at the national level. In 1937 and the years that followed, the Court backed away from major interference in national economic policy; today it is all but universally recognized that this is the province of Congress and the president. (There is one exception to this generalization. In 1976 the Court struck down a law applying the minimum wage to state employees as violative of the Tenth Amendment [*National League of Cities v. Usery*].)

This does not mean that the federal courts never make economic policy. Much economic policy making still occurs in the interpretation of statutes. Take the antitrust law as an example. In recent years the Court has held that it applies to cities and to professions. It is unclear to what extent the Court's decisions have helped consumers of municipal utility services or of professional services, such as those of physicians and lawyers. However, Congress can obviate any decision whose impact it deplores by amending the statute—as it did when the Court applied the antitrust law to the insurance industry.

In addition, judicial decisions in the field of administrative law may have economic impact. Martin Shapiro is a leading scholar of court-agency relationships. As we discussed in Chapter 6, his study of the Supreme Court's decisions in the 1950s and 1960s relating to the Patent Office and the Federal Power Commission showed that the Court had limited ability to generate, alter, or block basic agency policies and, moreover, that it seldom tried to do so.[52] (Studies by Joseph Tanenhaus and by Bradley C. Canon and Micheal Giles covering the same decades show that most agency decisions are approved when appealed to the Supreme Court.)[53] In later years, however, some courts have become more active in using administrative law to make economic policy, especially where it intersects with environmental or safety concerns. The Court of Appeals for the District of Columbia is particularly active in this respect. Some of its decisions have meant that consumers will pay more for goods and services (for example, *State Farm Mutual Automobile Insurance Co. v. Motor Vehicle Manufacturers' Association of the U.S.* [1982], which thwarted the Department of Transportation's withdrawal of a regulation requiring new cars to have automatic air bags), although not all of them have passed Supreme Court muster. In general, the Supreme Court under Chief Justice Warren Burger has more often than not disapproved of such activism, and the recent use of administrative law to intrude into economic regulation has been only modest and occasional.

Much has been written about the Supreme Court and the economy. However, there is little systematic and detailed study of the actual impact of Court decisions on economic activity. The paucity of data here is noted explicitly by one legal scholar, Arthur S. Miller, in his book *The Supreme Court and American Capitalism.* He writes, "Although much has been said about the power of the [Supreme] Court—of 'government by judiciary'—very little is in fact known about the actual impact of judicial decisions ... there is almost a complete lack of empirical data showing what connection there is between judicial decisions and group attitudes or behavior." [54]

On the state level, courts have not been so quick to retreat from the doctrines of substantive due process. John Schmidhauser and A. E. Dick Howard note that the state courts have continued to nullify state laws regulating businesses.[55] In so doing these courts have often relied on state constitutional provisions rather than federal ones.

(Reliance on the federal constitution could lead to a reversal by the U.S. Supreme Court. See *North Dakota State Board of Pharmacy v. Schneider's Drug Store,* 1973). It appears that state court reliance on substantive due process subsided in the 1970s, although there are no systematic studies on the matter.

State courts have also continued to make economic policy through applying and changing the common law. In the years after World War II most states adopted doctrines defining torts more broadly and making recovery of damages easier.[56] Bradley C. Canon and Dean Jaros did a study of one such liberalization, the abrogation of the doctrine of charitable immunity.[57] Beginning in the mid-nineteenth century, this doctrine prevented a person injured by a nonprofit institution such as a hospital from recovering damages. (The object of the doctrine was to protect and encourage charitable organizations.) In the quarter century following World War II, most state supreme courts abandoned the doctrine. In a detailed statistical study of hospital rates, Canon and Jaros found that the abrogation of the doctrine did cause hospital rates to increase, but only very modestly. James Croyle did a similar study of the impact of strict liability.[58] Under this doctrine, adopted by about three-quarters of the states in the 1960s and 1970s, manufacturers are liable for damages caused by defective products regardless of whether there has been any negligence in producing them. Again, product costs have increased only slightly in the adopting states. If these two studies are typical, it appears that state court common law decisions have a measurable but not very significant impact on economic activity.

There is another way of looking at the courts' economic impact. We can wonder about what would be different if the courts had not made the major decisions they did. Were the courts' economic decisions largely inevitable? Did they reflect economic movements, or did they generate them? The answer is speculative, of course, but we believe in the long run the courts reflected economic trends more than they generated them. Consider the early period. It now seems hard to believe that had the Supreme Court decided cases such as *McCulloch, Dartmouth College,* and *Gibbons v. Ogden* in a way opposite to how they did, such doctrines would have actually prevailed for any long period of time. Various aspects of the economy were becoming so nationwide in this era that the doctrines could not have suffered large degrees of state interference and still have remained viable. It is, of course, uncertain how opposite decisions would have been handled; perhaps the Court would later have weakened or overruled them, or perhaps Congress would have begun regulating interstate commerce much earlier.

Our speculation is buttressed by the fate of the Court's economic decisions of the early twentieth century. By the 1930s the Court's opposition to congressional regulation of labor relations and to minimum wage and maximum hours policies was clearly running against the prevailing economic needs and political trends. Eventually a confrontation occurred, with the result that the Court backed down and changed its ways.

Economic activity affects our everyday lives, whether we are functioning as producers or as consumers. Often the causes of economic situations are complex or unclear. Court decisions have an impact on economic life, although we are generally ignorant of its degree. For the most part, however, the courts are contributors to and legitimizers of ongoing economic trends, and it is less likely that they are progenitors of radical new developments in economic policy.

SUMMARY

Historically the Supreme Court has seldom prevailed when its policies in major areas have been in direct conflict with those of Congress and the president. The Court does make considerable policy in areas where Congress and the president are not so directly concerned, but there has been little clear measurement of its impact in these areas. We know little about the impact of state supreme courts, especially when they make policy in opposition to that of the legislature or the governor. If Dolbeare's study is representative, state trial courts engage in little policy making on their own, although they can delay other agencies' policies. By contrast, lower federal courts do to some extent initiate policy changes in certain civil rights and criminal justice areas. All in all, the impact of the courts on public policy in the United States is not well measured; the matter certainly calls for better conceptualization and research.

In four areas where the judiciary is thought to make considerable policy, its impact has been varied. The Supreme Court has certainly broadened the scope of freedom of expression in recent years, but it is not clear to what extent this freedom is more widely exercised nowadays. In the realm of sexually oriented material, court decisions may well have followed social changes as much as they have initiated them. Similarly, the courts are largely responsible for expanding the concept of due process of law over the last few decades. Undoubtedly, criminal suspects and prisoners are better treated now. There is little evidence, however, that the innocent are better protected or that, as critics sometimes suggest, judicial concerns for due process augment crime.

Perhaps the judiciary's biggest impact on modern America came in the *Brown* decision, which initiated the drive for racial equality. However, it took the active participation of Congress and the president to sustain this effort and ensure substantial implementation of such policies. The state of race relations in America might be quite different if the courts had ignored the issue, but it also might be different if Congress and the president had not joined the effort.

Courts do not always initiate pushes for equality. Equality of the sexes has largely been developed through congressional legislation. Judicial policy making in the economic area has often facilitated new developments or reflected changes in relationships. The courts' policies here, while not initiatory, have made economic change smoother and more legitimate. But the courts cannot make policies that stand in opposition to prevailing economic trends or doctrines. When courts try to do so, as the 1937 crises proved, the judicial policies will be overridden.

The courts have had and will continue to have an important impact on U.S. society. On occasion they will initiate fundamental changes in public policy. More often they will legitimize, enhance, or more fully develop policies made by other government agencies or by nongovernment institutions. At times courts will delay or even thwart completely the policy preferences of other agencies. On an overall basis, the impact of the courts on U.S. society will best be understood in conjunction with an understanding of how other government agencies—and even private institutions—affect society. Similarly, our knowledge of the impact of other institutions on U.S. society requires a better understanding of the implementation and impact of judicial policies.

NOTES

1. Finley Peter Dunne, *Mr. Dooley at His Best* (New York: Archon, 1949), 77.
2. Robert Dahl, "Decision-Making in a Democracy: The Supreme Court as a National Policy-Maker," *Journal of Public Law* 6 (Fall 1957): 279-295.
3. For the best development of this theory, see Walter Dean Burnham, *Critical Elections and the Mainsprings of American Politics* (New York: Norton, 1970).
4. Dahl, "Decision-Making in a Democracy," 285.
5. Ibid., 286-291.
6. For a debate on which elections brought national law-making majority coalitions to power and how long the new majority had to wait to dominate the Supreme Court, see Richard Y. Funston, "The Supreme Court and Critical Elections,"

American Political Science Review 69 (September 1975): 795-811; and Bradley C. Canon and S. Sidney Ulmer, "The Supreme Court and Critical Elections: A Dissent," *American Political Science Review* 70 (December 1976): 1215-1218.

7. Dahl, "Decision-Making in a Democracy," 293.

8. Ibid., 293, 294.

9. Charles Black, *The People and the Court: Judicial Review in a Democracy* (New York: Macmillan, 1960). Dahl also subscribes to the legitimization thesis; see "Decision-Making in a Democracy."

10. Arthur Selwyn Miller, *The Supreme Court and American Capitalism* (New York: The Free Press, 1968), 231.

11. David Adamany, "Legitimacy, Realigning Elections and the Supreme Court," *Wisconsin Law Review* 1973 (1973): 790-846.

12. See Funston, "The Supreme Court and Critical Elections"; and Canon and Ulmer, "The Supreme Court and Critical Elections: A Dissent."

13. Jonathan Casper, "The Supreme Court and National Policy-Making," *American Political Science Review* 70 (March 1976): 60.

14. There are a few exceptions. See James Croyle, "The Impact of Judge-Made Policies: An Analysis of Research Strategies and an Application to Product Liability Doctrine," *Law and Society Review* 13 (Summer 1979): 949-968; Bradley C. Canon and Dean Jaros, "The Impact of Change in Judicial Doctrine: The Abrogation of Charitable Immunity," *Law and Society Review* 13 (Summer 1979): 969-986; and Gregory A. Caldeira, "Changing the Common Law: Effects of the Decline of Charitable Immunity," *Law and Society Review* 16 (1981-82): 669-694. For a bibliography on state supreme courts, see Mary Cornelia Porter and G. Alan Tarr, eds., *State Supreme Courts: Policymakers in the Federal System* (Westport, Conn.: Greenwood Press, 1982), 201-209.

15. See Robert E. Keeton, *Venturing to Do Justice: Reforming the Private Law* (Cambridge, Mass.: Harvard University Press, 1969); and Lawrence Baum and Bradley C. Canon, "State Supreme Courts as Activists: New Doctrines in the Law of Torts," in *State Supreme Courts*, ed. Porter and Tarr, 83-108.

16. Bradley C. Canon, Robert Bradley, and Pauline L. Franke, "The Kentucky Supreme Court as a Judicial Policy-Maker," unpublished paper, Political Science Department, University of Kentucky, 1980. The state's highest court was called the Court of Appeals until 1975.

17. For a discussion of the general nature of state supreme court cases, see Robert A. Kagan et al., "The Business of State Supreme Courts," *Stanford Law Review* 30 (November 1977): 121-156.

18. Bradley C. Canon and Lawrence Baum, "Patterns of Adoption of Tort Law Innovations: An Application of Diffusion Theory to Judicial Doctrines," *American Political Science Review* 75 (December 1981): 977-978.

19. For a brief history of the California Supreme Court's policies in various areas, see Preble Stolz, *Judging Judges* (New York: Free Press, 1981), 76-82.

20. Baum and Canon, "State Supreme Courts as Activists"; and Mary Cornelia Porter, "State Supreme Courts and the Legacy of the Warren Court: Some Old Inquiries for a New Situation," in *State Supreme Courts,* ed. Porter and Tarr, 3-21.

21. Kenneth Dolbeare, *Trial Courts in Urban Politics: State Court Policy Impact and Functions in a Local Political System* (New York: Wiley, 1967).

22. Ibid., 3.

23. Ibid., 104.

24. Ibid., 105.

25. For an interesting study of the workings and political impact of a federal district court early in the nation's history, see Mary K. Tachau, *Federal Courts in the Early Republic: Kentucky 1790-1816* (Princeton, N.J.: Princeton University Press, 1978).

26. Note, "A Dilemma in the Public Schools: School Board Authority vs. the Constitutional Right of Students to Wear Long Hair," *Louisiana Law Review* 33 (1973): 697.

27. See Robert F. Kennedy, Jr., *Judge Frank M. Johnson Jr.: A Biography* (New York: Putnam, 1978).

28. Robert Carp and C. K. Rowland, *Policymaking and Politics in Federal District Courts* (Knoxville: University of Tennessee Press, 1983), 139, Table 21. For somewhat similar data at the court of appeals level, see Sheldon Goldman, "Voting Behavior on the United States Courts of Appeals Revisited," *American Political Science Review* 69 (June 1975): 491-506.

29. Carp and Rowland, *Policymaking and Politics in Federal District Courts*, 89.

30. See, for example, Donald Horowitz, *The Courts and Social Policy* (Washington: Brookings Institution, 1977); and Colin S. Diver, "The Judge as a Political Powerbroker: Superintending Structural Change in Public Institutions," *Virginia Law Review* 65 (February 1979): 43-106.

31. See Paul L. Murphy, *World War I and the Origin of Civil Liberties in the United States* (New York: Norton, 1979).

32. David A. Anderson, "Libel and Press Self-Censorship," *Texas Law Review* 53 (March 1975): 422-481.

33. See Kenneth C. Haas, "The Comparative Study of State and Federal Judicial Behavior Revisited," *Journal of Politics* 44 (August 1982): 721-746.

34. For a study of the comparative impacts of state-imposed exclusionary rules with that imposed by *Mapp,* see Bradley C. Canon, "Testing the Effectiveness of Civil Liberties Policies at the State and Federal Levels: The Case of the Exclusionary Rule," *American Politics Quarterly* 5 (January 1977): 57-82.

35. See James Q. Wilson, *Varieties of Police Behavior* (Cambridge, Mass.: Harvard University Press, 1968), esp. ch. 6-8; Albert J. Reiss, *The Police and the Public* (New Haven, Conn.: Yale University Press, 1971); and Jerome Skolnick *Justice without Trial: Law Enforcement in a Democratic Society*, 2d ed. (New York: Wiley, 1975).

36. See, for example, Malcolm Wilkey, "The Exclusionary Rule: Why Suppress Valid Evidence?" *Judicature* 62 (November 1978): 215, 224.

37. Canon, "Testing the Effectiveness of Civil Liberties Policies," Table 2, 72; and Bradley C. Canon, "Is the Exclusionary Rule in Failing Health: Some New Data and a Plea against a Precipitious Conclusion," *Kentucky Law Journal* 62 (Fall 1974): 703-707.

38. Comptroller General of the United States, *Impact of the Exclusionary Rule on*

Federal Criminal Prosecutions (Washington: Government Printing Office, 1979), 11.

39. Jonathan D. Casper, *American Criminal Justice: The Defendant's Perspective* (Englewood Cliffs, N.J.: Prentice-Hall, 1972).

40. Harrell R. Rodgers, Jr., and Charles S. Bullock III, *Law and Social Change: Civil Rights Laws and Their Consequences* (New York: McGraw-Hill, 1972), 75, Table 4-1.

41. Ibid., 71-81.

42. See Edmond Cahn, "A Dangerous Myth in the School Segregation Cases," *New York University Law Review* 30 (January 1955): 150-169.

43. Harrell R. Rodgers, Jr., and Charles S. Bullock III, "School Desegregation: A Multivariate Test of the Role of Law in Effectuating Social Change," *American Politics Quarterly* 4 (April 1976): 153-175; see also Frederick Wirt, *The Politics of Southern Equality: Law and Social Change in a Mississippi County* (Chicago: Aldine, 1971).

44. See Richard Posner, *Economic Analysis of Law*, 2d ed. (Boston: Little, Brown, 1977).

45. Miller, *The Supreme Court and American Capitalism*, esp. ch. 1-3.

46. C. Peter MacGrath, *Yazoo: Law and Politics in the New Republic* (Providence: Brown University Press, 1966).

47. Lawrence Friedman and Jack Ladinsky, "Social Change and the Law of Industrial Accidents," *Columbia Law Review* 67 (January 1967): 60.

48. Lawrence Friedman, *A History of American Law* (New York: Simon and Schuster, 1973).

49. Canon and Baum, "Patterns of Adoption of Tort Law Innovations"; see also William Prosser, "The Assault upon the Citadel," *Yale Law Review* 69 (June 1960): 1099-1147.

50. Histories of American law tend to end in the 1860-1910 period. See Friedman, *A History of American Law*; J. Williard Hurst, *The Growth of American Law* (Boston: Little, Brown, 1950); and Morton J. Horowitz, *The Transformation of American Law* (Cambridge, Mass.: Harvard University Press, 1977).

51. Cited in Miller, *The Supreme Court and American Capitalism*, 5.

52. Martin Shapiro, *The Supreme Court and Administrative Agencies* (New York: Free Press, 1968).

53. Joseph Tanenhaus, "Supreme Court Attitudes toward Federal Administrative Agencies, *Journal of Politics* 22 (August 1960): 502-524; and Bradley C. Canon and Micheal Giles, "Recurring Litigants: Administrative Agencies before the Supreme Court, *Western Political Quarterly* 25 (June 1973): 183-191.

54. Miller, *The Supreme Court and American Capitalism*, 3.

55. John R. Schmidhauser, *The Supreme Court: Its Politics, Personalities and Procedures* (New York: Holt, Rinehart and Winston, 1960): 83-88; A. E. Dick Howard, "State Courts and Constitutional Rights in the Day of the Burger Court," *Virginia Law Review* 62 (June 1976): 879-891.

56. See Keeton, *Venturing to Do Justice;* Prosser, "The Assault upon the Citadel"; and Baum and Canon, "State Supreme Courts as Activists."

57. Canon and Jaros, "The Impact of Change in Judicial Doctrine."

58. Croyle, "The Impact of Judge-Made Policies."

CASE INDEX

JUDICIAL POLICIES: IMPLEMENTATION AND IMPACT

INDEX

legitimacy of decisions - 194, 256-259
limits of judicial impact on - 261
in Little Rock, Ark. - 1, 160
lower federal court action and delay - 42,
47, 51-52, 62-63, 245, 257
"massive resistance" plan - 91, 157
mayors, role of - 101
media reporting about - 173, 175
in New Orleans - 100, 157, 175, 221
by northern courts - 52, 258-259
and private schools - 118-119, 131, 133
progress of - 256-259
psychological impact of *Brown* - 257-258
reaction against judges ordering - 62-63
resistance in South - 90-91, 157, 160, 179,
220, 256
school boards and personnel, role of - 98,
100-101, 218
and state legislatures' reaction - 157
at University of Mississippi - 80
and utility theory - 202-203
and white flight - 131-134, 219, 258
"with all deliberate speed" statement, impact of - 51, 86-87, 257
Dicta - 41
Dirksen, Sen. Everett - 146
Distribution of literature, and First Amendment - 43
District courts (federal) - 208, 244-246
and desegregation in South - 62-63
and patent validity - 68-69
and sentencing of draft evaders - 60
Dolbeare, Kenneth M. - 27 n. 33, 73 n. 22, 81-
82, 90, 99, 128, 137 n. 15, 167, 176-179,
210, 215, 240-244, 268
Dole, Sen. Robert - 148
Douglas, Justice William O. - 48, 149-150,
161
Downs, Anthony - 83

Easton, David - 191
Economic policies. *See also* Antitrust policies;
Labor policies; Workmen's compensation
Edelin, Dr. Kenneth (abortion defendant) - 9
Eisenhower, Dwight D. - 160-162
Energy conservation policy - 133-134
England, Robert - 98, 100
Environmental groups - 164, 169
Environmental theories of impact - 219-223
Equal employment opportunities - 260-261.
See also Affirmative action
Equal Rights Amendment (ERA), proposed -
262
Equality in American life
judicial impact on - 256-262
racial - 256-261
of the sexes - 261-262

Evasion of judicial policies - 15, 39-43, 129-
134
of busing - 131-134
by consumer population - 129-134
described generally - 15
by elites - 196
by implementing organizations - 85
by judges - 39-43
by police - 97
Exclusionary rule in search and seizure - 32-
33, 43, 86, 206, 219, 252, 254, 256. *See
also* Criminal justice; Police
and consumer population - 111, 115
and environmental theories - 220
interpretation by state courts - 52-55, 68
police attitudes about - 95-96, 214-215
police response to - 86, 89, 94, 97, 115, 216,
220, 254
public attitudes about - 24, 221, 254
Fair Housing Act of 1968 - 256, 260
"Fair trade" laws - 116, 215
Farber, Myron (*New York Times* reporter) -
129
Faubus, Orval (Ark. governor) - 160
FBI (Federal Bureau of Investigation)
interviews of suspects - 123
as source of information for police - 84, 88,
168, 175, 210
Federal Power Commission (FPC) - 95, 214,
266
Feedback behavior - 15, 25
attorneys' role in - 22
by consumer population - 124-125, 128, 140
by secondary population - 20, 110, 140, 196
Festinger, Leon - 197
Florida Supreme Court - 16, 42, 252
Ford, Gerald R. - 10, 150
Fortas, Justice Abe - 150, 161
Frank, Jerome - 192, 195
Franke, Pauline L. - 270 n. 16
Frankfurter, Justice Felix - 1
Friedman, Lawrence J. - 136 n. 14, 240, 264,
272 n. 48
Funston, Richard Y. - 269 n. 6, 270 n. 12

Gatlin, Douglas - 133-134, 203
Georgia Supreme Court - 41
Gibson, James - 60, 178
Giles, Micheal - 65, 69, 103 n. 1, 133-134,
203, 217, 222, 266
Glazer, Nathan - 218
Goldman, Sheldon - 75 n. 68, 271 n. 28
Gordon, James F. (federal judge) - 62
Government agencies as representatives of
consumer population - 112-114. *See also*
Organizations; names of particular
agencies